EDITOR-IN-CHIEF

# EDITOR-IN-CHIEF

### THE FLEET STREET
### MEMOIRS OF
### SIR DENIS HAMILTON

HAMISH HAMILTON
London

HAMISH HAMILTON LTD

Published by the Penguin Group
27 Wrights Lane, London W8 5TZ, England
Viking Penguin Inc, 40 West 23rd Street, New York, New York 10010, U.S.A.
Penguin Books Australia Ltd, Ringwood, Victoria, Australia
Penguin Books Canada Ltd, 2801 John Street, Markham, Ontario, Canada L3R 1B4
Penguin Books (N.Z.) Ltd, 182–190 Wairau Road, Auckland 10, New Zealand

Penguin Books Ltd, Registered Offices: Harmondsworth, Middlesex, England

First published in Great Britain 1989 by
Hamish Hamilton Ltd

British Library Cataloguing in Publication Data

Hamilton, Denis
Fleet Street memoirs.
1. Great Britain. Newspapers. Editing.
Biographies
I. Title
070.4'1'0924

ISBN 0–241–12591–X

Typeset at The Spartan Press Ltd,
Lymington, Hants
Printed and bound in Great Britain by
Richard Clay Ltd, Bungay, Suffolk

FOR OLIVE

# CONTENTS

# LIST OF ILLUSTRATIONS

# PREFACE

WHILE CHAIRMAN OF REUTERS I HAD ANTICIPATED RETIREMENT IN THE country, where I had a house and commercial apple orchard. Using the large number of papers and documents I had amassed in my career, I intended to write two books: a quasi-formal account of Fleet Street after the second world war; and a more personal anecdotal autobiography, recounting my own experiences from Middlesbrough to the *Times*, by way of the Normandy beaches.

However, the onset of cancer, first in the prostate, then in the bone, put paid to any plans for a work of scholarship – I simply did not have, given the radium treatment, many operations and intensive hormone drug therapy, the necessary concentration for a book of that kind – particularly as I led an outwardly active life, in charge of Reuters till 1985, a member of the Independent Broadcasting Authority, trustee of the British Museum, member of the British Library Board, a governor of the British Institute of Florence, trustee of the Henry Moore Foundation and a member of the board of the Standard Chartered Bank . . . . In the end I settled for the easier of the two tasks – a book of memoirs, which I could undertake with the help of my son Nigel, who was completing his *Life* of Field-Marshal Montgomery. Over some two years, using that most vital of aids for sick writers, the tape-recorder, we managed to get down a more or less coherent record of my career. I realise that it is incomplete, selective, and often out of focus. I haven't always paid tribute to those to whom I owe my success – particularly my mother and father and early colleagues. Nor have I been able to paint into the narrative the full personal background to my achievements, such as they are – the love of my wife, Olive, and of my four sons and their children. Without their understanding affection I could not have dedicated myself to my profession; without their support I could not have confronted and so far vanquished the disease. But those who have attempted autobiography will know the hazards of trying to do too much. I was not well enough to explore these elements; nor did I trust myself to do so at a time when the hormone treatment I was receiving made me deeply emotional. In the end I felt that any public interest in my life would centre on my experience as a journalist, and perhaps also as a wartime soldier – which undoubtedly left its mark on me.

In these acknowledgements, therefore, I would like to thank the friends and colleagues of my life – not all of them named in these pages – from my batman to my farm-manager, from journalists to doctors, nurses and relatives. I owe a particular debt to my secretary, Joan Crockford, for her loyalty and efficiency over the past thirteen years, and for transcribing the tape-recordings on which this book is based, as well as typing the manuscript. But above all I am indebted to my wife, Olive, who has loved me for nearly 50 years of active life and enabled me to set down these recollections.

                                                                    C.D.H

# CHAPTER ONE

# JUNIOR REPORTER

AT THE AGE OF 17 I LEFT SCHOOL IN MIDDLESBROUGH AND GOT MY FIRST job, as a junior reporter on the *Middlesbrough Gazette*. I was interviewed by the editor's brother, E.L. Thompson, a sub-editor and also sports editor. In some ways, Ernie Thompson was to feel that the greatest thing in his life had been the making of me into the journalist and soldier I became. On his retirement the newspaper gave him a preposterously low pension and when I heard about it I took steps to have it increased. Nor was Ernie alone: when my father retired prematurely with cancer of the lung, having worked in appalling conditions in the Acklam iron and steel works, making the Mulberry Harbour in the war and the like, he was given a pension of ten shillings a week. It shocked me that his employers – for Dorman Long was a big company – should behave in this way. I determined that if ever I had control of pension funds in my hands I would do differently – and I was instrumental, with a colleague, Lord Mabane, in persuading Lord Kemsley after the war to institute a proper pension scheme in his newspapers.

The *Middlesbrough Gazette* was owned by Lord Kemsley. He and his brothers had bought Allied Newspapers in 1924 and over the next thirteen years had built it up into the most substantial press empire in Britain, until Lady Kemsley died and his new wife – about whom I shall have more to say – insisted the empire be split, Lord Camrose taking *The Daily Telegraph* and the magazines, Lord Kemsley *The Sunday Times* and the provincial newspapers such as the *Newcastle Journal and North Mail*, and the evening papers in Newcastle, Sunderland, Hartlepool, and Middlesbrough.

My father was an engineer, like his father before him and three of his brothers. He had trained in the manufacture of gas turbines and had toured the world – travelling to China and Russia – before settling in Middlesbrough where he became responsible for the maintenance of Dorman Long's Acklam steelworks; if, for example, the blast furnaces failed it was his job to shut them down, repair and maintain them. But he was not an ambitious man – indeed, when he was offered promotion to London he declined the post. He was a quiet man, yet forthright, not one to suck up to anybody in his working life, or put improving his chances first – I am sure he could have gone further if he hadn't been so outspoken. He was devoted to my brother and to me and all our holidays were taken together, either at Scarborough or in Derbyshire at my grandmother Trafford's home. She was a tremendously strong lady who lived into her nineties, having married a prosperous farmer and general trader who died of pneumonia while still relatively young.

I don't think my mother, as a farmer's daughter, had any great personal ambition, but she was a very deeply Christian person, a great churchgoer and church worker, like her own mother. At home she undoubtedly 'wore the trousers' in the matter of family finances. There was no question of my father ever going off on a spending spree: she saw that every penny was allocated. If a bill came in in the morning, it had to be paid that day – an influence I have never been able to shrug off. It was not impressed on me, but was made apparent, that this was the way to behave and then you were in no danger of over-spending. My parents never, ever, spent anything they hadn't got.

I was to meet later in Roy Thomson someone the exact opposite – who thought that anyone who didn't borrow was mad. He thought me crazy not to borrow from him to buy Thomson shares to make myself a millionaire. But I didn't like owing money and I certainly would not have liked, as his Editor-in-Chief, owing money to a proprietor who would thereby have had influence over me. I could have been a very wealthy man if I had taken the value of the offers he made. My children may think I showed lack of foresight, but I was happy then in the decision I made and I have no regrets now.

I was the elder son, born on 6 December 1918 in South Shields in County Durham – shortly after the Armistice. In due course I won a scholarship to Middlesbrough High School. I wasn't a great student but I took up Scouting ardently, and became a King's Scout, attending jamborees in Holland and Hungary, hiking in Norway, camping across Britain – it amazes me to think today how supportive my parents were, given my father's income. It was in the Scouts that I learned my greatest childhood lessons; not so much the skills of tying knots or map reading, but of how to deal with people, and that to do so you had to know your stuff yourself. I was determined to learn all I could and to impart it to others.

Thus I did not relish, once in the sixth form, the idea of further years of study at university. Nor was I gifted mechanically like my father and my brother. I was a fervent reader of the local paper and the *Daily Mail*, which my parents took, and one day announced to my father that I would like to go into journalism. I had started to write Scouting notes and odd features for the local paper, and delivering them to the newspaper office. I had begun to sense a calling. My father spoke to Ernie Thompson. My headmaster could not have recommended me more highly. When I started I had no dreams of being Editor-in-Chief of the *Times* or of ever leaving Middlesbrough. At most, I dreamed of being editor of *this* paper – but my day-to-day drive was humbler still: I wanted simply to do the job well and to learn my chosen trade.

The trouble was, there was no tradition of training in journalism. So I trained myself by volunteering for almost every story that was going, particularly the ones involving 'unsocial hours' that the married men would not want to do. I then compared my own efforts with what went into the rest of the paper. No one ever explained to me, this is how you should write the story; there were no training sessions or anything at all formal in the way of advice. This sowed in my mind the seeds of an idea for a journalists' training scheme – this, and my later experience in the war, when I saw for example, how people from university were trained to be excellent Intelligence officers, or young men of nineteen into very good junior officers. I was able to start a training scheme for journalists after the war because Kemsley's was the largest newspaper group in England; within three years the demand was so great it became a national scheme for the training of all journalists. (Not that it went without a hitch. In my first attempt to put the concept over to the Kemsley staff I wrote a draft month's programme of training, using, thanks to my army experience, the 24-hour instead of the 12-hour clock. A great big Father of the Chapel, or local chairman of one of the printing trade unions, said, 'We're not having your army stuff here. You may have been a great soldier but we're not having it.' I protested, 'What do you mean? I'm not thrusting anything from the army down anyone's throat.' He said, 'Well, look at it; 1600 hours – what the hell does that mean?')

At school, I'd seen something of the divide between the sons of professional people – solicitors, engineers, doctors – and the scholarship boys from the industrial slums of Middlesbrough, the filth and squalor around the steelworks. The conditions in which people lived and worked were intolerable – indescribable smell, fumes and dust, side by side with shipyards where ships were built right through the winter without cover, or proper sanitation for the workforce. The

Acklam steelworks was already obsolete, and although I had no particular political motivation (my father was a member of the local Conservative Club), I did believe in 'progress' – and saw the job of a newspaperman very much in that light. I had no ambition to sit in a magistrates' court all day, and my shorthand, as a result, was abominable. People kept saying, what speed are you up to, how are you doing? – but I found it very hard. I wanted to investigate, and to do features. Most of my work was done travelling by bus or bicycle.

I had enormous luck in my first week. A friend of my father's rang, knowing I'd started on the *Gazette*, and told me the shipyard was going on strike. So I got that story, and soon afterwards, when there was a big explosion in the steelworks, and four or five people killed, I was able to get another friend of my father's on the telephone for the inside story. So, within three months I was established as someone who could get the stuff in the first edition. I had a number of other lucky breaks – a murder story, and an air crash in the Cleveland Hills.

My apprenticeship as a reporter did not go entirely without blemish. All this time the editor remained a rather remote figure whom I rarely saw – until the Tuesday when I was summoned to his office. It had been my lot to do the Church notes, and now the editor demanded to know if I had been responsible for those published on the previous Saturday. I said I had. 'Well,' he said, 'you're taking more and more space in the paper.' 'Yes', I acknowledged, 'but I'm getting more and more Church news.' He looked at me sagely, then lifted his chin and tapped a copy of the paper on his desk. 'Now this story you wrote about the late Vicar of Middlesbrough.' 'Yes,' I said keenly, 'I wrote that.' 'Well,' he said, 'the late Vicar of Middlesbrough is in the waiting room.' It was a useful lesson to me which I needed then.

Our home chancellor of the exchequer ensured that part of my weekly wage of seven shillings and sixpence was put into the Halifax Building Society. I lived at home and still maintained my interest in Scouting, persuading a local councillor, who was an auctioneer and estate agent, to donate a field outside Middlesbrough as a permanent camp site – my first foray into the world of philanthropy in which, over the years, I was able to persuade millions of pounds out of people for social and cultural causes.

In 1937 at the age of 19 I left home, having been given a better job in Newcastle. I bought a car for £20 and was one of the first to take a driving test. In the following year I joined the Territorial Army; I felt that war was coming, there would be conscription, and it made sense to get in first. I'd missed the war in Spain because of my age – one of my schoolfriends did go out and was killed almost immediately – and after all the scouting I'd done I supposed I had something to offer. Unlike the other Territorial officers at the Drill Hall in Newcastle I hadn't done any cadet training at school – Middlesbrough was Labour-controlled and the High School had no Cadet Force – nor had any journalist at the office joined the Territorials. But the Durham Light Infantry was doubling its battalions and needed thirty officers within a month, so I stood a reasonable chance. The DLI had had a magnificent record in the first world war – famed for putting more battalions in the field than any other regiment, and distinguishing itself in all its actions. Great numbers of the men had been pitmen, who, of course, were used both to danger and to taking care of one another.

Traditionally you got a commission in the TA not because of ability or leadership qualities, but because you were a friend of the colonel or the colonel's family, or you had been at public school or had played rugger for Durham or whatever. None of these requirements did I satisfy, but my name was appearing at the top of feature articles in the *Newcastle Journal* and I think this engaged the curiosity of both the commanding officer and the adjutant. I was the first journalist they'd met at close quarters and I arrived in my own car. I suppose there was a quiet determination about me in those days – once it had been suggested there was a chance of getting a commission nothing was going to stop me. I was used to interviewing and could hold my own.

Soon I found myself amongst solicitors, accountants, bank managers and men from minor public schools. The Territorial Army was living out its last days as a social club, really – though it is sobering to think that barely 20 per cent of those TA officers survived the war. The outstanding ones, to my mind, were the pit engineers, for they could handle the men so well – the men all looked up to them because their lives already depended on them. They went down the pit shaft together every day and the pitmen owed their survival to the engineers' sound judgment in driving new seams, to their safety measures and to their taking over when there was an accident.

In my own case it was my experience as a King's Scout and assistant scoutmaster that decided the adjutant in my favour. I was commissioned next day and assigned to a company at Birtley, one of the Durham coalfield towns. Our small drill hall was in the middle of long rows of back-to-back houses built by the mining companies. Within a fortnight I was on a firing range near Sunderland with thirty men, shooting out to sea, and a Regular sergeant, seconded from the father regiment, telling me what order to give. The famous 151st DLI Brigade had spawned another, the 70th Brigade, to which my battalion, the 11th DLI, belonged. Everybody was a volunteer and the cameraderie made for extraordinary discipline. I was given a batman, Private John Brown, who worked in a carpet factory in Durham city. His father was a police sergeant. After I had met him he said to his son: 'You stay with him for the rest of the war' – which the son did, though he would have made an excellent sergeant-major. When I became ill six years ago he put the telephone into his house in Durham, so that he could telephone me, and did so regularly until his death. That was typical of him and of the Durhams' spirit of loyalty.

I was Signals officer. I don't know if this was because I was a newspaperman or because my scouting had made me familiar with Morse code and semaphore – proficiency in these being part of being a King's Scout. I had a very good rate of tapping a Morse code buzzer. All members of signals platoons in the division had to pass a test under the inspecting eye of an officer and sergeant of the Royal Corps of Signals. We got 100 per cent of our men through, which was unheard-of in the division; I think it was partly due to my perfectionism in those days: if we were going to do it, we were going to be the best.

But perfectionism, that Northern conscientiousness about doing properly whatever job one tackles, can exact a price. It is, of course, the classic recipe for migraine. My mother suffered from it – 'sickly bouts' as they were called in those days – and I must have inherited it from her, for even at the age of eight I remember being brought home from school feeling very sick for no obvious reason. For the rest of my life I was to be tortured by migraine, sometimes three or four times a week. The curious thing is that although I had it in the war, during moments of great concentration on training, for example, I never once suffered migraine in battle.

Part of the Territorial Army was embodied about a fortnight before war was declared, and I was among those chosen. We knew we'd have to go to France very soon and, while wishing to be in as early as possible, we realised we faced the real prospect of slaughter. We were so ill-equipped. We'd left rearmament too late; we had only one Bren (light machine gun) per company when we should have had one per section; we had no anti-tank rifles and, of course, the rifles we did have were of first-world-war vintage, kept heavily greased in storage – laid down somewhat like wine, but without improvement. Just before we went to France early in 1940 we were issued with first-world-war telephones in great thick leather cases connected by miles of cable. Until 1942 there would be no wireless link with battalion or brigade headquarters – a recipe for chaos once Hitler invaded Holland and we had to move forward out of our prepared defences.

Before I go into battle, however, I ought first to recount a personal campaign, fought at home with my parents over the object of my romantic attentions, Olive Wanless.

# CHAPTER TWO

✺

# THE GIRL IN
# GREY STREET

IT WAS AS SENIOR FEATURE WRITER IN NEWCASTLE UNDER TERENCE
Horsley, the gifted news editor of the three papers – the *Newcastle
Journal*, the *Evening Chronicle* and the *Sunday Sun* – that I began to
perceive wider horizons. Often I would go away for two or three days
and develop a feature or series for one or other of the papers. Gradually
my cuttings book began to swell. I roamed all over the North of
England from Teeside to the River Tweed and over to Windermere. I
was also required, on occasion, to write stories for the *Daily Telegraph*,
which was owned by Lord Kemsley's brother, Lord Camrose.

Among those I interviewed was the then Bishop of Durham – also, as
now, one of the most controversial figures in the Church of England. Dr
Hensley Henson gave me a copy of his forthcoming sermon on some
great topic of the day, but what most impressed me was the size of the
type. Huge letters, typed by his secretary between wide margins, made
the Bishop's peroration resemble a poem rather than a sermon. It was
my first insight into the art of simplification when addressing large
numbers of people – whether in church or in the army, where Field-
Marshal Montgomery was to demonstrate such mastery. I also
interviewed Anthony Eden's mother, Sybil, Lady Eden; the family had
extensive interests in the coal mines. She told me a great deal about her
son. She was a bit of an eccentric, and I think (having got to know Eden
well in later years) that some of his outbursts of temper must have
related to that strain of the family.

Harold Macmillan was the Member of Parliament for Stockton and I
reported some of his meetings. He and his wife, Lady Dorothy, were
most helpful to a young reporter; I interviewed him on several
occasions on the prospects of the North-East moving out of the terrible
Depression, and this started a friendship which was to last until his
death in 1987. Unemployment in the 1930s sometimes exceeded 40 per

cent, and without the war, ironically, the North-East might never have been regenerated. To this day I can picture the groups of dispirited men hanging about at street corners and the rush to the volunteer mobile soup kitchens which came round at noon, particularly for the children.

There was also Hugh Dalton, the booming voice of the Labour party and member of Parliament for Bishop Auckland; and there was Archbishop Temple (then of York), who was the hero of my young life. Temple was a very rotund man but an intellectual giant, with a photographic memory – he could read through a book of verse and then recite it back. Because of his 'socialist' ideas – that banking and the resources of the nation should be made available for the nation, not for a few individuals to make fortunes – he was unpopular in certain quarters, and many thought he shouldn't be made Archbishop of Canterbury, which he became in 1942. It was Temple who restored my faith in the Anglican Church at a critical and impressionable moment of my life – which, in turn, was ironic because I had, by then, begun to court a Roman Catholic.

I'd met her while seeking an interview. I was aware that Roman Catholics could be difficult people to deal with from my experience in Middlesbrough, where I had been Acting Editor of the *Teesside Herald*, a rather high-sounding name for a 24-page newspaper, published on Fridays and bought mostly by the people of Middlesbrough to send to their relatives around the world. The contents had all appeared in the daily editions; what I did was to select material that would be of interest abroad, and measure up the photographs for the four pages of pictures. Now, each year there was a Corpus Christi procession through Middlesbrough in which about 20,000 Roman Catholics paraded before being addressed by the Roman Catholic Bishop of Middlesbrough. For this event an enlarged edition was printed, and special pictures taken.

I remember thinking I'd done a rather good job as I looked at the first Corpus Christi copy off the machine. But suddenly the editor of the *Gazette* and the circulation manager, a Mr Keegan, burst into the reporters' room, and cornered me in a pincer attack. The circulation man, a devout Catholic, screamed, 'You fool, you have spoilt the paper!' for under a picture of some rather splendid-looking men carrying a huge banner I had written that they were Knights of St Columbus when, of course, they were Knights of St Columba. 'We are ruined, we are ruined, we will be the fools of the world!' he shouted. But by that time I was half-way down the passage to the machine room where I had friends whom I prevailed upon to stop the presses while one of them chipped at the type so that there was a smudge at the end of

'Columb'. All this took less than a minute before the machines were running off their 50,000 copies. I had great pleasure – and relief – in rushing back upstairs to Mr Keegan and assuring him that all was well. After that I made sure I treated Roman Catholic affairs with the caution of a bomb-disposal specialist.

Soon afterwards I was asked to write a feature on scientific research at the Royal Victoria Infirmary, Newcastle, funded by the North of England Cancer Campaign, and went to meet its secretary, expecting some antiquated lady devoted to good works. To my surprise I found a most charming young woman in her early twenties sitting in the office overlooking Grey Street, one of Newcastle's architectural gems. For an hour I took notes while her secretary typed away in the adjoining room. Two days later I was back for more information, and that Sunday my article duly appeared in one of Kemsley's national newspapers, the *Sunday Graphic*.

Having by now passed my driving test, I had bought myself a rather nice Vauxhall 10, spanking new. In this I now returned to Grey Street to suggest a second article, from a different angle, for Newcastle's *Sunday Sun*. For me personally it was the beginning of the biggest story of my life. Olive Wanless, who came from Alnwick, in Northumberland, had been chosen to run the campaign under Sir Thomas Oliver, the famous physician of the North, and had become quite expert at speaking at meetings and getting potential donors to contribute. At that time no newspaper used the word 'cancer' except with the greatest caution, for the idea was widespread that it was incurable. I therefore suggested that we produce a booklet on fairly popular lines exploding the myth of incurability in cancer patients. I asked Mr Thurgar, surgeon in charge of treatment at the Royal Victoria Infirmary in Newcastle, and Dr Dickens, the research director, to write a text about the disease with illustrations that would be understood by reasonably intelligent people. An old friend of Middlesbrough Scouting days, who had joined an advertising agency, designed it. It was the first venture of its kind anywhere in the United Kingdom and we arranged for it to be sold on the bookstalls throughout the north-east. Soon it had sold out completely. (Years later, when editor of the *Sunday Times*, I asked one of the leading experts on cancer, Dr Ronald Raven, to write a series of articles about the need for early detection and the increased chances of survival; this breathed hope for many patients who might otherwise have given way to despair, by showing how important is the sufferer's mental attitude to the disease.)

Olive and I received leatherbound copies, blocked in gold, of our booklet, and the two thin volumes are among our most prized possessions because, apart from anything else, they marked a milestone in our personal lives. We had become inseparable, Olive often joining me while I was covering a news story, sitting in the car while I sought an interview, or consuming endless peach Melbas at a certain Italian restaurant in Newcastle. We were soon secretly engaged, and the day came when, having had to obtain the approval of her guardian, I felt I must inform my parents, and take Olive to meet them.

My father never had a car; he simply couldn't afford to run one. But he greatly enjoyed my coming home to Middlesbrough for the weekend and taking him round the Cleveland countryside, through the dales and over to Whitby. This time Olive came with me. They liked her, but my grandmother had been for fifty years president of her Anglican parish Mother's Union, and my mother worked tirelessly for the C of E in Middlesbrough – whereas Olive was a convert to Roman Catholicism, something that I certainly would never be. Moreover, Olive declared that she would have six children – and even announced she would go to early Mass next day. My father insisted on getting up to make her a cup of tea. It was a conciliatory gesture, but alas, she wasn't allowed sustenance before the service. All in all my parents were at their wits' end as to what would become of me in view of all this Popery.

We did think of getting married without their consent. But I was still not 21, and we needed to give three weeks' notice for the banns to be read. I was by now a full-time soldier, expecting to be posted with my battalion to the British Expeditionary Force in France at any moment. To wait until my 21st birthday in December 1939 was therefore impossible. Reluctantly we agreed that my parents' formal permission would have to be sought before the wedding could take place.

As I learned later, this caused considerable turmoil at home and there was a set-to between my mother and father. At first my mother was reluctant to give her consent. My father ended the discussion, however, by saying, 'Look, let them get married, because if he is killed we will never forgive ourselves afterwards.' In fact, my father fell ill with lung trouble and couldn't attend the wedding – which took place at a Roman Catholic church in Jesmond, Newcastle – but my mother came, together with my brother Ken and Olive's sister Maisie.

We'd thought – hoped – the wedding would be a very quiet affair, but we'd reckoned without the Durham Light Infantry. As we emerged, forty of my fellow officers formed an alley of drawn swords in time-honoured tradition. We were then forced into an old Austin 7 covered with suggestive posters, streamers and bathroom articles, and were towed through the centre of Newcastle - which was full of Saturday shoppers – into Grey Street and up to the Crown Hotel. There we realised what energy had gone into organising our wedding celebration rather than the war. We protested that a private family lunch had been arranged at Tilley's Restaurant nearby, but were told this had been put back while the ritual enactment of another wedding took place at the Crown. All the officers took part, with tablecloths used as surplices and the padre featuring prominently. It was as hilarious as it was unexpected. The officers became more and more inebriated and finished up at the Theatre Royal, from which they were eventually ejected for being disorderly. Thankfully, no one was run in by the police. It was a rumbustious occasion, perhaps the final outburst of innocent high spirits before the reality of the war overwhelmed us all – for within months most of the officers were dead, wounded or prisoners of war.

That night, our one honeymoon night, we spent at Barnard Castle. I was already on a signalling course at Darlington, to which I had to return. I still sometimes wonder whether Olive truly realised what she was letting herself in for, marrying an army officer after the outbreak of a world war. But her spirits never flagged in the long years while I was so much away – strengthened by our love, our marriage, and in time our children.

# CHAPTER THREE

# DUNKIRK

I RETURNED TO DARLINGTON TO MY COURSE, WHILE OLIVE CONTINUED with her cancer campaign tasks as well as working for the evacuation organisation, moving children away from potential German bombing targets and billeting them in the countryside. My signals platoon was the source of great pride to me, but while it was obvious we were mastering the art of Morse code transmission, I was getting to know very little about how to attack and occupy a position, or to defend it when the Germans approached. I was therefore sent to Catterick to take the Junior Leaders course. Here I realised that I had become a specialist without first learning the basic infantry skills which the other young officers, commanding infantry sections, seemed to possess. Nor did this deficiency look like being rectified, for the officer in charge of the course was an ex-Indian Army Reservist, and we somehow crossed swords the very day I arrived.

The whole first day was dedicated to an examination of how pickets worked on the North-East Frontier. Later in the afternoon, I asked how relevant this was to, say, eight Panzer divisions sweeping through Holland and Belgium, as even then seemed likely. This roused the veteran, and when he found out that I was a reporter working for the Newcastle papers, subsequent reference to me was accompanied by a sneer about 'yellow journalism'. Back at my battalion I was sent for and asked to account for my report, which expressed surprise that I had ever been awarded a commission and recommended that I should be moved out of the infantry to somewhere I could do no damage. My colonel was a wonderful Territorial – John Bramwell, whom I always think of with both affection and sadness, because having been a prisoner in the first world war he was to be so again a few weeks later. He laughed, but I thought it was a monstrous thing to have on my conduct sheet, and demanded to see the brigadier and, ultimately, the divisional commander. To each I expressed myself with the greatest force about the way I had been treated and the remoteness and stupidity of the course. The divisional commander ordered the report to be torn up. There was a sequel which we shall come to shortly.

Soon we were told to prepare to move to France, and we were warned that we would be under canvas. Once there I was involved in a daily competitive race to finish forward airfields. Some training was done but we still had little equipment. Early spring in France had a certain charm about it, and we spent some time picking up relics of the first world war, and learning with admiration how the War Graves Commission had so lovingly looked after the British cemeteries, as they were to do for those containing my own men killed not very far away four years later. My signal platoon was kept busy laying out lines to brigade and company headquarters and to adjoining battalions.

Early in May 1940 the Germans suddenly attacked Holland and Belgium, also surprising the French in the Ardennes and moving towards us. The best of the French army was left sitting underground in the Maginot Line while the British army had to abandon all its slit trenches and pillboxes and move into unreconnoitred Belgian territory as fast as possible, on foot, impeded by Belgian civilians streaming back from the German advance. Eventually the whole of our division was halted and we were told that we were to make the best defence we could against several German divisions, which were expected to attack in the next twenty-six hours.

Next afternoon, still with no sign of the Germans, I was ordered to take about 160 men to the selected defence line – a river – and man a bridge so that the brigade could cross in safety. On the way, we came across an officer from another battalion at a crossroads which was being bombed. In the darkness I said to him, 'I feel certain that your unit is taking the wrong direction – it is going in a circle and it is bound to meet the Germans in the morning.' Then we recognised each other. It was my ex-Indian Army friend, who clearly decided to dismiss my map-reading as being of the standard indicated in his report. He went his way.

At the bridge I put most of my men on the German side, but when dawn came there was no sign of anybody at all. Apparently, during the night the brigade had been given new orders, and the dispatch rider bringing them to me must have been killed. So there I was, in the middle of the French countryside, while unknown to me, the rest of my battalion was being attacked across open fields by a German Panzer division. Of a thousand men, only two hundred would return to Britain – the rest were killed, wounded or rounded up as prisoners of war, remaining in captivity until 1945. By incredible fortune I had missed this carnage. Long afterwards I learned that the Indian Army major, too, had walked into the Panzer division's line of attack. I never knew what happened to him, but the three hundred men he was leading had been butchered. Of four of us who had shared a tent, I was the only survivor. I vowed to remain in the infantry and, if possible, return to France one day to liberate the survivors. Twice, subsequently, I was nominated to the Staff College but on each occasion I went to the corps commander and asked to be allowed to stay in the infantry to fight.

Of the next few days I remember only what the army calls a shambles. With my 160 men I joined larger groups. From time to time we were scattered by German aircraft, or by orders that would then be countermanded an hour or two later. Occasionally we saw the crack Regular British divisions carrying out orderly withdrawals and, in one instance, our own 50th Division carrying out a counter-attack at Arras, which held up the Germans for a valuable twenty-four hours. We had only a rifle each, and there was little we could do. Eventually, we got to the Dunkirk area and helped set up defences around the perimeter while destroying transport and ammunition. I was still in charge of my group, mostly from our headquarters company: others had joined us, including the regimental sergeant major. I did my utmost to keep everybody together and to march in some semblance of the standard set by the Guards. We organised an attempt to get off by forming lines of swimmers and passing the non-swimmers along the line to the small boats. We managed to get numbers of men into boats to row out to the larger craft, but orders then came to concentrate on getting off at Dunkirk. So I took about threequarters of my men to the Mole where, tired though we were, we were kicked and shoved on to a naval minesweeper.

We were heavily dive-bombed about five miles from shore, and hit in two places, but somehow the captain was able to take evasive action and we got to the end of Margate pier. Most of us were a pretty disreputable sight. I had picked up an officer's greatcoat, which I had found on the sands at La Panne, to give me a little warmth after being in the water for so many hours trying to get men on to the small boats. We were glad to be alive and grateful to the captain and crew of the gallant vessel, which made straight back to Dunkirk. A few days later this minesweeper was bombed in the Channel and everybody was lost.

Meanwhile, we surged down the pier at Margate to find a very heavy police guard. Behind it there were thousands of people cheering us. I felt desperately humiliated that we had done so little and yet were being greeted as heroes. Without any attempt at organisation we were shuttled into two or three railway trains that were in Margate station and I was unable to keep my unit together. I shall never forget that as the train was starting to move off, a Salvation Army officer asked if he could send a telegram for me. I shouted something out of the window which, by some magic in the Post Office, reached my wife in Newcastle. I still have this telegram, framed, telling Olive I was safe; and she, in turn was able to tell my parents.

I remember passing through the outskirts of London with people cheering us all the way till, mercifully, I fell asleep and woke up on Nottingham station, where hundreds of civilians were waiting for us. The men were taken off to drill halls and schools to be looked after, and a kind couple gave me hospitality. We remained in Nottingham for two days, and were then told to assemble at Plymouth. Invasion, it was now believed, was imminent, and the 11th Battalion of the DLI was to defend an area of South Devon between Dartmouth and Start Point, the site of an important radio station.

At the centre of our defensive area were the famous Slapton Sands, where it was possible to bring a destroyer almost into the shore itself. The sands were clearly the key to our task and we set about positioning the three forward rifle companies almost on the beaches themselves. Each day various stragglers from the battalion reported in, plus a few officers. Soon our officer numbers were made up to thirty by the arrival of fresh men, some of them straight from training units. As Colonel Bramwell was a prisoner his successor became Lieut-Colonel Richard Ware, a first-class Regular who deserved far higher things than he received in the war. Yet no sooner had Colonel Ware begun than he was whisked off to form an Area command and the battalion was left in the hands of Major Fred Taylor, whose background was that of a lieutenant-quartermaster rather than infantry defence. However, Colonel Ware had promoted me to captain and had made me battalion adjutant, so I was able to exercise a great deal of initiative. We soon had a powerful battalion: three of our company commanders – all older Regulars – ultimately became major-generals. I grew a moustache in the faint hope that I too might look older. I was never to shave it off.

Our first defensive task was to demolish some small bridges over marshy land – the idea being that the area would be thus impassable to the Germans, particularly if they invaded at night. All were blown except one, just wide enough to take a motorbike for communication purposes. This left, standing alone in the centre of Slapton Sands, a very charming hotel, where it seemed that you could jump straight from your bedroom into the sea.

Shortly afterwards the forward companies reported to me that hundreds of civilians had arrived in lorries with shovels and spades and were digging long trenches from the sea back to the road. I hurriedly wobbled down on my motorbike to find out who was in charge of this excavation. I learned that the district council engineer had decided the sands were a perfect place for parachutists to land and, therefore, the beach must be dug up. I protested that this would simply provide ideal slit-trench positions for the Germans to sit in and fire at us, and quickly saw off this local invasion.

Next we laid about twenty boxes of mines along the beach and around the hotel. Within two or three nights there was an enormous explosion and every regiment along the South Coast stood-to in case this was the promised invasion. In fact, all that had happened was that a dog had wandered into the minefield – and up had gone the glorious hotel. Every day some bright spark would arrive from Command with an idea for the defence of this particular important stretch of sand. One of the strangest was hundreds of feet of what looked like well-perforated gas piping. The idea was that we should fill it with petrol, and then set this on fire by remote control when the Germans arrived. Another proposed device was a pioneer version of the Molotov cocktail, using a beer bottle with rags dipped in an acid solution. When the German tanks got near enough this was to be hurled through the driver's observation slit, or even lobbed into a tank via the hatch where the commander would be standing. Sentiment for beer bottles being what it was, this was one of the more popular inventions; but if it was used anywhere in the war it was certainly not to my knowledge.

One morning the left-hand company commander rang through to say that there was the biggest gathering of generals in red hats that he had ever seen in his life and they were asking for somebody in command. Again I did my motorcycle wobble across the narrow bridge, and sped on to the sand, where I halted neatly by going head over tail past the handlebars. This was the joke of the year for the generals, who were having a good look at Slapton Sands, again because of its tactical importance. I think it was General Auchinleck who, as the senior member of the party, asked me if I always reported so dramatically. Recovering what military dignity I could, I put him in the picture about the area and directed him to Area headquarters.

We stood-to each morning about half an hour before daylight, stretching our eyes across the distant Channel, looking for any strange ship. But by the autumn it seemed unlikely, from Intelligence reports, that the Germans would invade that winter. As a result, the whole brigade was withdrawn to the Totnes area, before moving to Liverpool docks and embarking for Iceland.

# CHAPTER FOUR

# ICELAND

LITTLE HAS BEEN WRITTEN ABOUT ICELAND IN THE SECOND WORLD WAR. It was first occupied by the Canadians in June 1940, when there were increasing reports that the Germans, having taken Norway, might try to seize the island. Its importance on the northern flank of the Atlantic convoys could not be overestimated and in time it not only became a base for the convoys to Russia but also provided vital airfields in the battle against the U-boats.

The whole of our brigade travelled on one ship – a Cunarder. As I was going up the gangway at Liverpool the movement control officer asked me if I was the adjutant of the 11th Batallion. I said I had that honour. He said, 'Well in that case you are adjutant for the whole ship.' I had never been on a ship of that size and had no idea what my duties were. Luckily Colonel Ware had, and with his help, and an orderly room clerk, I set about the business of running the 'passengers'. The greatest problem was to stop the soldiers throwing cigarette ends away, because of the risk of fire. One night some soldier did, in fact, drop a cigarette down one of the big air vents. It went right down to the hold where there were 4,000 kitbags, and a number of them were very quickly on fire before the crew managed to extinguish the blaze. It was a frightening but salutary experience. I had to appoint a court of inquiry to find out what had happened. There was little evidence of how the fire originated, and certainly no one owned up – but the court papers followed me around for at least two years, regardless of hostilities.

The voyage to Iceland took about three days, and we anchored in Reykjavik harbour. In the distance you could see the hills and Mount Hekla, but not a tree or any sign of vegetation anywhere. The brigade stayed on board while the adjutant of each battalion went ashore to arrange the taking-over of billets from the Canadian regiment, the Toronto Scottish, who were then to embark for England in the same ship. Their barracks comprised a group of huts built around a large parade ground made of lava dust and crushed stone. The Canadian colonel asked me to stand with him while his entire battalion was marched past, slow time, in single file. At first I thought the honour was for me – until I saw that they were marching past what looked like a corpse. On inquiry, I found that the 'body' was a still-unconscious private who, having run out of beer rations but desperate for more alcohol, had drunk anti-freeze from the battalion's vehicles. Whether the soldier recovered I do not know, but the colonel told me he was determined to give his battalion this lesson. Intrigued, as a good journalist I asked the colonel in the officers' mess what was his civilian occupation. I was hardly surprised when he told me he was the governor of Toronto prison!

Snow was already falling in Iceland and the hills were covered. Very soon our battalion took over the warm Canadian-built huts, many fitted out with stoves the size of two men. When you got them going you made the huts wonderfully cosy. And, of course, every excuse was used to brew a cup of tea laced with the frequent rum issue – hot Tom and Jerry, as I used to quote Damon Runyon.

The rough winter weather suddenly turned, in May and June 1941, to the most beautiful short summer – the only snag being the arrival of millions of mosquitoes from the inland lakes formed or swelled by the melting snow. Fortunately, Colonel Ware was an imaginative trainer, and very soon had every company out testing their ability to mount attacks and cope in defence, trying out different company commanders. A strong element of the old Territorial playboy attitude to soldiering still remained, however, in spite of the Dunkirk disaster. I felt we were only going to be in Iceland a short while and might be back in action very soon, so I took my duties very seriously – and soon fell out with our brigadier over discipline. Once again I was in danger of a negative report. Colonel Ware counter-attacked by putting me up for promotion to Major, as a company commander. Brigadier Kirkup sat on this for a whole week, until the colonel declared that this was not the way to treat someone who was rightly disciplining people for their playboy approach to war, and said he was going to take it to Division. Kirkup immediately backed down and I got my majority. I was 23.

As the new D company commander I was determined to make it the best in the battalion. The 11th DLI, still part of 70th Brigade, had now been absorbed into the 49th Division, which chose as its divisional sign a polar bear, shown on four legs, pawing the ground. The divisional commander, General Curtis, a delightful man, did not impress me as a commander. Nevertheless he did establish a course for officers of the rank of major, studying the various aspects of command. It was the first course I had attended as an officer – after two years of war. Two excellent divisional instructors arrived from England, and the seeds of a much more professional, thinking approach to war were sown.

I must admit that after almost a year of garrison duty in Iceland, I felt the time was drawing near when we would return to England and be sent somewhere to fight. But I had reckoned without our Prime Minister's fertile imagination. America still declined to enter the war. On his way back from a meeting with President Roosevelt in Newfoundland, however, Mr Churchill stopped off at Reykjavik to inspect our garrison. Walking down the lines of men, Churchill spotted several companies of Norwegian soldiers, who were expert in Arctic warfare. This was enough for Churchill – he now decided that the Durham Light Infantry, experts in coalmining, must become experts in Arctic warfare – so that we could re-invade Norway!

Our first invasion of that country, in April 1940, had been a disaster. If a second was to succeed we would have to be a lot more professional. So a group of about 30 officers of the rank of major from the different arms of the service – infantry, artillery men, engineers, machine gunners, medical staff and so on – were despatched to an area at the centre of Iceland where there were two glaciers, to study Arctic warfare in the raw. Two doctors from the Labrador medical service came to assist, and also two men who held the Polar Medal, having distinguished themselves in peacetime in the rudiments of Arctic movement and survival. I did not at all realise just how close to death I was to come. Once we had worked out some kind of battle drill for Arctic warfare we were to report to the War Office on the right equipment for such a campaign. Meanwhile, we would return to our units and train them. I have to confess that the thought of putting little Durham pitmen on to skis, when they had perhaps never done anything more wintry than to build a snowman, all seemed very funny to me. But indications kept flying back from Churchill's battleship that this operation really was going to be 'on' – so off into the Icelandic interior we drove, after a very smelly voyage around the northern coastline in a fishing trawler.

From our base camp we set off on skis and snowshoes, climbing up the side of a mountain. Once we had reached the designated glacier, the instructors decided there was sufficient ice to demonstrate how to build an igloo, using bayonets or a special knife. We were first shown how to cut blocks of ice, then assemble them in a circle round a pit, and build up the walls like bricks in a nursery, each new row just a bit thinner than the last, and tapering towards the centre. Eventually we got something about four or five feet high, and were shown how to fill in the cracks with snow, which very rapidly ices up and keeps out any outside air. A little entrance tunnel was also constructed so that you could crawl into the igloo.

Next, we spent a day or two examining the glaciers and learning how to cross them. There was also the rather frightening business of how to climb the icy cliffs near the top of these mountains. I didn't mind going up the rope to the top, but I was frankly terrified of coming down – you had to put the rope between your legs and throw yourself over the cliff until at some point you stopped, and then lower yourself slowly with your feet banging against the mountainside.

About the fourth night, I remember, we thankfully retreated into our igloos. We had all been issued with special white outer garments, tops and bottoms, which we put over our regular army uniform and were trying out before they were issued to the whole division. I was sharing an igloo with a man from my own regiment, Bill Kirkup, nephew of our brigade commander, and after some pemmican soup we turned the lights out, and fell asleep. I was awakened by what sounded like distant beating of drums and a pounding pain in my forehead. I shook Kirkup in his sleeping bag but got no response. I felt awful and realised that the 'noise' was, in fact, the pumping of my own heart. Something was grossly wrong. Clearly, we had used up all the oxygen – but how?

In a minute or two I heard ski sticks being pushed into the tunnel and shouts of 'Are you OK?' I said I could crawl out with a bit of help, but I was very worried about Kirkup, who resisted all my attempts to shake him into sensibility. I got out, and the two doctors went in to see if Kirkup was still alive. Thank goodness he was, although he had come very near to losing his life. What had happened was that an overnight snowstorm had blown up. The last part of building an igloo was to leave a tiny hole in the top into which you stuck a glove, as an air-vent which would let a little air in. Our glove, unfortunately, was under two feet of snow. It was a most unpleasant experience – but worse was to follow.

After more exercises with guns and sledges, it was decided that we would march across Iceland to Reykjavik to practice rates at which one could travel with full kit on snowshoes or on skis, and what problems one might meet. We were now issued with one small bivouac tent between two – you actually slept on the base part of the tent and your combined weight would in theory stop the whole thing blowing away. Icelanders, when they heard of the plan, were very sceptical indeed. None of them, they said, would ever attempt this journey unless he was highly qualified and knew the very few routes. One might have imagined that we would have taken a guide – but not so. Two or three days of marching and having discussions about how a platoon of thirty men would deploy in these sort of conditions brought us to a ravine which, to north and south, seemed to have no crossing place. The light was failing and there was nothing for it but to camp for the night. A small group would recce for possible crossing points the next morning. During the night, however, one of the most spectacular storms ever experienced in Iceland hit the capital, sinking many ships at anchor, blowing many of the Nissen huts to pieces, and very nearly ending our lives. All we could do was to lie huddled together in our bivouacs praying that the winds, which exceeded 120 miles an hour, would not blow us into the ravine. It took probably thirty-six hours before we were able to crawl out of the tent to find something to eat and, even more urgently, to cope with those natural functions that we had been able to hold back. We had been lucky to survive – and very silly to go without a guide. Reconnaissance revealed no possible crossing place over the ravine so we had to turn back.

Fortunately, there was a boat about to leave for Reykjavik. Leaving our instructors to ponder on the lessons of the last two or three weeks we thankfully waved them goodbye. Great was our astonishment on arrival to find the whole of our brigade embarking – the 10th and 11th battalions of the DLI and a battalion of the Black Watch*. Fortunately for us, another of the brigades had received orders to move back to Britain using a large troopship, and to take advantage of this our own brigade had been told to embark with them. To our immense relief Churchill's idea of reinvading Norway was scrapped, for the moment at least, and we left Iceland and Arctic warfare without regret.

In not much more than a couple of days we were home in Newcastle. Bill Kirkup and I had a bath at the Station Hotel and after breakfast I thought I would call at Olive's office in Grey Street. Stupidly, I did not telephone her beforehand but walked straight into her room, where she nearly collapsed. She was seven months pregnant with our firstborn, Michael.

All sorts of ideas were now in the air. New Churchillian ideas began to circulate. There was a very strong rumour that we were to be prepared to invade Sicily, the very opposite of Arctic operations.

To prepare for the harsh Sicilian terrain (that, or the Mafia), we were now ordered to Pontypool, in Wales. Pontypool was a typical small Welsh valley mining town, its residents intensely proud of their community. They were not a little anxious about the arrival of a north-country mining battalion – followed by an Indian mule team, complete

*This was the 12th DLI, until someone had the bright idea that if we changed the name into a Black Watch battalion it might encourage the Scotsmen living on Tyneside also to join up.

with Indian grooms. The animals were kept somewhere near Ponty-pool greyhound track and the first morning after their arrival all officers were told to report there at 7 am so that the commanding officer could give a demonstration of how to handle a horse. What none of us knew was that the Indian grooms always had their horses ready at least a couple of hours early, so as not to be caught out. By the time our colonel (a brilliant horseman and an experienced player of polo in Northern India) arrived, the horses were therefore frisky with cold. They all looked to be the most beautiful things from Newmarket, as they probably were.

Crisis number one came when the colonel turned to me saying, 'You are second-in-command of the battalion; and you are to have your own, personal charger. Up!' I did not dare admit, in front of my fellow officers and a growing number of soldiers, that I had never been on a horse before. The Indian grooms gave me a leg up, I grabbed hold of the reins (secretly looking to see how the colonel held his), then he was off, and so was I. The last race at Pontypool greyhound track had been over hurdles. These were still in place, about two to three feet high. My splendid beast did almost one circuit with me clinging to its neck and the reins, with my feet in the stirrups, and with the horse jumping each set of hurdles in what I assumed was an elegant style. It could not last. Suddenly the horse came to yet another of these hurdles, stopped – and over the top I went.

In going round the circuit I had had to keep my head low because of the overhead lamps; there was also a four-foot-high steel fence all round the circuit, which restricted manoeuvre. I now found myself sailing through the air towards what I thought was the middle of the steel fence, certain I was going to break my neck. Luckily, by the time I hit it I was on the way down and, although shaken, I was none the worse. Virtually the whole battalion had however, assembled to see the fun – which was only beginning. The commanding officer shouted out 'Adjutant and Intelligence officer next.' It was all rather crazy, for both of them were thrown very quickly, the Intelligence officer having a particularly bad time and I think finishing up in hospital. Within three weeks he wisely joined the Intelligence Corps. No more horse riding for him!

We spent a little time in Pontypool before being moved to North Wales, virtually under the shadow of Snowdon, to a tented camp in a place which was known to the troops as 'Penny on the Drum'. This was the area of Lloyd George's birth and was beautiful country, very near to an estuary and the open sea. At first the training was carried on at company level and occasionally I took my horse out for a short walk, watched over by my Indian groom. As the days went by and our confidence grew the brigadier felt it was time to have a three-day brigade exercise, even if no more than an exercise in movement.

Each battalion had, I suppose, something between fifty and a hundred mules, most of which were angry beasts. The troops were shown how to load them up with ammunition, machine guns and mortars. The brigade set off along a very small metalled road through the Welsh hills, with my battalion in the rear. There was hardly a stretch of flat road, it was up and down all the way. Suddenly a message arrived at the back of the column at which I was positioned as second-in-command. Would I mount and report rapidly to the colonel, at the end of the column? I got on board my horse, which also had my greatcoat and sleeping things, and away I went. With troops on either side of me waiting for the inevitable crisis, I got to the colonel but, unfortunately, there was no way of stopping the horse as it was, it seemed, a Grand National twice-round-the-course beast. I thus passed right through the brigade at high speed until we reached the head of the foremost battalion. Suddenly the horse had had enough and stopped very quietly. There I was, safe but extremely sorry for my performance, having been watched with amazement by several thousand men of the brigade.

Between horse trials I did get one or two chances of looking round the countryside and seeing Criccieth – where ultimately, Lloyd George was to be buried beside a most beautiful river. I also dined with the colonel at a restaurant in Portmeirion. That Mediterranean fantasy built by Clough Williams-Ellis looked strangely out of place in Wales, and in fact it was the nearest to Sicilian architecture my battalion would get in the war – for in the event it was decided to send a Canadian division to Sicily instead of us.

We had defended Devon and trained for arctic warfare and for the mountain heat of Sicily. What next did Mr Churchill have in store for us, we wondered?

# CHAPTER FIVE

※

# PREPARING FOR
# D-DAY

IT WAS NOT LONG BEFORE ORDERS CAME. OUR NEW ROLE WAS TO BE THAT of a motorised division which, I supposed, meant an ordinary infantry division but with sufficient transport to move rapidly. Once again we were sent to South Wales, where we did a great deal of route marching, exercises and river crossings. It was clear that we were now to prepare for the invasion of France. Colonel Sanders was succeeded by Colonel Nigel Poett, who had already made quite a name for himself as a Regular officer in the DLI. Very tall, he was an extremely forceful person, destined to finish his service as a full general. I admired him greatly, and named my second son (born the following year) after him.

Though we lacked battle experience, a new professionalism was sweeping the army at home, in the wake of General Montgomery's pioneering efforts in Southern England after Dunkirk. Not only did we rehearse and train for battle at every level from company to division, but the officers were sent on a host of courses. The first I attended was the London School of Street Fighting, set in Battersea. The commandant was Richard Fleming, brother of Ian – later to be one of my closest friends. Richard Fleming's instructors were mostly Guards officers and NCOs. The idea was that I and an officer from the Tyneside-Scottish, Major McGregor, would become commandant and second-in-command respectively of our own street-fighting school, which was to be set up in Birmingham. It was therefore imperative to get full value from our two or three weeks in Battersea.

The course included learning how to drive massive railway locomotives, and how to sabotage them; how to sabotage the railway line; and how to get over the top of a house (the drill being to throw up a long coil of rope with a four-headed spike which hopefully would find a place on the drainage system, or on the roof or chimney, and one would pull oneself up to the top and slide down on the other side). It was certainly a part of soldiering that didn't appeal to me, but I had to go through with it. Using a road in Battersea that had been heavily bombed, we also had to learn how to fight indoors, in a series of houses in which your reaction to sudden events was tested. Each house was rigged up with surprises which only appeared when the instructor, walking behind, pulled on a rope or pressed a button – and a man's head would appear out of a piano, or the like.

Immediately the course was over we went to Birmingham, part of which had been badly bombed, to requisition certain streets, brick them off and make them into a combat-training area in which live weapons and live ammunition could be used, particularly grenades and Sten guns. Soon officers and NCOs of every battalion were taking the course which McGregor and I devised. They, in turn, went back to teach their own soldiers. It was tricky work, and I had several narrow escapes when taking people round and having to cope when they panicked. I shall never forget, for instance, one stalwart sergeant from a Yorkshire regiment who was supposed to hold a grenade in his hand, already primed, for three or four seconds. This left only a second or two to fling it at the enemy while he got out of the door. Unfortunately, he dropped the live grenade. Such was his courage that he then tried to jump on top of it to save us from the explosion. I managed to get him off it and kick it down an escape hole, which we had provided in all the downstairs rooms for this very eventuality.

It was a gruelling time and I was frankly relieved to hear, some weeks later, that I was being posted back to my 11th Battalion. Colonel Poett had been promoted to command an airborne brigade (which was to earn immortal fame capturing, on D-day, the vital Pegasus bridge). But Poett had been succeeded by a lieutenant-colonel who must have come from some remote Staff job – he was physically unfit, he fell asleep during lectures and demonstrations, and Captain Donald Stephenson, the adjutant, had bravely gone to brigade headquarters and predicted catastrophe for the battalion if he continued much longer. This was one of the reasons why I returned to the battalion until they had decided who was to be the next CO. Fortunately for the battalion it turned out to be Lieut-Colonel J M Hanmer, a Regular officer of the highest class, no intellectual but devoted to the regiment and determined to make the battalion the best in the brigade. As he was some time in arriving, I was in command. Meanwhile the divisional commander, General Curtis, left to be replaced by General 'Bubbles' Barker, whose first action was to order every man (and vehicle) to change the feeble, pawing polar bear, head down, for a roaring animal. General Barker was a sort of Monty in miniature.

For some time, I suppose, I had been groomed for battalion command. Each division would put forward the name of an officer, usually of the rank of major, who was under consideration for immediate promotion to lieutenant-colonel and, if chosen, he would attend the Senior Officers School at Brasenose College, Oxford. In due course my name was put forward and I went to Oxford. The quality of instruction and the keenness I experienced during these three months were factors which persuaded me immediately after the war that if the army could do training and seminars of such high quality, there was no reason why journalism should not do something similar.

I also attended a commanding officers' course at Inverary, which was the HQ of the Combined Operations Training and Research Department, after which the brigade moved to the Clyde to get some experience of assault on enemy-held beaches by small landing-craft. To accustom the troops to jumping into six feet of water with rifles slung over their shoulders, the whole battalion embarked one day on a large paddle-steamer. We were in our oldest uniforms, officers as well as men all carrying rifles. The vessel's naval commander indicated, as I stood beside him on the bridge, that the moment had arrived when I should show an example to my battalion and jump. The drop was at least twenty feet. I cannot really recall whether I enjoyed the experience, but I do remember one of the hardest things was actually keeping your tin hat on.

Anyway, down I went, finally rising to the surface of that noble river and striking out for the sea wall at Rothesay. This was a popular weekend resort for Glaswegians taking the sea air, and a lot of people were on the esplanade watching the army getting ready for the Second Front, while I floundered my way towards the sea front. I had swum a fair distance and was beginning to tire a little when I thought I would turn round and see how close behind the nearest man was. It was then I realized I had been the victim of a friendly hoax – I was the only man in the water. The laughter soon turned to cries, however. The paddle-steamer had followed me towards the shore and all of a sudden the men had to start jumping overboard. I knew well from our training in river crossing that most Englishmen were, in those days, scared stiff of small boats and water, and loud were the screams as the men hit the surface, being non-swimmers and having no faith at all in the Mae West inflatable life-jackets with which they had been issued. Many shouted for the rescue boats, but they were told to get on with it. Only when a number became hysterical were they taken back on board and brought to shore.

There followed further rehearsals of assault landing, mostly done in the dark, or just as dawn was breaking which, of course, was to be the eventual plan.

Finally, just before Christmas 1943, we moved to Southwold in Suffolk. This was a delightful small coastal town which had been garrisoned in force ever since Dunkirk in case of invasion. In order to design route marches and exercises I had to travel a great deal around the county and this gave me a chance to look at some of the beautiful Suffolk wool churches, as at Blythburgh. The land, which I had always supposed rather flat, turned out to be rolling, unspoiled countryside in which you were never out of sight of a church with Saxon origins: a further irony as we prepared to invade Saxon-occupied Europe.

Thinking back on the years preceding our invasion, one thing stands out in my mind. Never for one moment did I think that the British Army could lose the war. Even after Dunkirk, standing-to every night along the Slapton Sands, night after night, week after week, for four months, I never had a single doubt that we would prevail. Similarly, I never had any doubt that I personally would survive the war. Not until later, after the bitter fighting in Normandy and Holland, did I recognise how extraordinarily fortunate I had been.

At Southwold I ran a course for company commanders, examining the sort of problems we would have to face, but it was at Thetford, where we were to take part in brigade exercises using live ammunition, that I first met Monty. He had recently been brought back from Eighth Army to command the four Allied armies designated for the cross-Channel invasion, and he was busy visiting his new 'parish'. He inspected the whole of our brigade, walking past each man, looking him straight in the eye with the utmost intensity. Having inspected us, Monty hailed his jeep, got on to the bonnet and, through a microphone, asked all the men to break ranks and gather round so that he could give them a talk. A great many of the men hardly knew how to react to this strange order, but the commanding officers had been warned beforehand and were able to give a lead to their own battalions. Sometimes Monty would do four of these visits in one day and I have since discovered that he used the same speech on every occasion. The main purpose of his message was to say how confident he was of success, that the fighting would be very hard at the start, that the remaining month or two had to be used for intensive revision and he would guarantee that not a single life would be lost unnecessarily. He was not a bloodthirsty general, and he even made a particular point about the respect that must be shown to all those who were killed early on: they would all, he promised, be reverently buried.

The men were then dismissed – and Monty inspected their leaders: the brigadier, battalion COs and seconds-in-command. I cannot begin to explain how much we owe to Monty for his leadership in Normandy and after; but the impact of his visit, early in 1944, was of profound importance to me and to the lives of our men, for we were saddled with a brigadier patently past his best; we all knew it – but no one seemed able to remove him. Most of us were terrified where he would lead us in the first weeks of the invasion. I don't suppose Monty was with us for more than half-an-hour, but in those thirty minutes he summed up each one of us mentally. I took a bet with one of my fellow-officers on our brigadier's prospects – and won it easily. That very same evening our brigadier was bowler-hatted. What counted, in Monty's eyes, were the lives of his men; and those lives were not going to be squandered by officers who were patently not up to the task. Instead, we were given a brigadier with two DSOs, a ball of fire to strike the fear of God into you if you failed to perform in battle; and battle was now only weeks away.

# CHAPTER SIX

# NORMANDY AND BEYOND

WHEN I TALKED TO GENERAL MONTGOMERY AND GENERAL MILES DEMPSEY, commanding the 2nd Army, in the month before D-day, they told me that my extra pip to lieutenant-colonel would not be long in arriving. 'I like young colonels,' said Monty, 'they fight better and tire less easily.' In the event promotion came sooner than expected – on the very beaches of Normandy, when for a number of reasons I had to take over command of the battalion.

In spite of the years of training and rehearsal, there were a host of surprises in store. It was hoped, for instance, that ex-Eighth Army divisions and brigades would leaven our otherwise inexperienced 2nd Army. Yet the battle in Normandy was to show that those divisions that had been fighting for years in North Africa and the Mediterranean were tired and resentful that, as they saw it, they were now asked to shoulder such a heavy burden of the renewed fighting.

We were appallingly deficient in working with armour. The Germans had better tanks and better anti-tank guns, and some Panzer divisions, despite the losses in Russia, remained in the top class. Heaven knows what would have happened if Hitler had not kept back so many of these tireless Panzer divisions in the Pas de Calais area.

It always angered me that armchair critics criticised Monty for being cautious when he knew from the start in Normandy how desperate was our shortage of British infantry reinforcements. Casualties soon mounted. Before long the replacement officers I was getting were Canadians – supplied under a system called Canloan – because we'd run out of British. I remember one second-lieutenant coming up at about five in the morning when I was in my command post. He shouted down to me, 'Colonel, my name is Gregory – I'm Canadian – I've come to give you a hand,' and I took him forward to show him the company he was to have to take over. He was killed that night.

There are times in war when the noise of artillery and shelling and aerial bombardment is very frightening, and the man who is utterly brave and foolhardy can be a menace. In a sense, the ideal officer or soldier is the man you might call moderately brave, neither cowardly nor full of bravado. For the ordinary bread-and-butter work of the battlefield you need determined soldiers who, while inwardly frightened, realise there's a job to be done. There were certainly, in my battalion, acts of extraordinary valour. I recall Sergeant Denham, wounded in a cider orchard in Normandy after I had sent out a patrol to see if the Germans were withdrawing. We had joined up at the same time and he too had survived Dunkirk. Now I saw him lifted on to a stretcher. I asked the bearers: 'What happened?' 'He went out to rescue somebody,' they said. He was horribly wounded and I comforted him, but I couldn't help asking why he'd risked his life. 'Well, Jack was out there and I went to pull him in.' – 'In daylight? What an incredible thing to do!' – 'Well, he comes from the same pit at Birtley. If it had got past the war and got known that I had left Jack out there, my life would have been finished in the pit. So I went out to fetch him in.' His reasoning says a lot about those pitmen.

Our 70th Brigade was in 49th Division, one of the first follow-up divisions into the bridgehead. I had landed on the second day. I was still only 26 years old but I'd often been in temporary command while the former CO was away, so that I wasn't alarmed at having to take over in the field. I felt I could stamp my own authority on the battalion and could give clear orders even when receiving, myself, rather tentative ones from above. I felt that I could think things through, and in moments of stress I could still provide sound decisions. The battalion came in on the following day and we went straight into action, on foot. We took bicycles – one platoon per company – but the troops were never really happy with them. It was tough going. Ordinary artillery didn't have that much effect on a pillbox, a strong point or even a house. In the bridgehead you had to call on the bigger guns to help. We had no tanks in the battalion – you were generally allotted them only for a considered attack where the enemy was holding firm.

Our early fighting was outside Caen, then we moved over the River Orne to thicken up defences west of the town, where the hammering was being done by the Panzer divisions, for fear that if there was to be a British breakout, that was where it would come. As a result there was tremendous fighting. The Germans got their second wind, bringing more seasoned troops into the line while we were learning the hard way. We had done miraculously well in getting two entire armies ashore, within days. Now we were faced by what Monty termed the 'dog-fight' phase – and this proved more gruelling than even Monty ever imagined. The shelling and mortaring was even more intense than the first world war as the Germans threw every man and gun into battle. Perhaps my worst memory is of the day when one of the battalions in our division ran away and for about four hours, on the orders of General Barker, I was involved in an on-the-spot inquiry, interrogating the survivors, particularly the commanding officer.

In warfare, you have to accept that mistakes will always be made or things won't always come off as you hope. If there are, say, three or four adverse things, they will be covered by ten things that go right. But this particular battalion, the 6th Duke of Wellingtons, had about twenty things go wrong. They had been badly sited, with too many men at the edge of some woods, so that when shrapnel started flying around it seemed more than it really was. There was a great concentration of German mortars – 'moaning minnies' – which went disturbingly on and on. An attempt to get hot food to the men failed, so they hadn't eaten properly for twenty-four hours. As a result they started digging deeper and deeper, which is always a sign that people are frightened. Then some started drifting back. They had suffered a lot of casualties among the officers, and one of the last straws was when the commanding officer's carrier was seen to be pulling out. Those that were left thought the CO – who was actually visiting the line – had run away. They all ran then.

I had to interrogate the CO, a very unpleasant experience, but in a quick report I set down that it was the sum of a number of unfortunate things that had led to the incident. I think it was the only battalion to break down in the whole campaign and the Duke of Wellingtons never talk very much about it. What was left of the 6th battalion was sent home, and replaced by a battalion of the Leicesters. Such are the fortunes of war. You need tremendous luck. Five or six things can go wrong – but you can't survive ten, certainly not twenty.

The fighting in Normandy was very bitter – first between hedgerows, then across vast cornfields without cover. Our casualties were alarming. But we knew that, in toto, we were winning – the bridgehead was inexorably expanding, and more and more American troops were arriving, many of them direct from the United States. Suddenly, in August, having lost so many men and inched our way forward, we found no one in front of us and were starting to move fast when the three battalion COs were summoned to a morning rendezvous. We assumed it was to receive fresh orders. To our chagrin, a letter from Monty was read out saying that in view of the number of British casualties and lack of reinforcements, he was having to break up whole brigades and divisions, our brigade among them.

I had the sad job, with my fine adjutant, Donald Stephenson, of working out where the men would go. As far as possible we tried to keep groups of men and formations together; many went to other battalions in the same division. From having had six DLI battalions in the field, all of a sudden we were down to one – which gives some idea of the casualties we took, and the adjustments necessary. Such 'shake-outs', however, are not confined to military life, and sad though my task was, it was a valuable if bruising experience. I made a particular point of talking to every man in every section – and I tried to see that every man went with his sergeant or officer.

Meanwhile, the battle itself had swept on to the Seine and I myself – having given instructions for what was to be done with the battalion funds, correspondence, silver and so on – was posted as second-in-command of the 7th Duke of Wellingtons. I also dropped down to Major. It could have been awkward, considering that I had been fighting as a lieutenant-colonel and battalion CO since D-day, but my new superior was being groomed as an understudy brigadier and it was assumed that for much of the time – as in England – I would be the effective commanding officer. I thus commanded the battalion as we moved into Belgium, past Brussels and up to the Albert Canal. Ambitious plans were hatched as part of the Arnhem battle, but we ended up defending a sector of the front beyond the famous Nijmegen bridge, and it was there, shortly before the Battle of the Bulge, that we were hit by a fierce German counter-attack.

On the night of 3 December 1944 we were on the water's edge at Halderan on 'the island' between Arnhem and Nijmegen. As commanding officer I must have been expecting something to happen, because I insisted on sleeping in my headquarters established in a cellar, with its telephone and radio communications with the rest of the battalion, back to brigade HQ and to the battalion on our left. When the attack came my driver and batman were in the sleeping cellar fifty yards away and were wounded as they tried to get over. We held a front perhaps three-quarters of a mile wide, littered with mines. We were strongest along the road that ran parallel to the river, but the ponds on either side had swollen to the size of lakes, so when the Germans hit the road in great concentration there was no way of stopping them. It was fairly clear they were aiming for the strategically important small town of Bemmel behind us, and prisoners later told us that they were then going for the Nijmegen Bridge a mile or so further west. The railway bridge was in the river but the road bridge, though damaged, was still intact. They'd sent frogmen already to try and blow it up, but the charges had failed to detonate.

I had a fair number of men in reserve but the volume of noise and telephone calls and radio messages at the start indicated to me something far bigger than a patrol attack. I knew I could cope with the initial thrust but I was more concerned – if it was going to be a big affair – to do something about the Germans forming up for the second wave. I therefore first got the brigade artillery to put down heavy defensive fire and then, in my certainty of the threat to the bridge, I insisted we call down the whole corps artillery of medium and heavy guns. I had a gunner major with me, and before anyone could query the authorisation for such a heavy concentration of fire, I ordered it to come down on a crossroads just behind the first German attack. Had we ourselves been attacking, I reckoned, that was where we would have formed up our reserves in readiness for the green light once the first attack was signalled a success.

Subsequently, I became notorious as the only battalion officer able to bring a whole corps artillery concentration on the enemy without permission. It certainly made a most incredible noise. Months later we found the wooden grave markers of hundreds of Germans who had been killed that night as they gathered to move forward, but all day following the battle, aerial observation reported endless ambulances removing the wounded.

It was an extraordinary battle, even the battalion's cooks joining in. The Germans who'd smashed through had seized the road, but any self-congratulation they felt must have turned to something else once they realised they were trapped, that there would be no support. I urged Brigade to order the battalion on my left to drive towards the river and bottle up the Germans inside our own lines. We then systematically mopped them up. None of them got away. When daylight came, they saw they could not succeed and began to put up the white flag. There were, though, some quite brave machine-gunners who had to be winkled out. All the time I was moving around with two signallers with packs on their backs, so that I could give out mobile orders – such was the concentration of the original German shelling that all our telephone lines were out of action. That apart, it was one of those nights when everything went well. Every wireless set worked, we took well over a hundred German prisoners, apart from more than fifty killed in their attack and the many hundreds dead or wounded by our artillery barrage. I was able to secure two Military Crosses, two Distinguished Conduct Medals, and numbers of Military Medals for my gallant comrades. My Battle of Halderan became a sort of classic defensive action and was used, I later learned, for training lectures and instruction. Within a fortnight I was notified that I had been awarded the Distinguished Service Order, in the field. It was written up in the Press at home – 'How the Nijmegen Bridge was Saved' – and in due course I received a personal letter from the owner of the Middlesbrough and Newcastle papers, Lord Kemsley himself, congratulating me. It was gratifying – but I could still not have imagined that I would be working as his personal assistant in London less than two years later.

# CHAPTER SEVEN

✳

# LIBERATING ARNHEM

WE SPENT THE FINAL WINTER OF THE WAR DEFENDING OUR ISLAND bridgehead beyond Nijmegen. But once Monty had cleared the Rhineland and crossed the Rhine the following April, we were ordered into the attack, first to clear the remaining Germans off the island, then to seize Arnhem itself. For this task I had at my disposal more guns than the whole of Eighth Army at Alamein. I was given field regiments, medium regiments, heavy regiments, heavy AA regiments, hundreds of rockets, a divisional support battalion, tanks, flame throwers, mine-clearing flail tanks, sapper platoons, air support – I could ask for anything out of the shop window and it was there.

In the end, however, it was an infantry operation once again, thousands of troops having to attack across minefields, with the help of the tanks and flail tanks – though the last couldn't be used because of the dykes and trees, and even the tanks could only operate on a one-company front. Where the Germans stuck it out in fortified houses or strong points I brought up flame-throwers and the opposition quickly crumbled. My job was to lead the Germans to believe we would assault from the 'island' to the south of Arnhem, while the rest of our division crossed the Rhine and then encircled the town from the east, across the river Ijsell. Once it had done so we were given the green light to seize the town itself and to open up the road network for a lightning Anglo-Canadian advance to Amsterdam. Unfortunately, one of our ammunition lorries blew up, blocking the main avenue of our advance, but I ordered the reserve companies in by other routes and we were soon in possession of the vital Arnhem railway station. For six months we'd been denied the town, after the gallant battle fought by 1st Airborne Division, and fired by a sort of historical excitement I remember stuffing wads of Arnhem train tickets into my pockets, taken from the booking office. I still have them today – the only 'loot' I brought back from the war.

We were in Arnhem only a few hours, for it was essential to keep up the momentum of our advance. We were heading along the main road to Amsterdam when, to my astonishment, our advance ground to a halt and we ran into heavy shelling which killed the officer and sergeant-major standing beside me. I ordered a rapid tank attack on a wood where we could see enemy infantry and some unusual and very un-German looking tanks. The puzzle was solved when the first prisoners were brought in – these were troops of the volunteer Dutch SS brigade. That they could go on fighting for the Germans, who were threatening to blow the dykes and ruin Dutch farmland for a generation, as well as starving the population of Amsterdam, was almost beyond belief. I had great difficulty in restraining my men from making short work of the prisoners we took.

Hitler had withheld food from Amsterdam in reprisal for a Dutch railway strike. We made rapid progress towards the city but were halted after thirty-six hours because Queen Wilhelmina sent a message that, with the end of the war so near, she didn't want the Germans to flood the low-lying country between the Rhine and the Zuider Zee, reclaimed after so many centuries. We had to swallow our martial disappointment and wait. When the time came to restart we advanced behind a squadron of armoured cars into the village of Baarn where the royal summer palace of Soestdyk was situated. It was guarded by some low-grade defenders, very quickly dealt with.                                    .

Many years later I was introduced to Prince Bernhard of the Netherlands. I told him I'd liberated his palace – to which he replied that he wished I hadn't done so much 'unnecessary damage'. This was, alas, typical of him. I replied that every life in my battalion was valuable to me, and if by a few shots from tanks or machine-guns I could frighten the enemy into surrendering, then that was done. I did not like Bernhard, and it was reciprocal. Monty, of course, did not trust him, and would not have him in his map room, even though Bernhard was C-in-C of the Dutch Liberation forces. Monty couldn't get over his suspicion of Bernhard's German blood.

More importantly than his palace, however, that afternoon, 6 May 1945, we led a food convoy into Amsterdam and began disarming the German forces left in Holland, some 100,000 men. They had signed a surrender document at Wageningen, a town which I had liberated. We organised a sort of assembly process. Prisoners came up with their transport and were guided into different fields; guns in one area, horse-drawn traffic in another, ammunition in another, rifles and small equipment in yet another. At about 6 pm I went to see how my battalion was faring. I left my jeep and signallers on the main road and crossed into one of the fields. All of a sudden there was a gigantic explosion.

What probably happened was that one of the Germans had thrown in a primed grenade which went off accidentally and ignited the whole ammunition dump. My driver assumed I must certainly have been killed, because of the magnitude of the explosion, but with extraordinary luck I got caught between two blasts. I was knocked over by their force, and deafened, but I was able to carry on and organise the rescue of the casualties. It was a ghastly sight because most of the dead were cut up into tiny pieces. I had the harrowing task in the next twenty-four hours of writing to the next-of-kin of these men, trying to gloss over the fact that they had died in such an unfortunate way, just when the war was over. It was such a cruel end, particularly for those Territorial volunteers who had been fighting since Norway in 1940 and had survived the campaign all the way from the Normandy beaches.

A few days later we held a victory parade in Utrecht. Then the entire division shifted south: I was now to command the Kreis of Gevelsburg, an area of the Ruhr on the southern boundary of the British zone of occupation. I was still barely 27 and for a while, I confess, I went through a bad patch wondering why I had been spared death when so many good and brave men had given their lives. But the soldiers of a battalion look to their CO for so many things – above all for inspiration – and I could not let them down after all we had been through. On the way to the Nijmegen Bridge I had said to Lance-Corporal Brown, my batman, about a fierce tank battle, "That was a bloody near squeak! What were the lads thinking?' 'Oh,' he said, 'no one round here was very worried. We all look at your face when anything's on. If you look all right what the hell's the point in us getting worried?'

It was a lesson in how important it is to look confident. I can't hide from myself the fact that on many occasions I was either uncertain of the outcome or plain scared. But as commanding officer you *had* to show yourself, and show yourself totally in command of yourself and the situation, for the troops instinctively get to feel whether the commanding officer is going to keep control or not. Quite a number of COs were removed, either because they lost their nerve through not being able to get enough sleep or clearly lost the confidence of the troops. Youth was on my side. I never felt the need for sleep – I could go for three or four days at times without sleep or with just a catnap, whereas, interestingly, some of the Regular COs, who would have been about 35 years of age, cracked very quickly. In two cases in my own division, brigadiers cracked – one a Guards officer, a huge fellow, whose nerve went; he had to be taken back very rapidly and didn't

fight again. In another case, in Holland, a brigadier couldn't relax
enough, and shot himself. Several times I was put in temporary
command of a brigade until a more experienced brigadier was found, in
circumstances about which you just kept quiet.

Given the way in which a CO had to perform, it was not surprising
that so many colonels were killed or removed. Practically all those in
my division were dead by the end of the war. Hence my period of
anguish in Germany. Why had I survived? I felt there must be some
high purpose – that the example set by those brave men of the battalion
mustn't be forgotten, or wasted. At the going down of the sun, I felt, we
*would* remember them, try to be worthy of their sacrifice in the lives and
careers that awaited us.

Although the CO was a father figure, in the second world war he
didn't dress particularly differently from the other ranks. In winter I
wore leather jerkins, the same battledress, the same black boots, and
very often shared the same slit trenches with my signallers or batman.
We ate the same food, from the same mess tins. I remember at the end
of the war we had a march-past in Baarn – the battalion cleaned itself
up and we looked like parade-ground soldiers. Every Dutch inhabitant
was determined to make friends with the soldiers that evening and to
entertain them. I was taken off by a charming young pair and given a
drink. The next morning they came to my headquarters in great
embarrassment, saying they'd no idea they'd been entertaining the
commanding officer – they thought I was a private soldier because we
were all dressed alike.

They, reasonably enough, did not understand that the business of
command depended not on badges or uniform, but on an officer's
ability to look after his men. The Greeks knew, and so did Napoleon,
that there are really no bad soldiers, only bad colonels who sometimes lead them. He also asked that famous question when assessing
a man's probable practical value: 'Is he lucky?' For three years
I was responsible for gathering officer material or talking to those
who wished to be considered. If I gave a talk I would often use this
text:

Xenophon asked Socrates what was the basis of discipline, and the
answer given then will still be the answer 10,000 years from now.
'Discipline is founded upon respect for the officer and confidence in
him'.
And then the soldier asked again. 'And what are the fundamental
qualifications of such an officer, the fundamental characteristics?'
Again, the old philosopher answered and his words are everlastingly

true: 'Such an officer is one who has at heart always the best interests of his men'.

I've often thought about these things since, for in spite of the vast literature that exists on the two world wars, almost nothing that I am aware of has been written about command of the infantry battalion. It is something so special, at once personal and yet with wise responsibilities, that it deserves to be better recorded and discussed. While I was at Brasenose College, for instance, being prepared for battalion command in battle, the only advice I ever heard on the personal side of command came from Field-Marshall Wavell. He stopped suddenly in the middle of a lecture and said, 'You can forget all this, all I've talked about, you know. What is far more important is your digestive system.'

A rifle battalion in war had nominally a thousand men usually divided into four rifle companies, plus headquarters and support companies. By the latter stages of the war, particularly during a big offensive, the total might swell to 5,000, for the CO would – as happened in the breakout from Nijmegen bridgehead – be expected to orchestrate artillery, machine guns, sappers for lifting mines, specialist anti-tank gun units, tanks, armoured cars for reconnaissance and aircraft on call via RAF liaison. He might also have batteries of rockets and flame-throwing, minelifting and bulldozer tanks, as well as reserve infantry under his direct hand – a mighty orchestra indeed, and led from the front. Conducting such an orchestra you had to know how to employ each section in harmony, getting the best out of them all. It was part of the mental requirement of a CO to be able to conduct this great team without internal disputes or differences.

You had to 'know your stuff', in Monty's phrase, but knowledge alone was not enough, at least when fighting an enemy as tough and resourceful as the Germans. The pressures of battle were immense, and to survive you had to be young and fit, mentally as well as physically. I've remarked how few colonels or brigadiers survived the Normandy battle. You had to be able to carry on commanding despite loss of sleep. The majority of officers could not cope after the loss of two nights' sleep, and very few people could cope at all after three nights' loss. COs were issued with a form of benzedrine injection to keep them going in an emergency; but you were far better advised to hand over to your second-in-command if you were getting utterly tired, and sleep - for if the CO can't cope, the battalion's performance in battle will collapse.

You also have to be sensible about bravery. Soldiers really get worried when a commanding officer is braver than the brave, and obviously out for a VC. Such behaviour can come from natural aggression, or from becoming 'bomb-happy' with strain, which can lead to acts of stupidity. One commanding officer in my own brigade refused, if there was shelling, to jump into a slit trench. He felt that this was undignified in front of the soldiers, and before long he was killed. I myself had no compunction about doing so. I once told General Barker, our divisional commander, when he visited our position, 'We're going to be shelled at any time, it's normal here. I shall stay with you but if you don't jump into a slit trench I'll push you in.' Refusal to get below ground, particularly in commanding officers, was plain foolhardiness – an abuse of your mission, which was to keep exercising command. If the CO is killed, demoralisation can very quickly set in; moreover, his job is, as 'father' of the battalion, to be seen by the men, to move among them, to know them and to take an interest in them. In battle, this means constant exposure visiting your forward posts and companies; it is for that daily and nightly task that the CO must conserve his courage and his life – not for reasons of pride.

Some Regular officers who were very brave used to quake at the arrival of brigade or divisional commander; they were really more scared of their future promotion prospects than was good for them. We Territorials had no 'hang-ups' in that respect. My future career didn't depend on impressing those in higher authority. I could therefore get on with my real job: getting the best out of the men.

Inside a great number of people are hidden qualities which often only war can bring out. Wisdom certainly grows with age, but in war you have to make snap, firm decisions – and the power to make them, I found, exists already from the age of 19. Young officers might be sent up to battle looking as if they had not had their first shave, yet within six months they would be commanding a company as if they'd been doing it for a decade, with great authority. Nor is there in battle any feeling amongst the older soldiers about a young officer, as long as they realise that he has leadership qualities and decision of mind and really cares for them. It is extraordinary, too, how after heavy casualties private soldiers can suddenly become corporals and sergeants, and cope with their new responsibilities.

In battle, the colonel exercises command through his company commanders, so he has to know them well, their strengths as well as their weaknesses. Some are good at holding out in difficult situations, but ponderous and slow in attack, or poor at getting the best out of the supporting arms. If you have an excellent company commander with plenty of dash and who doesn't need his hand held, of course, you tend to overwork him; there are others who want half their orders written for them. And after casualties you must be able very quickly to assess the suitability of your surviving officers for new positions. Just as important as a top-class company commander is the battalion adjutant, the chief staff officer. I was fortunate to have two excellent adjutants running the HQ Company, doing the administration, organising food and supplies, as vital in war as in peace.

Then there is the chaplain. It is essential that padre and commanding officer get on well together, for a first-class padre is as essential to the morale of the battalion as the CO, particularly if he too is battleworthy. Some of the quietest padres I met were the bravest, and had a profound influence on the men. On the whole, men are less frightened of death and wounding than of letting themselves down in front of their comrades. They need to know that the padre will see that prayers are said over them and their families are comforted – a job also shared with the company commander or even the battalion commander, depending how much time he has.

During the war I had three chaplains serving with me. The first, at the beginning of the war, was a Roman Catholic. As we retreated towards Dunkirk I suggested that we hold a short service in memory of those we'd left behind, either dead, wounded or prisoners of war, before we broke up or met whatever was waiting for us on the beaches of Dunkirk. The padre said, 'Yes, I think it's a very good idea, I'll have a service for Catholics and if you Protestants want to stand and watch at a respectful distance, I will have no objection.' I was deeply shocked. 'Surely you're the chaplain of the battalion?' I said. 'Oh no, no,' he answered, 'I'm a chaplain of the brigade and I go to the other battalions of the brigade if they want a Catholic service. I just happen to be attached to you.'

Later, in the Normandy bridgehead, I had a man who was quite different, having won the MC already at Dunkirk. And when I went to the Duke of Wellingtons the very remarkable padre was Stephen Chase, the most gentle of men, yet brave as a lion in rescuing wounded. I really had to keep my eye on him. When I told him that his attempts to fetch in the wounded were a great strain on me, and that there were stretcher-bearers, he said, 'Colonel, I am attached to you for rations and transport, but otherwise I am under Higher Authority.'

In my experience church parades, if held in the open and with a certain amount of military ritual (we always had a band playing in England before D-day) always attracted good public attendances. In fact, as part of my plans for battalion entertainment at the end of the war, I illicitly arranged for a three-tonner to go home and fetch the band's instruments and red uniforms from store. We had a nucleus of the band who were stretcher-bearers and a colour-sergeant who was a half-trained band master. Within weeks we had several thousand Germans turning up to our performances in Gevelsberg. Suddenly an army edict was issued ending compulsory church parades. The Sunday afterwards only about ten people attended the service.

I was rather irate. I felt that if ever a padre deserved a decent congregation, it was Stephen Chase. He was a deeply active Christian, caring for the battalion and families, in every possible way, and his sermons were always very moving. I was anxious as to the effect this snub would have on him. On the following Sunday, therefore, I went round all the barrack rooms, saying, 'Now, come on, I'm going to church and I think you should make the effort, too, if for no other reason than that, if you had been killed, you all wanted to be buried by him. Don't look round to see who else is going, have the courage to make your own decisions.' That way I managed to turn out several hundred men, and we kept it going every Sunday until Stephen Chase was demobilised. But the problem was one I would find myself up against time and time again in later life, with trade unions and in so many other areas, this British fear of being your own man, always looking round to see if someone else is going to lead.

The other non-combatant officer who is vital to the well-being of a battalion is the doctor – and many successful partnerships have been forged between padre and MO. In battle, ambulances would come up to collect the wounded. In the meantime, one doctor had to cope. I have seen 200 people lying on stretchers waiting to be tended. Of course, if the colonel in charge of the field ambulance was any good he would realise the extent of the casualties in a battalion area and would send up more doctors.

Montgomery always insisted that field hospitals should be as far forward as possible, because of the effect that nurses had on the men's morale. He used to visit field hospitals, but he told me it was bad for him, because it could sap one's resolution, as a commander, to see too many casualties. Of course, in Normandy, thanks to field-ambulance aircraft, wounded could be patched up and flown to places like Southampton where there was a full medical service. Field hospitals in the bridgehead were being shelled all the time, and the nurses would be in slit trenches, but emergency operations, of course, had to go on.

At a battalion level in the thick of the fighting, the problem was different: how you were going to get reinforcements to replace the wounded. Though I have mentioned one instance of lost nerve it is extraordinary, looking back, how few cases we had, even during the very heavy casualty period in Normandy. I think we learned a lot of lessons from the first world war, with its eternal trench duty: then it was held to be almost essential to have the threat of execution hanging over a man if he failed to do his duty. We were much more mobile, and, didn't have all the horrors of having to operate in two or three feet of rat-ridden mud. Once or twice drivers who had to bring up the food in darkness, night after night, said they'd had enough: you just gave them a couple of days' rest, trying to forestall trouble – getting them a bath and clean clothes, the respite of an army entertainment if it was available, a little peace to write letters home. I think in our war we were a lot better at man management.

Sex was always a problem. As a result the CO was faced with some awkward problems, sometimes more awkward than fighting the Germans. I had never, for instance, encountered homosexuality. It was the rule, when overseas, that the men could write one 'green' letter a week which was censored at base, thus avoiding the embarrassment of its being read by their officer. One day in Iceland a Military Police sergeant came up from base with a letter which he wanted me to read. It was from a Private Smith to some stoker in the Royal Navy giving very great detail about what they were going to do together when eventually they got leave. Having led a quiet life, my knowledge of buggery was nil. It was a great shock. The sergeant said a charge would have to be prepared against the man.

I summoned the platoon commander and asked him what he knew of Private Smith, whether he'd noticed anything exceptional. 'No, no, he's quite a good soldier, quite harmless' – it was obvious that Lieutenant S was on the same level of ignorance as I was. There was nothing for it but to send for Private Smith myself, not on daily orders, but privately. I said, 'It's one thing your having a love affair with this stoker, but what is going on in your barrack room? Are there people like you in your platoon or your section?'

'Oh no, absolutely not!' he answered. 'For a start,' he said, 'I rather feel that if they knew this was going on I would get bashed to death.' He was not a northcountryman or a pitman. I said, 'Have you had any relations with any of the officers?' He was utterly indignant and said no, it was a personal affair. I was satisfied from our long talk that he was not a corrupting influence, and I refused to put him on a charge, but once back in England I carefully had him transferred. This incident made me much more aware of the problem. I had to talk to all the officers without naming Private Smith, and I had a talk with the regimental doctor.

Heterosexual problems could be just as difficult, however. While the fighting was going on I don't recall a single case of VD. The biggest problem was what the wives and sweethearts might be getting up to while the boys were away. A soldier might suddenly get a letter from his wife saying that she'd run off with an American or that she could not wait for him to return. The padre would discuss it with me and sometimes we would ask for investigations at home, after which I would recommend seven or ten days' compassionate leave to see if the soldier could talk his wife out of it. The army was very sensible about this, at least once the first weeks of fighting in Normandy were over and the bridgehead had been securely established. Quite a number of broken marriages were patched up by a man's going on leave. But you needed a very good combination of the padre and the CO to decide what action to take. If you were over-generous about it, you lost your fighting strength. But you can imagine the problem for a soldier if he got a letter from his wife saying she was pregnant by another man: he'd be a pretty useless soldier until it was sorted out.

Once the war was over it was the other way round; how to send your soldiers home in a clean condition. One of my personal staff went to Paris and afterwards wrote to his wife that he'd been egged on by his pals to visit a brothel; though it was too early to know, he might have VD. It must have been a thirty or forty-page letter, full of shame, and saying that if the tests proved positive he would expect her to divorce him or he would shoot himself. It was a serious case because this man was no fool. I decided I must talk to him about the letter, and said, 'I strongly advise you to tear it up. Let's await events and then see. It doesn't happen every time and there are some things you have to keep within your breast in life, and I think this is going to be one of them.' I added, 'I'm sure you'll be all right, you may have found someone who was clean.' He looked at me with reddened eyes. I said, 'I think it's time for me to take action'; and I tore the letter to shreds. 'It's the right course,' I assured him. And he never got VD. I later met his wife, and I had one or two letters from him after he was demobilised saying he could never thank me enough.

It is a bigger problem when a fellow-officer actually catches the disease. In one such case I immediately ordered the officer home to the regimental depot. He had to have hospital treatment, and I felt it was impossible to have that in the battalion, if I was to maintain its esprit de corps. He was a brave officer, who had the Military Cross – but an officer must show an example.

As far as the men were concerned I talked to the whole sergeants' mess, appealing to them for their support and example. About two weeks afterwards I was told that the RSM had been found dead – he had shot himself. I went straight to his quarters and saw there a letter addressed to me expressing his deep regret and saying he didn't wish to go into his reasons, but the doctor would confirm why he'd done it. I had already sent for the MO, to whom I said, 'You'd better examine him very closely to see whether he's got VD.' I assumed that in view of my line on responsibility, the RSM just dared not face life. But the doctor said, 'There's nothing there.' The man shot himself prematurely; certainly nothing had yet manifested itself.

When I gave evidence at the brigade court of inquiry I was, as the phrase now goes, economical with the truth. I did not disclose that he'd left a letter for me. I just said that his was a pure and simple case of utter exhaustion, that it had all got too much for him and he'd shot himself. This ensured his widow got his pension. I wrote to her saying he'd been through so much fighting, and then the responsibility of running the garrison, that it had become too much. And I let it be known in the battalion that the RSM had just got overworried. In fact, he'd never spoken to the doctor about his problem. To this day I've no means of knowing for certain; but his case has helped ensure that in business life, I've always tried to be alert to those colleagues who were obviously having home or financial problems. People may actually shoot themselves, and you then feel the most awful responsibility yourself.

In all these matters there was no text book, so far as I know, for infantry battalion commanders – you just muddled on. The Army would say that the main job of the commander is to get on to the objective but, in retrospect, it seemed a gap which might have been filled. As it was, we Territorials had to work by instinct. The Regulars had some of this drilled into them, though often in a rather stereotyped way, and did not always realise they were now part of a citizen army whose front-line soldiers were longing for it all to end – fortunately not without a sense of humour about it all.

I remember one very dark night I was checking that the front-line men were alert. We were very near to the V1 launching sites in Holland. Suddenly one came over with its spluttering engine, and flames indicated an imminent fall to the ground. For a moment it seemed that it would hit the forward posts themselves. There was a short revival, though, and it actually came down at a point everyone judged to be the battalion headquarters. The cheers could be heard back to the Channel. The lads had no idea I was with them enjoying the fun.

# CHAPTER EIGHT

✵

# PEACE-KEEPING
# IN GERMANY

SINCE THERE WERE NOW NO GERMAN POLICE, PART OF OUR ROLE AS occupying troops was to maintain law and order in the Ruhr. Training continued, in order to marry the experience of the veterans with the newcomers from home, most of them very green aged 18 or 19. Of course, at the start of the occupation no one realised what tensions there would be with the Russians, although the brutality of their officers towards Russian PoWs in our zone soon astonished our men. There were several cases where Russian troops misunderstood an order; the officer would draw his revolver and shoot them. At that time our troops had a certain respect for the Russian army and, perhaps, for the Soviet system. But the brutality of these commissars, and the slaughter of the PoWs later when they were repatriated, often just after they'd got across the border, was grotesque. We had no inkling ourselves at that stage; we put them on lorries which went to the railhead and had no idea what was going to happen to them.

Our occupation area, the Kreis of Gevelsburg, was the size of a small English county. In it we had every sort of refugee, slave worker, PoW and displaced person. Our first task was to start sorting them out. The Poles were mad for revenge and desperate for food, and the battalion was out on patrol every evening with radios, trying to protect the German villages and isolated farmhouses from being raided by them – raping any female between 12 and 70 wherever they went. Some of them had been away from home for six years. We had to try to collect them into camps or German barracks, and put a guard on them so they couldn't get out at night.

It was also decided to concentrate practically all the Yugoslavs in my battalion area. At various times I had between twenty and forty thousand, practically all Regulars of the Royalist Army. I had about forty generals, including the Chief of the General Staff, and almost all were either aristocrats or from families with a long tradition of military service. As a result, the Yugoslav troops were well-officered and caused no problem to us or the Germans; the difficulties arose in connection with their homegoing. Once a week, at night, I used to get all the senior Yugoslav officers together and, through an interpreter, give them a description of how the war in the West had gone. Their questions were always very much to the point, and by common agreement among them avoided awkward political points such as why we had switched our support to Tito. Then King Peter came out from England and they all cheered him at a parade. He was a weak-looking character who seemed to like his liquor, judging by the quantity he consumed in the two days he was in our area.

I discussed with officers from the British civil side what was to become of these Yugoslavs. Various suggestions were made that as soon as barracks could be got ready for them they would be brought to England. It was also suggested that the Canadian and American governments, and even the Australian, were ready to take a certain number. However, several of the generals came to me one night and said that they were going back to Yugoslavia, they were so desperate to see their families. I didn't want to get into a political discussion, but I felt certain that if they did they would be shot; this was, anyway, the view of the specialists in repatriation with whom I had spoken. But some half-a-dozen decided to go it alone: they got lifts to the Yugoslav border and soon news filtered back that they had indeed been shot. After that, any heroics were at an end. I have to say I was very impressed by them – partly because I never had so many generals saluting me.

As for the Germans, we found no concentration camps in our area, but we did have a number of manufacturing plants which had been run on slave labour. What I saw at one steelworks was frightful enough; two or three hundred living skeletons locked up in a barrack room which might have taken a dozen men in the British Army. There were a couple of pails, hardly any food, and they were just dying where they stood.

I sent for the German manager of the plant, and demanded his explanation. He said, 'I was totally unaware of it, totally unaware. My job was to run the factory, somebody else marched in the labour every morning. I never came to see this, it was not my job.' I became very angry with him: 'Surely you must have realised people were dying?' I took out my revolver, not to shoot him, just to hit him with it. Then I suddenly pulled myself together and realised it wouldn't have done any good. The answer, whenever I asked the burgomasters to explain, was always 'We didn't know', or that it was a military thing.

At the start of the occupation, of course, there was a policy of strict non-fraternisation and I would speak to the burgomasters only weekly – meetings that were largely taken up by protests about how their citizens were being looted and raped. One couldn't help but say at the first meeting, 'We didn't start the war, this is what you brought on yourselves,' for the manner in which they had treated their subject 'races' was now being visited on them with a vengeance. But as things settled down, once we got the displaced persons into camps, the problem became one of organisation on such a large scale. Sometimes Nazis were brought in by other citizens; we simply conveyed them to central depots to be handled by our civil side – for very quickly, you had to come to terms with your priorities. Keeping the battalion, or very often, the whole brigade, up to scratch was my prime responsibility.

After the first world war men had been so desperate to get home that there were mutinies in which officers were killed, including one or two generals. As a result, we were advised to be wary. In fact, we started demobilisation very quickly, all things considered, and I do not recall anyone, soldier, NCO or officer, ever complaining to me that the system was unfair. What *was* unfair was the Customs duty we had to pay when we arrived in the home port. Because I had the badges of a lieutenant-colonel I had eventually to pay full duty on a single bottle of liqueur – all that I brought back, after two years of continuous fighting and occupation duty. Fortunately, they were less hard on the private soldier – but it certainly reminded you that there were going to be no concessions or perks just because you'd risked your life on behalf of those at home.

In the meantime our 49th Division, as a long-established Territorial formation, was kept up to full strength, whereas many of the wartime divisions melted away. To keep the battalion up to scratch as a military unit I ordered quite a lot of drill. It was taking something of a chance, for most of the Territorials had been in uniform for five years and weren't anxious to become Guardsmen, but I always found that, on the whole, the troops rather enjoyed drill when it was well done, with a good sergeant-major. Once a week I gave a prize for the best company drill, and I organised varied training with scope for the imagination – sending companies and platoons off in vehicles, doing imitation terrorist-operation exercises, and holding shooting competitions. With the spring, we started a great deal of sport. I also organised entertainment by night, and as demobilisation approached, prepared the men by day for civilian life. With three officers who had been schoolteachers we worked very hard on vocational training – a man could do a month's course as a motor mechanic, or plumber, bricklayer and so on.

My battalion became a showpiece of resettlement and entertainment throughout the Occupation Army, so that all the newspaper correspondents who were sent out to see what the Army was doing in Germany ended up with me – General Martin, military correspondent of the *Daily Telegraph*, and Joe Illingworth of the *Yorkshire Post* and others. I wrote to various publishers and got books sent out. I suppose it was all of a piece with my Scouting and Sunday School past. I worked very hard and got very tired – and that's when the migraine emerged.

I had, truth be told, just about had enough. The Scottish doctor who'd been with me through most of the war said, 'You are absolutely worn out. You're the only CO who's fought right through, from the beginning to the end, left in the division; you've put in all this effort – what's the point of staying on for another month?'

The divisional commander therefore consented to my going home a month before my official demobilisation at York. Our own Brigadier Henry Wood had been posted to the War Office and I had been commanding the Brigade Group until his successor, a Regular, arrived from the Far East. I met him only once but I knew there was going to be a clash which would probably finish with me in the guard room because I thought him so insensitive in dealing with the men. It was a civilian army; I had always been able to get soldiers to tell me everything about themselves, either singly or in groups – I suppose this is where my journalistic training came in. I'd have a beer with them at night and ask them what they thought of things, and explain the problems, taking a chance that most Regular officers would never dare to do. In my view, this was part of the CO's job. I'd been with them quite a time. Those who'd been in action knew me as their battle commander, knew my motives were genuine, that my concern was with their welfare – which is why later, during all the troubles in Fleet Street, I was so deeply disappointed that whenever you built a bridge of trust and understanding with the printers on the shop floor, the political activists came along and kicked it over.

I got a great deal out of that period in Germany, having to handle a transitional period from war to peace. For many of the men the second world war would be, in retrospect, the peak of their lives: the comradeship, the willingness to help others, risking one's life to do so, and the fact that we were all fighting for a common goal, understandable to all. Later, the wreckers in the factories were able to say, 'All you're working for is the boss to have a Bentley, a yacht and three mistresses. . . .' I do, in fact, feel it is an outrage for the boss to go to the factory in a Rolls Royce, to dine only in posh executive dining rooms; the success of Japanese firms shows that the opposite approach is much to be preferred.

It was a terrible wrench to leave my uniformed family. Nearly two hundred men had preceded me in previous weeks and a great number had written to me saying they had settled into civilian life. Now, in March 1946, it was my turn to go. I had asked my second-in-command to arrange for me to slip away from the battalion very quietly. I thought I could. But suddenly, from behind nearby houses and a requisitioned school the whole battalion appeared and the band was playing 'Auld Lang Syne'. I didn't – I couldn't – stop; I waved farewell.

The demobilisation boat decanted us at Harwich. I hurried down the station platform. Suddenly a Customs officer moved forward from behind a pillar. I declared my bottle of Benedictine, paid up and boarded the train. I was home from the wars.

# CHAPTER NINE

# FLEET STREET

IN ONE STRIDE I STEPPED DOWN FROM BEING A LIEUTENANT-COLONEL commanding a thousand men, sometimes an entire brigade, to being a reporter and feature writer in Newcastle; from £2,000 a year to £400 – or £8 a week. It was a considerable climbdown, particularly with a wife and three children to support, two of them twins I hadn't seen since their birth before D-day. Even my eldest son stared at me when I arrived at our house in Alnmouth, and asked, 'Who are you?'

I didn't last long as a post-war reporter for the Kemsley papers in Newcastle. Trying desperately to remember the maximum number of words permissible in the opening paragraph, I penned a series of feature articles on contemporary themes and historical subjects relating to Northumberland. I got interviews with VIPs and found my recent military rank a great advantage. But was it the right career after almost eight years of command, from second lieutenant to acting brigadier?

I considered going to university. But with three children and a fourth expected, this seemed a financially frightening prospect. Meanwhile I was offered a staff post on the Manchester *Evening Chronicle* at £12 a week, with the prospect of eventual editorship. While I was debating whether or not to accept, a telephone call came through from London. It was from the office of Lord Kemsley himself. I was told to report there the following morning. Taking the sleeper, I obeyed. Lord Kemsley needed a new Personal Assistant, and Lady Kemsley recalled hearing of me on a visit to Newcastle years earlier. After a brief talk it was clear that he wanted me for the job. 'How much did they pay you in the army?' he asked. I told him two thousand pounds a year. 'Well, if you were worth that to the Army,' he said, 'you're worth that to me.' Thus, literally, I moved overnight from the Newcastle *Chronicle* to the heart of Fleet Street as PA to the owner of the largest newspaper group in Britain.

Next morning I reported for duty at the grim headquarters of

Kemsley Newspapers, in an unfinished, war-damaged office block surrounded by bomb sites, in Gray's Inn Road. The arrangement was that I would go home to Alnwick for a long weekend each fortnight, until I found a house. In the meantime, I lived in the Mount Royal Hotel. Lord Kemsley had a private secretary (Major Botterill) and a social secretary, Miss E.V. Morgan, who handled most of his entertaining. The entrance to Kemsley House used by the family and the senior staff was a dingy door in Coley Street, where the commissionaire would be warned by telephone – usually at about 9.45 am –that Lord Kemsley had left Chandos House, his beautiful home in Queen Anne Street. From that moment the lift was held for his arrival. Some mornings he took a short walk on the way, checking whether the newsagents were carrying stocks of the *Daily Graphic*.

I was introduced that week to all the members of the Berry family on the board: Lady Kemsley; Lionel (the deputy chairman), who had been invalided out of the Army and had been a Tory MP until the 1945 Labour landslide; Denis, whose main activity seemed to relate to the group's plant and building; and Neville, who had no fixed job but had been in charge of Glasgow before the war. (Neville and I had corresponded in Germany where he had started a Guards Armoured Division newspaper and I had founded one for the 49th Division). Lord Kemsley's nephew, Ewart, whom I had known since 1938, was in charge of Newcastle. Then there were the non-family directors: Sir Robert Webber (Cardiff), W. Veitch (Aberdeen), J.R. Oldham, Eric Schofield and N.H. Booth (Withy Grove, Manchester), H.J. Staines (Sheffield), W.W. Hadley (Editor, *Sunday Times*), W.H. Teasdale (Advertising), H.N. Heywood (Editorial), E.P. Francis (Circulation) and William Mabane, a National Liberal Minister knighted and made a peer after the war and a sort of minister-without-portfolio for Kemsley.

Kemsley's daughter Pamela, the Marchioness of Huntly, who divided her time between London and Aberdeen (where Kemsley owned the two-centuries-old *Press and Journal*), and Oswald Kemsley did not join the board until the 1950s. Oswald's role was unknown to me, but he was an unhappy man who told me all he wanted to do was to run an antique shop (he was to die in a yachting accident off Cornwall after only a year or two on the board). Lady Kemsley came into the office only for board meetings – which seemed to be singularly occasional. Another son, Douglas, had been killed in Italy in the war. All had served in one or other of the Guards regiments. The youngest, Anthony, was about to go up to Christ Church, Oxford, from Eton.

Lord Kemsley's daily regime began with dealing with the post with

Major Botterill (who was rather under-employed) and Miss Morgan. The major tried to sell everyone the idea that I was under his command: as a lieutenant-colonel I soon disposed of that. Learning to cope with his lordship's newspaper and political correspondence I found that Kemsley had his own ingenious system. Much of his mail simply disappeared into a drawer on a side table – which he opened once a month. Nearly all Kemsley's correspondence, by such delay, answered itself.

Kemsley owned a vast newspaper empire; but he had become largely preoccupied with the flagship of the group, the *Sunday Times*, of which he styled himself Editor-in-Chief. The event of the week was, therefore, the newspaper's Tuesday editorial conference, which I attended from my first week. Those attending sat to the left and right of Lord Kemsley: Lionel and Neville Berry; the editor, W.W. Hadley; Valentine Heywood, managing editor; H.V. Hodson, assistant editor; Leonard Russell, literary editor; Bill Mabane; and Ian Fleming, group foreign manager, whose contribution ranged over the whole paper. It was a rather solemn affair and too much of a post mortem, as a Royal Commission on the press shortly afterwards observed. I was more than a note-taker and, from the start, was encouraged by Lord Kemsley to speak up. I was anything but shy, and the staff members were naturally sensitive to outside criticism and very anxious that the initiatives for the following week did not slip out of their hands. Territorial possessiveness and complacency were the hallmark of the *Sunday Times* at that time, and remained so until David Astor took over the editorship of the *Observer* from Ivor Brown in 1948, when its circulation started to move noticeably up, in direct competition with the *Sunday Times*.

Since the *Sunday Times* was to become, in later years, my particular 'baby', it may be as well to remind ourselves how Lord Kemsley had acquired the newspaper and, indeed, who Lord Kemsley was – for when Roy Thomson succeeded him as owner of the paper in 1959 there were many cries to the effect that a semi-literate Canadian should not be allowed to acquire the flagship of Britain's Sunday newspapers. Such people obviously had no idea of Lord Kemsley's origins, confusing his big country-house parties, his Rolls Royces and London mansion with nobility. In fact, Gomer Berry had probably been as ill-equipped by birth and education to own a great national newspaper as was Roy Thomson. Like Roy, Gomer Berry left school at 14, the son of a Merthyr Tydfil estate agent. His first job was as assistant in a haberdasher's – a fact which he tried hard in later years to cover up. His early success he owed to his elder brother, William, who had become an apprentice on the *Merthyr Tydfil Times*, and then moved to London at eighteen. Within four years William Berry had launched the *Advertising World* from a shared third-floor room in Fleet Street. It prospered, and William summoned Gomer from the haberdasher's shop to London. They could not afford to go out for meals so they bought a secondhand gas burner and cooked sausages over it, taking turns at the frying pan.

With a third brother – Seymour, who became an industrialist – all of John Matthias Berry's sons were destined to be millionaires and peers of the realm, each in his own right; a truly astonishing story of rags to riches. Meanwhile Gomer Berry's first job, under his brother's guidance, was to build up the circulation of the *Advertising World*, then to sell advertising space. After four years the Berrys sold out at a profit which enabled them to found *Boxing World* and other successful periodicals. In 1915 they bought their first real newspaper, the *Sunday Times*, founded in 1822.

After the first world war the Berry empire expanded enormously. In 1924 the brothers bought the former Hulton Group of Manchester newspapers from Lord Rothermere and, with Sir Edward Iliffe, formed Allied Newspapers. Hulton's *Daily Sketch* and *Illustrated Sunday Herald* were in due course acquired by Allied, together with newspapers in Glasgow, Sheffield, Newcastle, Middlesbrough and elsewhere. Within a handful more years, the two Berrys and Edward Iliffe had become masters of a vast periodical publishing house, the Amalgamated Press, Kelly's Directories, the *Financial Times* and, in 1927, the *Daily Telegraph*, sold to them by Lord Burnham. William Berry was elevated to Lord Camrose, Gomer Berry became Lord Kemsley and Edward Iliffe, Lord Iliffe. The Berrys had vanished, transformed as in some fairy tale into renamed peers of the realm.

Lord Kemsley parted from his brother and Lord Iliffe in 1937, six years after his second marriage – a marriage that was to have a profound effect on his career. Kemsley's first wife had died in 1928, a homely woman who bore him six children. Many times Kemsley would tell me the story of what it was like losing your wife – a nostalgia heightened by its sequel, for into the lonely widower's life drifted a beautiful divorcée, Mrs Edith Dresselhuys. Her first husband had been a Dutch diplomat; now her eye fell on the Welsh newspaper magnate, a rich, eligible widower, and she surmised that he would get a further title (brother William's barony arriving in 1929). She was both remarkably attractive and an accomplished hostess. Kemsley – reaching his fifties – fell for her. They were married in 1931 and it was largely at ex-Mrs Dresselhuys's urging that Kemsley insisted, at the last minute, on retaining possession of the *Sunday Times* – for being a woman of social ambition she saw, as Kemsley did not, how important ownership of this great national newspaper would be to their – and her – social standing. Kemsley had intended to keep only the provincial newspapers. 'But Gomer,' she said, 'if you lose the *Sunday Times* you will have no position in London. Who will you be, owning a lot of provincial newspapers?' So he became owner of the *Sunday Times*, with the agreed stipulation that Camrose's *Daily Telegraph* would print it – a contract that was to be of critical relevance to me some years later.

Kemsley was not a journalist, as we have seen. But his skills at circulation and advertising stood him in good stead. He relied on old-fashioned, able journalists to bring out the papers. In his plush offices above the private lift he could pore over the circulation, advertising and finance figures – which were never shown to anyone else in the organisation, not even the directors. Eventually this would be his downfall, but in that twilight of the age of Victorian and Edwardian newspaper barons he played his role exactly as Lady Kemsley had dreamt. At the great country estate they acquired, or his grandiose London mansion, he regularly gave dinner parties for thirty guests. The Berry sons were all in awe of their father – who held the family purse strings – and even more so, it seemed, of their stepmother. I was very fond of the eldest son, Lionel, an intelligent, reflective man of good if overcautious judgment. But his father crushed almost any initiative he took.

As a journalist myself, of course, I could not resist passing on some of the news stories which entrée to Fleet Street now brought me – particularly through my army contacts. Montgomery had recently been made Chief of the Imperial General Staff, and had an ambitious vision of a small highly-trained army, relieved by National Servicemen at home so as to be able to fight wherever required. Within weeks, I had exclusive front-page stories on defence in the *Sunday Times*, an important hurdle in getting the co-operation of its naturally suspicious staff towards the new young PA in the room next to the chairman and editor-in-chief. But in my eagerness to shine, I was working too hard.

One morning Kemsley announced, 'You are the source of great trouble between Lady Kemsley and myself.' I said I was very sorry but didn't know why that should be. 'Well, what is happening about your family coming to London?' I was still travelling up to Alnmouth every other weekend, and too busy to go house-hunting in London. Olive, with three children and a fourth on his way, could hardly be expected to come down to look for a London house either. The answer, therefore, was 'Nothing.' 'Well,' said Lord Kemsley, 'I've got to report something to Lady Kemsley tonight. Can I tell her I'm making arrangements for somebody to help you look for a house? You can have any car you want and someone will get hold of an estate agent – but you must be within ten minutes of my house in case I want you. Either we will buy you a house and rent it to you, or somehow you must rent a house and we'll pay for it until you sort yourself out; but you've got to get your family down here, otherwise I'm in trouble with Lady Kemsley.'

Arrangements were made, and a house near Hampstead Heath was found. For all this solicitude, however, Lady Kemsley had not the faintest idea of what made up a newspaper, or how it was produced. Her obsession was entertaining – which at least kept her from too much meddling. At her chosen art, she was undoubtedly highly successful. One day Olive, having joined me in London and been invited with me to Dropmore, said to her, 'How is it, Lady Kemsley, you can get thirty interesting people for dinner whenever you choose?' Lady Kemsley looked at her. 'Oh, it is quite simple. In England you hang a ham outside the back door and they all come! I have the best cook in London and the best wine; they all come.' It was true, as I can vouch. I don't think I ever went to one of those thirty-guest dinners without there being at least one, if not two, Cabinet ministers present. People on the way up *wanted* to come, wanted this opportunity to meet the luminaries of politics and the press – for the *Sunday Times* had become virtually the official organ of the Conservative Party, a national newspaper which could be counted on to support the party line with *Pravda*-like fidelity, a very powerful organ at election time or in crisis. On the way out from one of these great dinners – I think there had been thirty-six guests in the lovely dining room designed by Adam, with its Raeburns, its silver, the women in their beautiful evening gowns – I remember saying to Lord Kemsley, 'Don't you feel this is all a bit ostentatious now, after a world war, when there's still rationing?' 'If you were a Viscount you'd do it!' he snorted.

I could see, however, that there was something irritating him so I asked him what was wrong: 'Have you had the wrong people sitting next to you?' He looked at me wistfully. 'I was thinking of the dinners I used to have in the 1930s when I would look down the table and I would see eighteen men and eighteen women; each woman would be wearing a tiara, there'd probably be two princesses there . . . . All those men in beautiful white ties – that's what I would like to come back!' To me this semed incredible. 'There'd be a social revolution if you went on like that,' I said. 'And if you expected some of your literary reviewers [he always had one or two notable writers on the paper to come along and give intellectual weight] to dress up like that, there'd be a mutiny!' He looked surprised. 'Well, that's what I'd like to see back. In my view there should be a court order [by court, he meant Buckingham Palace] that we should all wear white ties.' I said, 'My goodness, Lord Kemsley, it would put me in some difficulty – we've already got to do the laundry for four children in our house.' 'Oh,' he replied, 'I just buy new shirts every week.'

Kemsley always dressed formally, even for the office – striped black silk tie and pearl tie pin. Stiff collars were worn by all his sons and I had to conform. One day, at the last minute, I put on a new tie, a present in a pleasant shade of khaki. It was not well received. 'Shades of the Desert Army?' Lionel inquired sardonically. The only exception to Kemsley's strict etiquette was Ian Fleming. He always wore blue shirts, black ties and very dark blue suits. He never conformed, thank goodness, and it relieved the stuffy atmosphere. The *Sunday Times* editorial staff were jealous and terrified of Ian's influence with the Kemsleys. 'K', as he initialled all his memoranda and as he was known behind his back throughout the organisation, boasted he never took any work home when he left at 5 in the evening, or at weekends. Every night was bridge or canasta night with Ian Fleming and Micky Renshaw, who were both to become dear and loyal friends of mine, and to die long before life had run its race for them. Stakes were always set but, in view of my lamentable distaste for card-playing, when I took part they were set at the minimum level. Micky made an enjoyable profit at card with the Kemsleys, who needed luck but often could not recognise it when it came. He and a select few – mostly women – always referred to 'K' as 'Groucho', as Kemsley had a distinct facial resemblance to the great American comic.

Though he would not take work home with him, Kemsley liked to feel in charge. Chandos House was connected to the office by teleprinter and private telephones. A news service was prepared and transmitted to him by a special Kemsley editorial staff. He greatly enjoyed reading this out to the table, the guests silenced while some important news item was arriving. These minor trappings of power were important to him, as were the elaborate efforts made to get all the London papers to him if he was abroad. It was like the court of some minor principality at which I had been appointed, so to speak, his highness's private secretary. As such, I went with him in December 1947 to South Africa, and there met a truly great man, whose integrity and moral purpose have remained to me a shining example all my life.

# CHAPTER TEN

# MEETING SMUTS

WE TRAVELLED ON THE ATHLONE CASTLE, A 25,000-TON LINER; PRINCESS Alice and her husband the Earl of Athlone were also passengers, and one of my jobs was to play deck tennis every morning with the Princess. It was my first contact with British royalty and instructive – indeed, I doubt if I would have been able, later, to employ Princess Margaret's husband at the *Sunday Times* unless I'd become acquainted with the Alice-in-Wonderland world of obsequiousness and genuflecting, beyond which are ordinary human beings. Fortunately, I had my green DLI blazer which gave me a certain ADC sort of status. The Kemsleys pursued their obsession with card games, losing more money, thanks to their poor play, than will ever be known.

But perhaps the most interesting person aboard, and the most simple and sincere, was Sir Simon Marks of Marks and Spencer. Old Thomas Spencer had been born in Middlesbrough, where his widow still lived in her nineties. Marks and Spencer had run their first stalls in Leeds market, she told me after the trip, wheeling their own barrows with the motto 'Don't ask the price – it's a penny'. Since those days in the 1890s the firm had grown into the most extraordinary retailing chain ever known in Britain, with Simon Marks at its helm. Of all those I have met he was the most outstanding as an employer. I learned a great deal from him – though there was a profound difference between our problems, in that he never had trade-union troubles. Later on I got him to give talks on humanity in industry and what was wrong with management in this country. When I told Lord Kemsley what we had been discussing so animatedly on our perambulations, he dismissed it as 'bunk' – which, sadly, was to prove the case in Fleet Street where generations of inter-union rivalry and obsession with the pecking order simply destroyed hopes of modernisation, expansion and goodwill between employers and employed.

Another passenger on this voyage was Lord Norman, the controversial Governor of the Bank of England. In these days of supersonic travel such chances to meet and get to know some of the most distinguished men and women of the age have become rare. I wasn't awed – responsibility for the lives of a thousand men or more in battle quickly washes off the make-up – but I was intrigued. My horizons were enlarging daily and if Lord and Lady Kemsley were stuffy, indeed tedious, figures to others, I shall always owe them a debt of gratitude for putting out the carriage step for an ex-Middlesbrough High School boy feeling his way in Fleet Street and the wider world. In South Africa, however, an even greater encounter was in store: with the Prime Minister, Jan Christian Smuts.

It was my privilege to be befriended by Field-Marshal Smuts, only two years before he died, and a matter of months before his extraordinary demise as Prime Minister in the South African general election of May 1948. He had once invited the Kemsleys to visit South Africa and therefore considered us his guests when we arrived in Capetown. He overwhelmed me with his vitality, austerity, incorruptibility and statesmanlike vision. He had devoted his life to the healing of divisions between English and Afrikaner communities in South Africa after the Boer War – in which he'd fought against the British. As a lieutenant-general he had next helped the British to conquer German South-West Africa, and to evict German troops from East Africa. He had been a member of Lloyd George's War Cabinet, an organiser of the Royal Air Force in its metamorphosis from an army flying corps, and later a British field-marshal advising Churchill on strategy in the second world war – in fact it was Smuts who, as Prime Minister, had ensured that South Africa supported Britain rather than Hitler. After the war he had written the preamble to the Charter of the United Nations  a man stamped with integrity and firmness of character, a man as unforgettable as Monty in his wiry, bony physique, his steel-blue eyes and the current of seemingly electric energy driving him from early morning to his early nights.

Smuts had come to Capetown from Pretoria only forty-eight hours before our arrival – for the Union of South Africa in 1910 had exacted, as its price, a system of moveable government administration by which Parliament sat in each city for six months. We had been invited to stay at Smuts's Capetown house – the Groote Schuur estate bequeathed by Cecil Rhodes as official residence of the Prime Minister of the Union in 1910. Amid perfect lawns ringed with hydrangeas in bloom, it stood in a magnificent setting before Table Mountain. Smuts himself allocated the bedrooms, I remember. Lord Kemsley was placed in Rhodes's old bedroom. I was put next door 'so he can growl at you,' Smuts explained. There was no running water (though hot water was produced for shaving). We ate lunch off Chelsea china with the Union crest in a dining room that could seat twenty-four; a simple meal with much fruit.

'It is a benign country,' were Smuts's first words to me as we admired the landscape, 'though it has seen much spilling of blood.' By 'benign' Smuts was referring to the climate and soil, which made farming so extensive and profitable, not to speak of the fabulous mineral wealth below. Smuts's range of conversation was awesome. He scarcely ever referred to internal South African matters – what exercised his mind were the affairs of the world: its literature, its international relations, the business of war. George VI had visited South Africa the previous winter. 'The war has worn him out', Smuts observed of the King – thirty years his junior. 'The weather in England was appalling while he was here and the King, of course, fretted at being away from home, not sharing the hardships of his people in the way he'd done all through the war.'

In spite of sympathy of this kind, Smuts retained the ruthless clarity of his legal and military apprenticeship. He woke me at 5.30 to take me with him around the grounds (his habitual quasi-botanical perambulation), wearing his battledress. I photographed him like this – and the photograph not only became his favourite, but remains to this day in his farmhouse-home near Pretoria.

Not only did Smuts still dominate all conversation despite his 76 years, but all conversation halted at 6 o'clock when he turned on the radio to listen to the BBC news bulletin, relayed by the Capetown radio station. No matter who was staying in the house, the BBC News took precedence, and was usually followed by lively comment and discussion. Smuts said that the motto which most guided his everyday life was an Arab one: 'The dogs may bark but the caravan moves on' – observing shrewdly, that unless one learned to ignore unfair criticism, one was lost, in spirit and often in health. He himself seemed immune to low spirits. Unlike Churchill he appeared to suffer no 'black dog' moments, but like Monty woke each day refreshed and ready for battle. He often talked of Lloyd George and of Churchill – though he refused to be drawn when I suggested that Churchill's captors during the Boer War might well have been relieved, even prepared to turn a blind eye, at the escape of a war correspondent who had been caught carrying arms and was thus liable to execution by firing squad.

Smuts had organised an extensive tour for us, often with himself as guide. We visited Stellenbosch, his birthplace, with its traditional Dutch architecture and the university he had attended and where he had met his wife before going on to Cambridge and a double first in law. Everywhere Smuts went he was called the 'General' – save by political opponents who nicknamed him 'Slim Jannie' for his cunning. The truth was that with one exception, that of his tragically short-lived political heir, Dr J.H. Hofmeyr, Smuts outmanoeuvred and outshone all his parliamentary colleagues by his intelligence, his stamina, and his ability to marshal his facts on great issues. 'Remember, politics is the art of the possible,' he would say, quoting Bismarck.

Societies do not follow great men indefinitely, however. Churchill had called a general election in Britain before the war against Japan was over. To his surprise, and indeed chagrin, Churchill was defeated – and in the spring of 1948, following our visit, Smuts would go the same way, even losing his own parliamentary seat. In both cases, they brought their countries through a world war but then, in their seventies, found themselves out of touch with the grass roots of democracy. Yet I accompanied Smuts on several visits to constituents that winter, in Stellenbosch and elsewhere, and heard him 'sounding out' local political feeling; moreover I was present when Lord Kemsley entertained five of South Africa's senior newspaper editors in April 1948 in London – and the only question was the size of the likely increase in majority for Smuts's United Party. Certainly none gave any inkling that he might lose.

Meanwhile, after a tour of the Kimberley mines and surrounding veldt, we stayed with Smuts again at his farm at Irene, a small township near Pretoria. Smuts had flown home to be with his wife – a small, three-quarter-size lady with early French ancestors, curly hair and blue eyes. In native language she was known as 'Ouma', and he as 'Oubaas'. They had lived on the farm since the Boer War. In all she had given birth to nine children. She refuted my suggestion (based on rumour) that some of her children had died in a Boer-War British concentration camp; in fact she had been held under house arrest in Pietermaritzburg for a year-and-a-half while Smuts played serious havoc as a Boer commando in the veldt. Perhaps it was this early military experience which gave rise to our friendship, bridging almost fifty years between our ages. One day, in the car, I confided to him that I still found it impossible to pass a settlement or geographical feature without asking myself how I would attack it – a wartime habit that was hard to kick. To my astonishment he said he still found himself making the same mental study half-a-century after his commando raiding was over.

Smuts's farmhouse reflected the man. Originally it had been a British officers' mess, part of Kitchener's headquarters at Middelburg in the Transvaal. When the Boer War was over Smuts bought it from 'the enemy' and re-erected it at Irene: a square, single-storey residence with eleven bedrooms and a broad stoep or veranda. The roof was made of corrugated iron, giving it a somewhat shack-like appearance. He'd intended to build a more modern farmhouse farther up the hill with a better view, he said, but had never had the time – or the money. He never accepted offers of financial help and even the £300 he paid the British for the building came from his fees as a young lawyer.

Until late in life he would sleep on the stoep outside his bedroom, on a narrow hard bed with a kitchen chair as his bedside table. Mrs Smuts's bedroom was as narrow as a ship's cabin, with a simple army-issue iron bedstead. The pride of the house was, of course, Smuts's library – some 10,000 volumes, now at the University of Witwaters-rand.

At Doornkloof, and again at Johannesburg in the ensuing weeks, I was able to talk at length with Smuts. He did not see racial problems between black and white as being the great problem in South Africa. Rather, it was the tension within the white community. 'The white man alone created our dilemma,' were his exact words. 'The Dutch and the Hottentots arrived in the Cape almost simultaneously. Then the British took over with greater resources.' This capitalisation of South Africa had brought great wealth but, equally, great problems. 'The situation today with all its perils was not created by God when he created the earth and its first peoples,' he commented. 'It is no good expecting God to sort out something that is not of His making. It is beyond the capacity of Parliament as it stands in South Africa today to find a ready-made quick solution which will please everyone. We must await the pace of events.' He had himself brought about the enfranchisement of the Coloureds, and certainly his deputy, Mr Hofmeyr, took the view that before long moderate blacks must be allowed to vote – a controversial attitude which led to calls for his resignation, all strongly resisted by Smuts himself who saw in Hofmeyr his gifted successor. Certainly Smuts himself was an enemy of apartheid – an arbitrary and unnatural segregation of races.

Because we were the guests of the Unionist Prime Minister, Lord Kemsley refused to meet any Nationalist politicians. So when invited to meet the editor of a Nationalist daily newspaper, *Die Burger*, he declined – but sent me in his stead. The discourtesy of the Nationalist journalists came as a considerable shock to me. They spoke Afrikaans with each other at table and clearly disliked the fact that I'd spent more years fighting the Germans than in journalism – for South Africa's decision to enter the war on Churchill's side in 1939 by only one vote and the subsequent arrest of politicians who supported Germany had been deeply unpopular in Afrikaner circles. Even the shy, agreeable general manager declared his hobby to be the devotion 'of every spare moment to finding new evidence of British atrocities in the Boer War'. When I inquired 'And Boer atrocities?' he shook with rage.

The Nationalists duly won the general election. On both occasions when Smuts subsequently visited England I met him. He was appalled by the Nationalist Dr Malan's approach, as his successor, to the white-and-black equation, but his chief concern still lay in the higher sphere of international relations, especially in the gathering Cold War. Hofmeyr's death in November 1948 at the age of 54 was an ominous tragedy for liberalism in South Africa. For Smuts personally it followed a domestic tragedy: the death from meningitis of his eldest son Japie – who had won a double first in engineering at Cambridge – in October 1948. 'So fine in character, so brilliant in intellectual promise,' Smuts wrote to me. For him character was of greater value than ability – 'I regard character as one of the great values of life. You can buy ability, but character is something quite different' he once said of Hofmeyr.

Many years later I paid my own respects to Smuts's memory by taking Olive to Doornkloof, which had thankfully been bought by the ex-servicemen of South Africa and made into a museum. We saw Mrs Smuts's handwritten calendar with the date of birth of each of her children and grandchildren. Through Japie's name she had drawn a sad line. I remembered again Smuts's letter: 'We cannot but accept in silence and pass on. My wife was stunned but is now her cheerful self again.'

'Oubaas' had died in 1950, 'Ouma' in 1954. It was now 1981. In the main drawing room hung the photograph I had taken of Smuts in the garden at Groote Schuur. I told the caretaker the story. It was the middle of the morning and I asked for three teas and three buns. 'But there are only two of you,' she protested. 'The third is for my driver' – a splendid well turned-out man, highly knowledgeable about the area, – I explained. 'If he is black then I cannot serve him,' she warned. I told her Smuts would have been shattered to know of such a thing happening in his house. 'That may be so,' she replied, 'but if I agreed and someone saw it happen, we could be arrested . . . .' It was a sad commentary on how low South Africa had sunk since the death of Smuts – in my opinion the greatest statesman, after Churchill, of the twentieth century.

I remember when Smuts was visiting London, he was without secretarial help; I lent him the services of my very able personal secretary. When Smuts – who accepted requests to make speeches throughout the world 'if the occasion appeals to me and I can write the outline of the speech within 48 hours and lay it aside' – departed, he gave my Miss McPhail a handsome cheque, with a note of apology: 'I am not a good shopper.' But for Miss McPhail, the chance to meet and be of service to a man of such human dignity and character was in itself sufficient; she never cashed the cheque, preferring to keep it with its signature.

Smuts was certainly an inspiration, and the trip with Kemsley to South Africa, after the sombre years of war and post-war rationing, a tonic. Beside the greatness of character Smuts and his wife displayed, the Kemsleys were, I suppose, a superficial pair. But Kemsley listened indulgently to the ideas I poured forth concerning his newspaper organisation, while Lady Kemsley, with her still-heavy French accent, remained a snob with extraordinary charm, and sometimes touching solicitude – 'I like Gomer to have two freshly cooked vegetables with every meal,' she declared. She judged other women in the same fashion – 'by the creases in their husband's trousers'. Of a certain couple, in which there was a rather domineering wife, she remarked contemptuously, 'He lives in his wife's navel,' unaware of any irony, given the manner in which Gomer deferred to her.

He deferred, but was never her pawn. She had saved him from surrendering the *Sunday Times* when the newspaper empire was divided between the Berry brothers, and she certainly ensured that he enjoyed the full prestige which London newspaper ownership gave him. Without her he could not have acted the grandee of Fleet Street. In that respect, she was indispensable to him.

The journey home, in the spring of 1948, brought to an end a memorable trip. As we reached the final stretch, with the ship steaming up Southampton Water, Lady Kemsley asked me to accompany her on deck. From her handbag she produced a Bible. 'I want you to take an oath,' she began. Surprised, I agreed. 'You have seen my passport,' she said. 'You therefore now know my true age. Swear on the Holy Bible that you will never reveal it!'

# CHAPTER ELEVEN

# TRAINING KEMSLEY'S
# JOURNALISTS

LORD KEMSLEY WAS NOT A VERY CLEVER MAN. SOME YEARS BEFORE THE war, one of his cronies had unwisely suggested that every Kemsley newspaper should bear an emblem of the group. Thus, 'A Kemsley Newspaper' appeared beneath every one of our titles. In post-war socialist Britain this was like holding a red rag to a bull. Herbert Morrison brought the matter up in Parliament and by 1947 a Royal Commission on the Press was set up and for the next two years took evidence.

Since part of my job was to help draft all Kemsley's articles, speeches and memoranda, I soon had to advise him on how to face the Royal Commission. In turn this gave me an unexpected leverage, after only a year with Kemsley, to do something revolutionary. I was disturbed that, as in the British army before Montgomery took a hold, there was virtually no organised training. As Monty would have said, there was no plan, no policy, journalists just drifted into battle. But with Kemsley very much on the defensive before the Royal Commission, I was able to suggest a scheme which, at any other time, he would have slipped into the side drawer in the hope that it would go away. Thus, the Kemsley Editorial Training Plan was born. It was expensive, it demanded enormous energy, effort and concentration, but it laid the foundations of professional training in journalism, being taken up and copied not only by all the press in Britain, but in many foreign countries too. Having started as the chief whipping boy of the Royal Commission – owner of the 'gramophone press' in Herbert Morrison's phrase – Kemsley emerged the standard-bearer of his profession.

It was not an easy metamorphosis, but I was certain it would work. During the war every Regular and Territorial officer, and thousands of conscripted leaders had to be trained and troops prepared to meet the most efficient soldiers in the West, the Germans. It was achieved by a

brilliant system of training potential leaders, specially selected – often to
their astonishment – for rapid promotion. If the army succeeded, why
shouldn't journalism, too? I was a missionary-cum-evangelist, with
much resistance and derision from the pre-war ranks who had not been
in uniform.

The plan was unique in concept anywhere. It consisted of four parts,
three covering editors, executives and qualified members of staffs, and
one covering regular courses for juniors and new entrants. The plan had
its own finely printed magazine, and a regular editorial competition
which I supervised, in which members of staff received commendations
and cash awards for outstanding work. It encouraged the interchange of
editors and visits abroad. Soon it became evident that a textbook was
needed and I organised and edited one, *The Kemsley Manual of Journalism*,
the product of a team of newspapermen, in the aftermath of a world war,
which was to become the standard work on our profession. W.L.
Andrews, editor of the *Yorkshire Post*, later wrote of 'one of the most
momentous changes in the practice of journalism . . . the change from
the casual way of learning journalism without clear standards of what to
master, to the discipline and curricula of the Kemsley Editorial
Plan . . . .' Senior staff were trained to undertake managerial responsibility, while courses for executives below the rank of editor helped create
a pool of journalists fully equipped to take over the most senior editorial
posts. General reporters, sub-editors, sports staff and photographers
were covered by a course that concentrated on the nuts-and-bolts of the
editorial scene, from copy-handling to typography, with insights into
advertising and circulation. Alone among newspaper groups Kemsley
had tackled the problems not only of in-house training for journalists
who wished to rise in their profession, but also of educating entrants to
the newspaper business, setting a pattern to the world.

We offered Kemsley scholarships for Commonwealth journalists;
meanwhile, hundreds of Kemsley juniors were trained under new
directors of studies in Manchester, Glasgow, Sheffield, Aberdeen,
Newcastle, Cardiff, Middlesbrough, York, Blackburn, Stockport and
Macclesfield, with university extension lectures on international
relations, economics, European history. A centralised library was
established, available to any member of staff, with a free lending service.
All the costs were borne by the company. And, as a service to journalism,
representatives of other newspapers outside the company were encouraged to attend.

The whole programme, enthusiastically backed by Lord Kemsley
himself, was steaming along by the time the 1949 Royal Commission on
the Press said this about recruitment and training:

The problem of recruiting the right people into journalism whether from school or from university and of ensuring that they achieve the necessary level of education and technical efficiency, is one of the most important facing the Press, because on the quality of the individual journalist depends not only the status of the whole profession but the possibility of bridging the gap between what Society needs from the Press and what the Press is at present giving. The problem is the common interest and the common responsibility of proprietors, editors and other journalists . . . .

Of course, this was not a new problem. As far back as 1890 the Royal Charter of the Institute of Journalists spoke of examinations or tests in theory and practice to establish journalistic proficiency. In 1946 the National Union of Journalists had approved a draft national scheme and the Newspaper Society and the Guild of Newspaper Editors had many discussions on a formal training system. But it was not until 1952 that the National Advisory Council for the Training and Education of Junior Journalists was set up, and three years later was changed to the present title of the National Council for the Training of Journalists.

The whole industry eventually became involved. I was an early chairman of the Council and, for fifteen years, I chaired national and international conferences on training and wrote a great deal on the subject. Proficiency examinations were introduced in 1953, and since 1954 two tests have been held each year. In retrospect, one might have supposed that a large newspaper company would then have abandoned its own system, but rather than follow that course, our staff training schemes continued, although the Kemsley plan was integrated with the national scheme in some respects. We always had a higher standard for newcomers than the national scheme, and our own entrants, whether school leavers or graduates, were trained by ourselves and were presented for the national certificates. Disenchanted with day and block release, we opened two basic training centres, one at Newcastle and the other at Cardiff, with permanent staffs of journalists as tutors. This relieved editors and senior staffs in various offices of the responsibility of putting over the basics. Thus, when newcomers joined they could get down to practical work immediately.

I also visited all the universities to see whether I could set up a national scheme offering employment to graduates who would bring improved intellectual quality to newspapers, and we formed a small annual interviewing panel with Lionel Berry in the chair. I recall one very confident performer, much backed by his Oxford tutor, telling us proudly that he had never seen the *Sunday Times*! 'I am an *Observer* man,' he announced without the least embarrassment. In one year, more than 1,900 graduates from British universities applied to our organisation for posts, over half of them as journalists. On average, we recruited thirty trainees each year. Many of the 1948-58 intake went on to high positions in journalism and newspaper management, after moving on to other newspapers or organisations after we had trained them.

Was the cost to Kemsley worthwhile? From the narrow standpoint of a company accountant, it was perhaps difficult to justify. But at a critical moment in the history of the press, with the age of television about to dawn, it gave a new professional status to the industry and helped ensure standards of reporting and writing that saved the press in Britain, both nationally and locally. Students and teachers all benefitted; and the pool of journalists and executives from which to choose editors and managers increased enormously. All in all it was something to be proud of – and an extraordinary punishment to Lord Kemsley for blazoning his name across his newspaper empire.

# CHAPTER TWELVE

# EDITORIAL DIRECTOR

LAUNCHING THE KEMSLEY EDITORIAL PLAN AND STEERING LORD KEMSLEY through the tricky waters of the Royal Commission were rewarded, in 1950, by a directorship of the company. I was – it seems astonishing when I think back – 31 years old. One of our board, H.N. Heywood, was retiring. He had styled himself chief London editor but when Kemsley indicated that he wished me to succeed Heywood, I decided to aim high. 'I suggest, perhaps boldly, the title of Editorial Director,' I wrote to Kemsley in a memorandum. 'It has the merit of falling into line with the others – Advertisement, Circulation and soon, Publicity. It does not, of course, alter the existing direct access of editors to the chairman.' Kemsley concurred, and on 25 October 1950 the announcement was made. I was no longer Kemsley's shadow; I was a director in my own right, charged with the editorial policies and supervision of the largest newspaper chain in Britain, controlling five Sunday newspapers, five mornings and eleven evenings.

Having said that, one has to admit that, in the words of one of our best provincial editors, Alastair Dunnett, it was 'a crumbling and preposterous empire', ruled by a deeply conservative Conservative who had succeeded in life by clinging to his brother's coat-tails and was then saved from real competition within the industry by the war. Nevertheless I was actually very fond of Lord Kemsley and his wife, and never once considered moving to another employer. In many ways they treated me almost as a son, lending us their flat in Paris on numerous occasions, paying for holidays when they felt I was exhausted, handing me each Christmas a generous cheque which helped me educate my four children. Beneath their stuffiness and social pretensions one had to admit that Kemsley's heart was in the right place – a man with a deeply paternalistic sense of responsibility, and an anxiety always to be seen to do what was right and proper. The trouble was, it was this very paternalism that drove him to pack the Kemsley board with his offspring, who were not noted for their talents either for journalism or big business. All were dominated of their father, to the extent that I was often used as a channel of communication. Such nepotism was, to me, immoral as well as self-defeating, and I think my worst arguments with Kemsley – in so far as anyone dared argue with him – were over the Berry boys.

Kemsley's sons were each given a Rolls Royce, jobs in the organisation, and expense accounts, as well as seats on the board, but only Lionel was a moderating influence. When I later remonstrated against Kemsley's decision to place his nephew's son in charge of our Sheffield office, Kemsley was enraged. He went purple. 'CD, you've no right to address me like that.' 'But,' I said, 'if I'm going to be of any value to you I'm going to be the one person, the way your board is constructed, that can say these things to you.' 'Of course you can say it,' he replied, 'but I will tell you that your job in life is to look after those four boys of yours, that is your prime purpose in life. And,' he went on, 'one day you may wish to put your four children in this group.' 'Never, never, never!' I said. 'Nepotism! I don't agree with packing the board with your family. I don't think it does your credit any good, and anyway, he lacks the necessary experience.'

Kemsley still wouldn't listen. 'I shall leave him there. His name is Berry, he is the son of my nephew, my nephew has died and he shall have a job.' 'A job, yes', I said, 'if you want, but not in charge of one of our biggest offices, which makes a million a year – a boy with no experience at all, none whatsoever!'

Here was the irony, the essential contradiction at the core of Kemsley Newspapers – for the proprietor who had authorised the revolutionary Kemsley Editorial Plan to ensure higher standards of leadership had himself so packed his board with cronies and family that any storm at that time could have driven us on to the rocks. Kemsley's talent had been for advertising salesmanship; but in the hostile post-war world, with labour disputes and growing competition for advertising, Kemsley Newspapers needed a board with powerful financial minds and administrative abilities, as well as the editorial certainty of a man like Northcliffe. The mix was wrong, and Kemsley's own editor-in-chief role quite misguided, since he had never had the remotest direct editorial responsibility or experience before the break-up with his brother in 1935. The situation, in some ways, was laughable. Kemsley's lack of judgment could be near-incredible – as when he decided to launch a new political party of the right, the Freedom Party.

Unfortunately, Kemsley himself was a man without ideas. Over the years he had collected a stable of writers to whom he paid a retainer, both to advise him and to write things for him. He engaged people like the politician Lord Woolton, the historians Arthur Bryant and G.M. Young, the journalist R.C.K. Ensor (who wrote under the pseudonym 'Scrutator'), the poet Edward Shanks, and others. From time to time these people drafted articles, wrote book reviews and acted as a rather elderly think-tank to Kemsley.

One of the star writers of that period was the novelist Charles Morgan, for many years theatre critic of the *Times*. One day he wrote a leader-page article with Kemsley on 'England in Chains' – the nation run by a lot of reds under Attlee and Bevan. It ended with a clarion call: England must cast off its chains and every man must wear a white tie again. That was the gist. Letters poured into the office, and Kemsley told me one morning, 'Call a conference in an hour's time, I am going to head up a Freedom Party.' So I called a conference and to the astonished senior members of the *Sunday Times* and others Kemsley announced that the Conservative Party was drifting backwards because Churchill was too busy writing his books instead of leading the Opposition, and that Attlee was a red, Bevan was a red and he must, therefore, lead this new political party. Kemsley then lifted the phone and started hiring all sorts of ancients who were to answer the letters and to produce the literature. Morgan was there, beaming away at the publicity this would all give to his books . . . And, of course, by the end of the conference everything had been dumped on my desk to follow up.

Literature in great quantities was printed and sent out to people who wanted it, branches were created up and down the country. Field-Marshal Lord Alanbrooke, the former CIGS, was invited to Gray's Inn Road, where Kemsley pleaded with him to become the leader of the movement. Naturally, Alanbrooke refused to have anything to do with it – so Kemsley asked Monty, the then serving CIGS, if *he* would become the leader. It was a very funny episode. I suppose when you remember that Kemsley had been an appeaser in the late 1930s, and had even gone to meet Hitler, it was all of a piece, but in post-war England it was risible.

The whole thing came to an abrupt end when Churchill – alerted no doubt by Monty – rang up and said, 'Lord Kemsley, I think it's about time Lady Kemsley, Mrs Churchill and you and I had a talk about this matter.' That finished it. Kemsley's crusading bubble burst, and the question became how, having got into top gear, you could get down to bottom.

Churchill played Kemsley like an adroit fisherman. Nothing could be done in Opposition at that stage, because the Conservatives were not ready for an election; he himself, he confided, was holding his strength, and anyway, the *History of the Second World War* had to be written, and only he could do it. Kemsley, by this tremendous show of attention, was entirely won over – so completely, it has to be said, that he decided to give the annual *Sunday Times* prize, worth £1,000, to Churchill for the very *History* for which he had supposedly been neglecting his political role.

Of course, we had a most eminent panel of judges who normally chose the winner, Osbert Sitwell, who had previously got the prize for his autobiography, and Richard Church among them; but all other contenders than Churchill were brushed aside by Kemsley himself. At this there was something of a rebellion, with cries of tyranny – a rebellion I was left to sort out and then cover up. My reward was that I was detailed to negotiate with and meet for the first time Mr Churchill, who was certainly a cunning old bird. Only when I'd confirmed that he would not have to pay tax would he agree to accept the prize – and then announced that he'd received it once before and, having got me to find a copy of the acceptance speech he had given on that occasion, proceeded to give the same one again.

My new brief, as editorial director, was really to help shore up this crumbling empire; to bring some sort of coherence to the group's editorial side and ensure the survival of as many of our newspapers as possible in an increasingly forbidding commercial world. My first act was to go and visit my new parish, and size up the editors, all of whom I had met when setting up the training plan. I had no intention of interfering with editors' prerogatives or tasks, but I did want to have editors in place who could do the job, so I visited each centre for two or three days and weighed up the staff. I remember saying to one editor, with quite a reputation, 'Anthony Eden was speaking yesterday at your big Festival. What did he say about the Middle East?' 'Oh, Mr Hamilton, I didn't go,' the editor replied, 'it had rained two days beforehand and I was frightened of getting a chill; and I couldn't find my galoshes.' He didn't last very long after that. One by one I promoted men with judgment and independence of mind. Those who had clung to their jobs by being obsequious and deferential to Kemsley were retired; I got them as good a pension as I could and put in younger men. And as soon as I put in a younger man as editor I set about finding him a deputy so that there was always someone coming up, having one day a week actually editing while the editor was having a day off.

I greatly enjoyed it, I confess. In some ways it was like being in the army again, in command; selecting your company commanders, making sure the battalion as a whole functions properly. We supplied common services from London, and twice a year invited all the editors to a conference, getting the heads of departments to talk to them about their jobs, arranging for them to meet the Prime Minister, discussing matters of common concern to us as editors. I soon realised what a fund of talent we really had in the organisation – men of real calibre who, if encouraged to broaden their horizons, were not only editors but potential business managers and leaders; and would one day prove themselves as such. I don't remember ever having to give an order to an editor. If I talked to them on the phone about an issue I'd always finish by saying: 'At the end of the day it's your decision, not mine.' Having said that, I did want to give as much help as I could. Very occasionally I was able even to provide them with a scoop. I shall never forget, for instance, the death of King George VI in 1952.

Leadership, I have said, depends on the exercise of judgment. But to be successful, you also need luck and instinct. It was instinct which, at the battle of Halderan in 1944, persuaded me to spend the night at my battalion headquarters instead of going to my billet. And on the morning of 6 February 1952 I again had a presentiment. I'd arranged to have my hair cut at nine before going to work. Instead, at the top of our road in North London a voice said to me 'You should be going to the office.' So I drove straight to Gray's Inn Road, and cancelled my haircut.

Within two minutes my telephone rang. Bill Taylor, our picture editor, wanted to see me. To my astonishment he then announced, in the privacy of my office, that the King had died. It was about ten past nine. I said, 'How do you know this?' Bill said, 'From an absolutely impeccable source, impeccable.' 'Well,' I asked, 'why hasn't it been announced by the Palace?' Bill explained: 'Because they're having to make all the arrangements with the Garter King of Arms to don his uniform and make the proclamation, and they have to inform the Commonwealth Prime Ministers and so on. Even send for black clothing for the royal family – that sort of thing.'

So I personally telephoned every evening paper editor in the group, saying, 'Prepare a special edition that the King has died.' Most of them didn't know whether their leg was being pulled or not. The King was known to be unwell but recuperating at Sandringham, and had been out shooting the day before. Princess Elizabeth, his heir, had not been recalled from Africa. But they did as they were advised, whatever their reservations.

The minutes then ticked by. By ten o'clock still nothing had happened, and I may say I was starting to get windy. The evening papers had to go to press by 10.30 am. At 10.15 Manchester rang and said, 'We're all ready and can have the machines running in two minutes – we'll beat the opposition hollow.' Glasgow said the same thing. Ten-fifteen passed, 10.20 came. I said to Bill Taylor, 'Your bloody leg's been pulled and my career is over.' Bill said, 'No, I've faith in this chap – don't panic, don't withdraw the order.' I said, 'I'm not panicking, Bill – I'm not used to panicking. But what will K say when it's splashed all round the world that Kemsleys made a boob – either announced it prematurely, or had the information and didn't announce it?' I couldn't contain myself any longer. Off I went to the wire room, which was a huge hall fitted with teleprinters. I looked at the tapes, clattering away – no mention of the King.

Ten-twenty-nine came, and 10.29½. And then suddenly, I shall never forget it, the teleprinters, one by one, stopped – about forty of them. There was complete silence. Then the memorable, energising word so well known to journalists of that era came stuttering out: 'Dynamite, Dynamite, Dynamite . . . .' It was a wire from the Press Association: 'The following statement was issued from Buckingham Palace and No 10 Downing Street: "It is much regretted that His Majesty passed away at 8.30 this morning . . . ."'

What would have happened to me had it all gone wrong, I still do not know. But it didn't. Fortune, for the moment, was still on my side. I'd survived. The question was, in an increasingly competitive post-war world, with restrictions on newsprint being lifted and the rising challenge of commercial television, would Kemsley Newspapers survive? Ought our newspapers to go for more news to fill the growing number of pages that could be printed, or should we go for features? And if commercial television really threatened our lifeblood – advertising revenue – ought we to diversify into television while we still could? On both these issues I held strong convictions. On one, the chairman backed me, leading me to an unprecedented recovery in the declining fortunes of the Sunday Times; on the other he would chicken out at the last moment, with consequences that would eventually force him to sell out to someone who didn't: Roy Thomson.

# CHAPTER THIRTEEN

# 'NO' TO TELEVISION

I THINK IT WAS IAN FLEMING WHO – AS IN SO MANY THINGS – WAS BEHIND the idea. Early in 1952 Kemsley summoned me to his office. 'We've got to keep an eye on the Americans,' he announced. 'We want to get some idea of where they're going, what moves they're making.' I was therefore despatched for a month to study the workings and future of the American Press – and I came back convinced that the Kemsley group should go into television. I'd found almost all the American newspaper owners I met frightened by the advance of television, which was creaming off their profits from advertising. Some believed that newspapers were finished as a business enterprise, but all accepted that television was the communications medium of the future, and that if you couldn't beat the TV business, then it was best to join it.

In Britain, there were already moves to break the BBC broadcasting monopoly. Rediffusion, Associated News, Granada Cinemas and Associated British Picture Corporation were already moving to get in on the ground floor and benefit from the Television Bill about to go before Parliament. Kemsley himself was interested but far from enthusiastic. He was nearing seventy and was really too old for such a drastic step. He read my report and did not discourage me from sounding out various contacts in Parliament and elsewhere. But he remained sceptical until an unexpected voice joined mine; that of his step-daughter, Ghislaine Alexander. She was a 'beautiful egghead' who took part in the highly successful television panel game, *What's My Line?*, then being shown by the BBC. In a chance conversation with her I mentioned my trip to the States and my conviction that Kemsley should go into commercial television. Ghislaine immediately suggested a lunch with Maurice Winnick, the former bandleader who leased *What's My Line?* and other panel games to the BBC.

Winnick was certain that commercial television was coming to Britain and would be a 'pot of gold'. But he was reticent about involving another partner in his own schemes, for, with a 'very powerful' backer, he was setting up his own company to run a station. Nevertheless, he could see the advantages of having the biggest newspaper group in the country behind his bid, so I offered to set up a meeting between Winnick and Kemsley – though I had to know who his 'powerful' backer really was. Happily, it turned out to be Sir Isaac Wolfson, the owner of Universal Stores; a fact which I felt would impress Lord Kemsley. Winnick warned that a great deal of capital would be needed, and that they might have to run the station for years before recouping the outlay. To set up station and studios might cost £2½ million, or even £3 million; an enormous sum in those days. I was sceptical about the need for such a high investment, until the BBC later confirmed the figures to the Independent Television Authority.

After much controversy, the Television Act became law early in 1954 – a great deal sooner than expected, for the Government seemed, at the end, anxious to remove the issue from the floor of the House – with an Independent Television Authority under Sir Kenneth Clark. In due course, a discreet official advertisement appeared, inviting applications for two separate stations, London and the Midlands-and-the-North. In the meantime, Maurice Winnick and Sir Isaac Wolfson had each met Kemsley. With Ghislaine Alexander's help I was able to persuade him to opt for one of the possible stations, and with this assurance, I called on Sir Kenneth Clark and Sir Robert Fraser (director-general of the ITA) with Winnick and Mrs Alexander, hoping to sound out our prospects of success.

To our surprise, Clark and Fraser were most welcoming. The original twenty-five applications had shrunk to five when the scale of investment became clear. The stability and prestige of the Kemsley empire were exactly what the ITA wanted, and we were more or less guaranteed that if Lord Kemsley were to be chairman, the licence was ours. Flattered by this, Kemsley took the decision to join Winnick, Wolfson promised financial support, and on 14 October 1954 our formal proposal went in. Studio and broadcasting equipment were estimated at £300,000; the paid-up capital of the company would be between £250,000 and £500,000 pounds, and we had assurances of banking facilities for up to £3 million. As our Manchester offices at Withy Grove were the largest newspaper offices in Europe, we proposed Manchester for the site of our studios, with subsidiary studios in Birmingham and London. Specimen programmes included Winnick's programmes hitherto leased to the BBC – *What's My Line?*, *Twenty Questions*, and *The Name's The Same*. Kemsley-Winnick Company was immediately granted the licence to supply the programmes for weekend television in the Midlands-and-North. At the same time, the other franchises were also announced: Association Rediffusion for London weekend television, and weekday programming assigned to The Norman Collins Group in London, and Granada in the North.

There was, naturally, a great deal of public bickering over the contracts. The sums required and the risks being taken meant that only the most powerful groups in entertainment and newspapers could conceivably stay the course; Kenneth Clark had little option but to grant the licences as he did – indeed his decision to exclude Prince Littler and Lew Grade (backed by Warburgs) on the grounds that they would exercise a virtual monopoly over available talent (Grade's theatrical agency, Littler's Moss Empires Theatre Group and Harry Alan Towers from commercial radio made a powerful combination) backfired – for Norman Collins soon ran into difficulties and had to bring them into his company with Clark's consent.

The problem was, that the four companies looked conspicuously Tory; indeed, the *Daily Mirror* christened the new independent broadcasting service 'Toryvision'. Randolph Churchill referred to a 'pernicious cartel', and Lady Violet Bonham Carter questioned whether the newspapers themselves would dare criticise TV programmes put out by their own groups. Whatever happened in the general run of programmes, however, we were determined to have non-partisan independent news broadcasting and thus I became one of the first four directors of Independent Television News (ITN) and appointed Aidan Crawley as our first editor. I wrote the first agreements with Reuters and the Press Association news-gathering agencies, and made Robin Day and Christopher Chataway our first newsreaders.

Meanwhile Cecil King of the *Mirror* Group and Lord Beaverbrook of the *Express* both attempted to stifle the new medium at birth – King in the hope that he could himself enter the fray 'after the second bankruptcy' as he later confessed, Beaverbrook because it was rumoured his own application for a franchise had been rejected by Clark. The licences had been granted for only ten years, and there was considerable anxiety whether we would get enough viewers to pull in the necessary advertising to pay for the start-up and running costs. Winnick was convinced we would have to spend double what the BBC was paying in order to get viewers – involving almost £1 million running costs in our first year. At ten shillings per minute per thousand viewers this would give a profit of over £1½ million in our first year if the audience reached 2.2 million. But if the audience only reached one million and we filled only two-thirds of the advertising space, we would lose over a quarter-of-a-million pounds in our first year (running losses). If the audience fell below one million the loss would exceed £800,000 . . . .

No one could predict audience figures or the willingness of advertisers to take up television broadcasting as a medium. Nervously, Winnick raised his advertising rate by a quarter, but it was a slippery slope and Kemsley was already getting cold feet. Sir Isaac had expressed his doubts; worst of all, Kemsley's own sons, except for occasional support from Neville, were all hesitant, having deplored my idea from the start. They disliked Wolfson; and Kemsley himself got on badly with Winnick. Bill Mabane, who was very close to the family and influenced by outside pressures, violently opposed the scheme. I remember a whole day's meeting being taken up with an argument as to whether the company should be called Kemsley-Winnick or Winnick-Kemsley. Winnick was touchy and suspicious, quarrelsome by nature, and lacked the ability to ingratiate himself where necessary. Kemsley, for so long King of his own castle, had not had to deal with a character of this sort before and felt he was not getting the respect his peerage deserved.

Then Wolfson decided to pull out. At first, Kemsley – who called me into his office to tell me the news – appeared quite sanguine, but later he telephoned his friend, Lord Rothermere, who sounded very gloomy about Associated Rediffusion's prospects. Impulsively, Kemsley decided to call off his invasion of the airwaves. It was now February 1955; the first programme from our Birmingham studio was due to be transmitted at the end of that year, and we had already spent £2 million. Vainly, I tried to convince Kemsley that it was too late. Whether or not it had been right to go into commercial television in the first place, it would be wrong to bail out at this stage, for withdrawal would cost a fortune and bring undoubted loss of face. Lady Kemsley said the same, worried about her pride. Kemsley, uncertain what to do, dithered – and then attempted to hedge his bets. He told Winnick he would limit his share in the company to £90,000 and would resign as chairman, allowing Winnick to use his printing plant for his television programme magazine nevertheless – a clear attempt to encourage Winnick not to sue him for breach of contract.

To Kemsley's chagrin, this compromise was unacceptable to Kenneth Clark, who quite rightly insisted that Kemsley's chairmanship of the company was a condition of the licence. So Kemsley had to agree to continue as chairman – but had reckoned without the pressure of his sons, who must have seen their inheritance at risk to Kemsley-Winnick's gargantuan debts. In June 1955 a family council was held, with Kemsley's wife and her stepsons all taking part. By providing his

sons with their guaranteed jobs for life, their Rolls Royces, and even
their Scotch beef conveniently supplied from Aberdeen, Kemsley had
signed his own commercial death warrant. At the behest of his sons,
and without reference to the Kemsley board of directors or to me, he
made the decision to get out completely, cost what it might. I think they
were finally convinced when Rothermere bailed out of the London
station, which was to go on the air first (though he later returned,
becoming a major shareholder in Southern TV).

Maurice Winnick, heartbroken, had now lost both his partners and
was forced to go to the ITA to say he could not proceed with his
franchise. Fortunately for him and the ITA, Associated British Picture
Corporation stepped back in; having turned down an original offer of a
franchise they now accepted, and ABC Television, with Howard
Thomas as managing director, took over from Kemsley-Winnick and
bought much of the equipment Kemsley had already ordered. After a
High Court action, it was left to me to sort out an agreement with
Winnick over the damages. We settled for £30,000 on the basis that
Kemsley had not used his best efforts. With this sum poor Winnick
went abroad to live, certain that in time he would have made a fortune if
Kemsley had not pulled out. History would prove him right.

It was a sorry episode, though an instructive one. Kemsley would
have become, without doubt, the greatest newspaper and broadcasting
magnate in the land, making untold fortunes for his sons. But it was not
to be. Luck had enabled him, clinging to his talented brother's coat-
tails, to become a peer of the realm, as well as a social and even political
power in the land. But behind the glittering façades of Chandos House
and Dropmore, his historic country house, he remained the cautious,
upright Welsh estate agent's son, out of touch with the lives of ordinary
people and the commercial development of Britain. His ramshackle
empire was doomed, and by pulling out of his television franchise at the
last moment, he himself had nailed its coffin.

# CHAPTER FOURTEEN

# THE 'BIG READ'

KEMSLEY'S FAILURE TO SEIZE THE OPPORTUNITY TO EXPAND INTO television had an immediate effect on his newspaper empire. Overnight, national advertising (for such items as soaps, detergents, and household cleaners) moved from the pages of our 'popular' newspapers on to the screen. Without the flair of Beaverbrook or Rothermere, Kemsley was powerless to fight back – and one by one, his national popular dailies and Sundays succumbed, leaving me, ultimately, to wield the executioner's axe; the *Daily Sketch*, the *Daily Graphic*, the *Empire News*, the *Sunday Chronicle* .... Nothing can be more soul-destroying than laying off good and loyal employees. Wherever possible we arranged alternative work within the Kemsley group, or outside. Certainly, the pension scheme I'd helped introduce after the war was a boon. But it was a heartbreaking job, and I insisted, as during demobilisation in the Army, on seeing every man myself, whether in Manchester or London.

There was no alternative. By rejecting television Kemsley had hoped to remain safe within his established empire. Instead, he became a man under siege. I did my best to strengthen and rationalise our provincial newspapers – encouraging them not to look to Kemsley House in London for their bread and butter but to concentrate on their primary task: to satisfy the expectations of their region or locality. With better training, a better intake of trainees and judicious promotion we were able to trim our sails and ensure the survival of almost all our regional titles, while all around them well-known papers went to the wall. But in London Kemsley would eventually be left without a single national paper except the ailing *Sunday Graphic* and the *Sunday Times*. And to Kemsley's consternation even the *Sunday Times* incurred the ultimate indignity; in 1956 its sales were surpassed by those of its rival, the *Observer*, under its young editor, David Astor. This was galling, for Kemsley had built up the circulation before the war from 300,000 on purchase to half-a-million by 1939. In its wartime straightjacket its sale had stabilised at that figure, and in 1950, with a circulation of 535,000, its revered octogenarian editor, W.W. Hadley, had retired and H.V. Hodson had been appointed his successor.

Hodson – a pre-war fellow of All Souls – was selected in preference to Hadley's deputy, Valentine Heywood. Heywood was a real 'pro', a news editor of great experience and skill, but not, we felt when we gathered at Dropmore one Monday afternoon to discuss the succession, the right man to be editor. In rejecting Heywood we were surely right – he was a fussy character with ulcers and an excruciating habit of announcing at our weekly editorial conference that he'd found some new restaurant or other near his home in Berkshire where you could get a three-course meal for a half-crown less than anywhere else. He simply lacked the stature to be editor of a great national newspaper – whereas Hadley's number three, Harry Hodson undoubtedly possessed it. But though Hodson could write an excellent leader at great speed, he was not by training a professional journalist – indeed, the true story of his accession to the Sunday Times reveals, I think, the doubts he himself harboured about such a career.

Our Dropmore meeting had extended through dinner and into the night. We ought, perhaps, to have looked outside the *Sunday Times* or even Kemsley Newspapers for a candidate, but I had only just been appointed editorial director, and was still a relative 'new boy' in Gray's Inn Road. In the end, it was decided to offer Hodson the job on the principle of 'the devil you know . . . .' Kemsley undertook to make the offer the next day – but Hodson could not make up his mind to accept. It was an extraordinary situation. Even Hodson himself later recorded how 'heartbrokenly disappointed' Heywood had been – 'Heywood would have given his right hand to end his journalistic career as editor of the *Sunday Times*, even for a month,' Hodson wrote. Yet Hodson himself hesitated. He was in his mid-forties and uncertain whether he wished to devote the remainder of his working life to Sunday journalism. Like Kemsley, he believed in discussing such matters with his wife Margaret who, like Lady Kemsley, was a most accomplished hostess; some would say that also like Kemsley he deferred too much to his wife's opinion. Certainly Kemsley became outraged when day succeeded day and Hodson failed to give an answer. Kemsley told me to speak to him – but Hodson responded that it was a private matter between him and Kemsley and that I, therefore, could know nothing of it.

Finally, on the Thursday or Friday night, I went to dinner at the Commons Press Gallery with our correspondent, James Margach. My assistant, Donald Stephenson, knowing that that was where I had gone, rang me up, saying, 'The old man [Kemsley] is desperate to speak to you', and from one of the press phone boxes I eventually got hold of Kemsley at Chandos House, announcing myself as usual, 'It's CD here.'

'Lady Kemsley's in a roaring state!' Kemsley declared petulantly. 'I'm very sorry,' I replied, 'what is the problem?' 'Well,' he said, 'I have been insulted. Lady Kemsley considers it perfectly clear I've offered the editorship – the plum editorship in London – to a man about whom we have reservations; and after an entire day he still hasn't responded. You are to ring him up and say, does he wish the editorship or not? And if he doesn't tell you what he wants, I am withdrawing the offer of the editorship to him.'

I had now to find Hodson, and having done so asked him why on earth he hadn't rung Kemsley to say he'd accept? 'Well,' he said, 'I was having long discussions with Margaret.' He did of course accept, but Lady Kemsley remained beside herself with rage. Even at the weekend when we went down to Dropmore she said privately to my wife: 'The idea of my Gomer, *my Gomer*, being insulted by this . . . intellectual! The trouble is, my dear Mrs Hamilton, he can't make a decision without his wife.'

This was unfair. Hodson was a brilliant man, with outstanding abilities as an academic and as a civil servant (he had been reforms commissioner in India, then a head of department in the Ministry of Production during the war). But before the *Sunday Times* he had had no experience as a newspaper journalist other than editing a Foreign Office journal. He was by far the most educated editor we had ever had on the *Sunday Times*, but one could not say that he was therefore the best. Under David Astor, sales of the *Observer* rose inexorably. Under Hodson sales of the *Sunday Times* dropped for almost four years. Finally, in September 1956 sales of the *Observer* actually passed our own. There was panic at Gray's Inn Road and Kemsley convened a special Monday conference – 'Black Monday' it was later called.

What had gone wrong? We had a fine team of journalists working for the paper, what emerged each Sunday was solid, respectable – and predictable, like its owner. The paper had failed to evolve with the times and the results showed in our readership surveys; for the *Observer* had an enormous sale to younger professional readers, whereas our profile was distinctly elderly. To a large extent the fault really was Kemsley's own. His influence was negative and restrictive, however well meant. He never really read the newspaper, any more than he ever read books. At most he cast an eye over headlines and the leader – yet he subjected Hodson to a constant barrage of petty complaints, often inspired by Lady Kemsley. Their prudery was legendary – as when

Lady Kemsley exploded one night, glancing through the first edition of another of our papers, 'Gomer!' she howled, 'this is horrible! This headline "Princess Margaret to have Bachelor Flat!" Our readers will think she is becoming a whore.' And in front of half-a-dozen guests, I was told to get hold of the editor and alter it. She could see sexual implications around the sharpest of corners – the best known being the order to remove from the photograph of a fine British bull the equipment he used to raise the standard of dairy farming.

The combination of Kemsley and Hodson simply couldn't match David Astor's flair, and neither of them knew what to do. But they were saved by two things: Suez, and the 'Big Read'. Midway through the Suez crisis, in October 1956, David Astor printed an extraordinary leader – a complete *volte face* in the newspaper's attitude. It was courageous and doubtless sincere – but it outraged thousands of readers and cast doubt on the paper's credibility. Overnight, its sales plummeted, whereas our own remained firm. It was time to uncover our secret weapon: serialisation.

I have often been asked how the Big Read began. In fact it began soon after the war, but was restricted by the shortage of newsprint. As controls were relaxed the question arose, as I have observed already, whether the newspaper should use the extra pages for more news or more features. Ian Fleming, as foreign manager in charge of our hugely expensive Mercury Service, naturally wished to see the fruits of his foreign correspondents splashed across the pages of Kemsley's provincial press as well as those of the *Sunday Times*. Yet I knew from the provincial editors that Fleming's service, however attractive in theory, was of scant interest to local readers, who wanted local news. Even syndication of our national political news or views was a dangerous step – the Royal Commission having slapped us down on learning that we circulated our *Sunday Times* leaders in advance to our other papers.

Disappointed, Fleming took to writing the *Sunday Times* gossip column, Atticus, and to his latest brainwave: James Bond, for the writing of which he was given two months' leave a year, spent in Jamaica. For myself, though a newspaperman to my fingertips, I was not downcast by recent developments in journalism. The shift of popular advertising to commercial television was not after all so different from the rise of popular newspapers themselves after the first world war. To compete against television, newspapers would have to do what television didn't do. More and more I was convinced the *Sunday Times* should analyse and amplify the news and what lay behind it. Like many of the staff, from Ian Fleming to Leonard Russell, I was self-educated, anxious to learn more – and I knew we weren't alone, that there were millions more among our potential readers who, with greater leisure and affluence, would respond at the weekend to a newspaper different from the dailies. On a busy weekday people wanted newspapers with well organised, instantly accessible information. But on Sundays they wanted something more.

Unfortunately, Hodson was not innovative. Harried by Kemsley over details, he resented interference, and any contribution I wished to make had to be made via Kemsley. My influence could, therefore, only be indirect, in sowing ideas or suggestions for staff appointments. It was galling to see David Astor relentlessly catching us up, but although I was impotent to direct the *Sunday Times* in battle, so to speak, I was able to furnish it with a secret weapon – a weapon which, once perfected, blasted the *Observer* out of the water.

Life as Kemsley's personal assistant and then as editorial director had given me unparalleled contacts not simply in Fleet Street, but in the world of British politics, finance and publishing. Great men in different walks of life opened up to me, telling me of their childhood, their struggles in life, their successes and failures. My curiosity was always aroused since I was a self-made man, having started without advantages of wealth or education. It was the life-stories of such men and women, I was certain, that would appeal to a wide audience of readers. If *Reader's Digest* could command a readership of millions for its books-in-a-nutshell, why not our Sunday newspapers?

At first, there were doubts. Could readers really cope with long extracts in news type? Only time would tell. One by one I started buying serial rights, far ahead of publication date, in some of the best post-war books, as well as helping to commission them. Newspaper editors are generally so busy they cannot plan years ahead. My position as editorial director enabled me to think ahead, as well as giving me a unique overview. Some books might take five years before they were written and ready for serialisation – a very long-term investment. The question was: would people read them? Luckily for me they would and did. The Big Read was born. Today it may seem surprising that readers would not only read four or five pages of serialisation extract, but would go on reading such extracts for perhaps fourteen consecutive weeks. Yet such was the explosion in the public's reading appetite that we were unable to satisfy it. The 'opposition' scorned the exercise – but the proof was in our circulation figures. Very soon, the 'doubters' in Gray's Inn Road were turning to me, anxiously wanting to know what else I had up my serialisation sleeve.

It was an enormously interesting task, negotiating with world-famous personalities and writers from Charlie Chaplin to Alan

Moorehead, Nicholas Monsarrat and Somerset Maugham. However, it took time to gain Kemsley's trust in my judgment. I remember buying serial rights in *The Wooden Horse*, by Eric Williams, which was to prove the most popular book of the period, recounting the true story of an escape from prison camp. I had intended it should be serialised in the *Sunday Graphic* but at the last moment I had to suffer the indignity of selling it to another newspaper because Kemsley thought that at £2,000 it was a waste of money. In fact, it proved an unprecedented success, and the film version has been seen repeatedly on television.

We were all excited when I bought Nicholas Monsarrat's *The Cruel Sea* for the *Sunday Chronicle*, for it was a masterly evocation of those wartime convoys by a writer who really knew his stuff. We spent a great deal of money on advance publicity for it, and then some clever person sent a copy of the book in advance to Lord Kemsley. It contained some fairly celebrated passages in which the men on the bridge were thinking what they'd do to the missus when they got home, if ever they did get home from those dreadful North Sea convoys to Russia. Kemsley said, 'I can't stop you from serialising it, but not a word of *this*' – these passages – 'must appear.' I protested, 'Well there's no point to the whole thing if you take out what ordinary people were thinking at that time of stress.' 'Out!' 'Well', I said, 'it's money down the drain, it won't sell a copy.' He said, 'THOSE ARE MY ORDERS.' And as orders were orders, I obeyed.

With Charlie Chaplin, whose autobiography ran in the *Sunday Times*, there was no such problem, or rather the problem was his, not ours. As he himself said: 'You can't imagine how difficult it is, if you've had five wives and you're very happily married to the present one, to write about the previous four. There's some really good stuff, but I daren't put it in.' In fact, the story he produced was riveting, without the wives. Alexei Adzhubei, Kruschev's son-in-law and editor of *Izvestia*, rang me from Moscow and asked if they could buy the Russian serial rights. I said I'd ask Mr Chaplin. I knew they never paid except in unconvertible roubles. When I told Charlie of the offer he was tickled. 'Of course they may,' he said – 'providing they pay me in Russian caviare' – which they did. When I asked why they bothered to pay at all, as the Soviet Union did not observe the Berne Convention on copyright, Adzhubei replied, 'But Mr Chaplin is a good communist.'

One of my approaches was to suggest to people that they should write their memoirs – and then be prepared to wait years if need be, as in the case of Alec Guinness. I put my idea to him ten years before he actually wrote his life story, and I got a letter from him saying he would only do it for Hamish Hamilton and the *Sunday Times*, which he honoured, as Chaplin had done – in fact, with Chaplin we never even had a written contract, it was all done on trust. Laurence Olivier was one who didn't deliver, but most people did.

Fleet Street editors generally would look round on Thursday to see what they could announce on the Sunday for the following week. I realised that was not the way to do it; you had to think ahead. Of course, all this cost money and you had to be careful – you could run away with great sums. It all depended what your object was. If it was to increase sales, you could do it by various methods, from bingo to going editorially down-market, or broaden your appeal in the way we chose to do with our serials. But there had always to be a plan, and the timing was critical. If you went flat out for sales without a plan you could end by bankrupting yourself, both in 'buying' the extra circulation and in extra production costs. It had to be planned with advertising, circulation and production staff, almost like a military campaign – and even then, you had to allow for the vagaries of fashion and chance. I bought several books which flopped, at least in terms of our expectations. But, as Monty used to say, as long as 51 per cent of your decisions are right, you will succeed.

I persuaded Alan Moorehead to write a marvellous account of the Russian Revolution, and following up one of Ian Fleming's suggestions we got Somerset Maugham to do a ten-part series on the great novelists. But I suppose, if I am remembered for anything in the 1950s, it will be for the big war serials, starting with Peter Fleming's *Invasion 1940*. For twenty years there was an avid audience wanting to know more about the war we'd just fought; how it had been run, by whom – the inside story. Lord Camrose had done a deal with Churchill whereby Churchill's residence was bought for the nation while Churchill's wartime story went to the *Telegraph*. But the *Telegraph* still had no Sunday edition and because of my friendship with Arthur Bryant I was able to buy serial rights in his version of the Alanbrooke diaries – *The Turn of the Tide*, and later, *Triumph in the West*. These were the first major works by a contemporary of Churchill which convincingly painted Churchill's strengths – and weaknesses. Alanbrooke had kept a nightly record of his life with Churchill, and the picture of this ageing monster, at once brilliant and exasperating, was riveting. Leonard Russell, literary editor of the *Sunday Times*, was responsible for the cutting and shaping – a masterly exercise in itself. I have never met anyone else with gifts to match Leonard's in serial-editing. It was a *tour de force*, compounded by Eric Cheadle's circulation drive and publicity campaign. We ran so many extracts, I remember, that Arthur Bryant rang up one day, enraged, and asked were we going to serialise the index, too?

People used to say to me, 'Why are you giving all this space on

Sunday to so-and-so, instead of giving us more news?' And, probably
with a smile, I used to say, 'Well, I'm really looking for very high-class
gossip.' I didn't want to go over every military detail of the campaigns.
As a reader I wanted to know if there'd been great rows between
generals, or funny incidents, or so on. I wanted the story larded so that
on a Sunday a reader would finish by saying, 'That was a damned good
read.' Serialisation of *The Turn of the Tide* in 1957 added tens of
thousands of readers to our newspaper, while the *Observer*'s sale stuck
for almost two years at their pre-Suez figure. We had built a
commanding lead when, in 1958, I was able to reveal my biggest coup:
serialisation of Monty's *Memoirs*.

I'd struck the deal with Monty some four years before, in the summer
of 1954, subsequently bringing in William Collins to handle the book
publication. I'd kept close touch with Monty since moving to Kemsley
Newspapers. He liked young men with ideas and while head of the
British Army, and then at Nato, he liked the idea of one of his erstwhile
infantry colonels in a senior position in Fleet Street. But by 1954 he was
approaching seventy, and was plainly under-employed as Deputy
Supreme Commander in Europe. It was obviously time for him to start
writing his memoirs. Over the years I had worked out quite complex
deals whereby famous personalities could minimize the tax on their
autobiographies, but Monty liked neither the complications nor the
suggestion of tax-avoidance. What he really wanted was not money but
security in his old age, so a single deal was worked out whereby the
major portion of our payment would be spread over future years, as an
annual fee, until he died. Given his age, this seemed something of a
gamble on Monty's part, especially as he had virtually only one lung
after being wounded in the first world war. But Monty's will to live was
as strong as his will to win his battles – and for the rest of his long life he
would have enough money to maintain his beautiful converted mill in
Hampshire.

Such was the sum involved that I had not told Lord Kemsley the
figure, when the deal was struck in the summer of 1954; but by the
winter of 1956, with the *Observer* hard on our heels, Kemsley would have
paid anything. Monty, however, suddenly decided to delay his
retirement from Nato until the autumn of 1958, having worked out that
he would by then have spent fifty years in the army – the longest period
of active service by any officer in British military history. Patiently we
waited – and once I saw the early chapters I knew we were on to a
winner. Our campaign, with vast advertising and wooing of newsagents by Eric Cheadle – we even handed out free Toby jugs in the form
of Monty wearing his famous black beret and two badges – was

probably the largest ever mounted. It is no secret that the serialisation brought us more than 100,000 extra readers overnight – readers who then remained. Such was Kemsley's gratitude that he even gave me a £5,000 bonus that Christmas – whittled down to £2,000 after tax!

In this way, the challenge from Astor's *Observer* was scotched, and the *Sunday Times* streaked ahead in sales. Then, in the summer of 1959, with the second volume of Alanbrooke's diaries cementing our advantage, Kemsley dropped his bombshell. He was selling.

# CHAPTER FIFTEEN

※

# KEMSLEY SELLS OUT

KEMSLEY'S SELL-OUT TO A FOREIGN BUYER, A CANADIAN, WAS ONE OF THE more extraordinary episodes in British newspaper history. It was certainly a most extraordinary event in my life, and I suppose it began in Switzerland in 1958. I was staying with Olive in Gstaad, as we did every February, for a fortnight with Monty. Monty had conducted the writing of his memoirs like a military campaign, all to a set schedule. Now, months before the due date, he handed over the typescript and, excited, I rang Lord Kemsley in Montreux in the valley below. It was then I learned that a facial operation on Lady Kemsley had gone wrong. A nerve had been trapped – and for the rest of her long life (she outlived Kemsley by eight years) this once handsome society hostess was to live in a darkened room with half her face covered, in continual pain and consulting every available doctor, and even a faith healer, without success.

This accident – though we didn't realise it at the time – must have sapped Kemsley's own nerve, especially when, to his chagrin, he learned at the end of that year that he was not going to be made an earl. After much hard work and string-pulling I had managed to get him a GBE to add to his viscountcy – in fact I was in his office when the letter from the Prime Minister arrived. He threw it down on the table, 'Huh, GBE!' 'But how marvellous, Lord Kemsley,' I said, 'most people would dearly love to get the Grand Cross of the British Empire – you will be able to wear a great sash at official functions.' 'I am already a viscount,' he cut me short, 'it is entirely proper that I should now become a nobleman.' 'But,' I said, 'you *are* a nobleman – the first Viscount Kemsley!'

'I wish,' he pronounced, 'to be the first earl! I should have been given an earldom for this' (I had assiduously ballooned up his generosity and public spirit in promoting the Kemsley Flying Trust and Kemsley Empire Journalists' scheme) 'and I shall keep on trying.' In vain I pointed out that the last newspaper earl had been created a long time ago, and no prime minister now dare risk the political flak that would ensue from such an award. 'I am going to get an earldom,' Kemsley interrupted, 'and you have got to help me!'

In its way it was as comic as Evelyn Waugh's portrait of the archetypal press baron in *Scoop*. We watched such antics with disbelief – but we recognised, too, that his heart was in the right place, that he, as much as we, wished to ensure the survival of good newspapers run on moral principles of truth and fairness. Even Kemsley's nepotism could be construed as unselfish, an extension of the same paternalism with which he governed his newspaper empire. But unknown to us – to anyone save his family – Kemsley's loyalty to that empire had begun to weaken. In the early summer of 1959, without informing non-family directors, he began to buy shares in his own company at the market price (forty-two shillings) using nominees. Then, when he had increased his shareholding from 30 per cent to approximately 42 he telephoned Roy Thomson, the new owner of the *Scotsman*, and Scottish Television, in Edinburgh. Still nothing was said to the non-family directors of Kemsley Newspapers. He asked Thomson to come to Gray's Inn Road the following morning, where he would learn something to his great advantage.

I happened again to be on holiday with Olive, this time in Greece. We'd gone to Mykonos and intended to visit Rhodes and Athens, but there was a sudden controversy in the Greek press about some remarks I was said to have made in a restaurant – I was upset by the killing of some DLI men in Cyprus. Anyhow, our holiday was cut short. No sooner had we landed and returned to our house in North London than the phone rang. It was Sunday night and it was Lord Kemsley himself.

Kemsley was not a man who telephoned a great deal. Now he announced in great excitement, 'I've achieved it!' I said, 'What have you achieved, Lord Kemsley?' 'I've succeeded in dialling your number myself!' he said. 'William [the butler] is having a night off.' He went on to say that he had been waiting for my return, and I was to lunch with him next day. As it happened, I had an appointment in Whitehall with a Cabinet minister. 'I don't care if you are lunching with the Prime Minister!' he said, 'I wish you to lunch with me.'

I didn't quibble. I didn't see him all morning, and at lunch we congregated in the luncheon room – my fellow directors Eric Cheadle, Angus Burnett-Stuart, Michael Renshaw and Kemsley's eldest son, Lionel. We had a notably quick meal, with just two courses. Then, when the two waiters went out, Kemsley began.

'I'm very sorry I had to interfere with your arrangements, but what I have to say I've been holding back until you returned.' I thought: perhaps the old boy is going to announce his retirement in favour of

Lionel. Then came his bombshell. 'You all know Lady Kemsley's been ill. Worst of all, each day somebody is buying our shares, and I'm frightened that if this goes on we may wake up one morning to find that somebody very undesirable has got 51 per cent and will control the organisation. Therefore, I have taken steps to sell it into hands I can trust, to someone who has given me various guarantees.'

There was complete silence. We were all stunned. 'Now come on, CD, you've just had a holiday, you're very bright; you guess who's bought it!'

'Well,' I answered, pretty bowled over by all this and thinking hard, 'I always knew the other side of your family wanted the *Sunday Times*. Is it your brother's family, Michael Berry?' Kemsley flushed – for there was, indeed, an unwritten understanding in the family that if ever the *Sunday Times* was to be sold, Lord Camrose or his heirs would have first refusal. 'No, no, that's not the case at all!'

'Then,' I went on, 'the only other person who would be suitable to meet the terms you mention is Lord Rothermere.'

'No, it's not Rothermere!' came his reply. 'I'm going to give you one more guess.' Everyone was as puzzled as I was – but they could all see Kemsley was rather enjoying my predicament. He kept saying, 'Come on, come on, give me the answer. He's not a stranger to you . . . .'

'Well,' I said, 'the *Financial Times* and Lord Cowdray; they have provincial papers – he has plans to make them into one big group.' Kemsley was intrigued. 'Actually that would make a very good idea, the *Financial Times*, the *Sunday Times* and the provincial papers. But it's somebody else. One person, CD,' he said, 'you've met him several times.'

I said, 'It's not Roy Thomson is it?' He replied: 'Yes; it's Roy Thomson - I've sold it all to him.'

Looking back thirty years later, I am surprised that I was then so taken by surprise. Kemsley was 74 – a very fit 74, admittedly – but lonely without Lady Kemsley to come home to every night and discuss the day. He showed no faith in the potential of his sons. His first taste of strikes in Gray's Inn Road – where the unions refused to rationalise their nineteen different union organisations, with sixty-five separate 'chapels' or branches – had shocked him, and he expected more. Although the *Sunday Times* was expanding, the group was shrinking and he had no appetite for new developments. He must have realised that his nephew at the *Telegraph* might prove troublesome and perhaps start a rival Sunday newspaper – as he did. I should have been more alert to the sale of the shares, and to the fact that at least two sons were also ready to move on. But I was blinded by my loyalty to Kemsley, who also fogged the picture by increasing the number of *Sunday Times* future-planning conferences. The target was a circulation of one million each Sunday, he declared. But even as he announced this, he knew it was a charade: he himself was abandoning ship.

Kemsley now gave an outline timetable. He wanted the deal announced within a fortnight and said both he and Roy Thomson were worried about leaks. We were told we would meet Roy soon. We did so some days later, one at a time, in the boardroom.

Eric Cheadle was our circulation director, and largely through the Monty serialisation and his promotional campaign the *Sunday Times* circulation was now about 850,000. Cecil King, owner of the *Daily Mirror*, had told Roy that if ever he got a London newspaper, Cheadle was the man. So Roy was particularly anxious to meet Cheadle, and offered him a very good contract to stay, as deputy managing director. The rest of us all sat awaiting our turn, like men queueing for a job. I went in half-an-hour later.

'Well, Denis,' Roy opened the proceedings, 'remember when we met at Dropmore? I was interested in buying the Aberdeen and Middlesbrough papers and you quoted figures that were absolutely crazy? I got the message: Kemsley didn't want to sell. Well, I won't hold that against you. Nor that you refused to join me as editor' – he'd once made me an offer to go over to him as an editor and general manager. He went on, 'I haven't made up my mind about the editorial side of things. Eric Cheadle has agreed to stay, but I'd like to leave your own position open for a few months.'

'You won't,' I said. He asked what I meant. 'You're not going to insult me like this.' He was a bit startled. I said, 'I think I'd better go and consult my fellow-directors. But you may find yourself in some difficulty.'

Thomson looked nonplussed, and I went straight along to Lionel Berry. I said that I was upset at the thought of a row with his father, who had shown me considerable kindness for over twelve years. Nevertheless, I'd had the most insulting interview of my life. 'I've served in the forces,' I said, 'I've served you as well as I possibly could and you have sold me like a piece of furniture. Well, you've made a very great mistake. You may think that because you've got the majority of the shares you can get away with this. But you can't get this through legally without my signature. And I'm not going to sign as a director of the company recommending the sale. I'm going to draw up a public statement on your behaviour and how you've dealt with a faithful servant like myself. I think it's intolerable that you've sold out for at least five million pounds – and made no arrangement whatsoever for me or any of my colleagues, except for Cheadle. Well, you're not going to get away with it. I shall make it clear to the Prime Minister and to all my contacts and friends what your behaviour has been – and your determination to scrape every penny for yourselves.'

Lionel was very defensive. 'As we've got the majority shares you can't hold it up,' he countered. But that was the point. Kemsley was selling about 40 per cent of the shares and needed 11 per cent of the other shareholders to follow him if Thomson was to have a real majority. A fly in the ointment such as I was threatening to be, saying it was not a just deal, that the money was insufficient and that no provision had been made for the directors who ran the company, might well ditch things. Certainly it would complicate them.

'Well, what do you think is appropriate?' asked Lionel. I said, 'I'm not trying to blackmail you for money but you have given me no contract. I have four children, I am 40 years of age. After all I have done for you and this organisation, what is my entitlement? Another three months' money? It's preposterous!'

'What are your demands?' I said, 'A three-year contract.' There was a pause. I went on: 'I can only suggest that you tell Roy Thomson what's happened, and see that he doesn't see the other two directors yet.'

So, Renshaw and Burnett-Stuart were told to go back to their offices, and Roy Thomson – my secretary told me – went in to see Kemsley. At 4.15 the commissionaire arrived with an urgent letter, to be given into my hands only. It was from Roy Thomson: 'Dear Denis, I think, on reflection, I have mishandled the situation. I hope you will come down and see me immediately because I wish to offer you a three-year contract.'

I went to see him, and he apologised: 'I'm sorry, I should have seen I couldn't put a man like you, the editorial director of the whole organisation, into such a position, especially as I understand you have four children at school. So I'm arranging a three-year contract.'

'But what about the others?' I asked. He replied, 'I don't feel so strongly about them.' But I did. 'I'm very sorry,' I told Thomson, 'but I'm not taking a three-year contract if they can't. I'm not just fighting for myself, but for all three of us.' I didn't blame Eric Cheadle for having made his own terms – he was a brilliant salesman and deserved recognition for his talents.

Roy had to go back to Kemsley and eventually it was agreed that Renshaw, Burnett-Stuart and myself would each be given contracts. Angus Burnett-Stuart was a dependable lawyer who went on and retired to Scotland at 60; Micky Renshaw was brilliant in the advertising field, and Roy could never have built up Thomson Newspapers without him.

About ten minutes after seeing Thomson I got a letter from Kemsley saying he hoped I was now satisfied, and wouldn't prevent or delay the deal from going through. I again went to Lionel and repeated that I did not want an argument with his father. Ironically, Lionel and his brothers had also been in the same boat. It was only when Lady Kemsley, in her darkened room, had heard the terms of the deal that she realised her husband had done nothing to safeguard their careers or expense accounts. 'Gomer – what have you done for the boys?' she is said to have asked. 'What will they do with their time and who will pay their expenses? Gomer, you must do something.' Whereupon Kemsley had dictated an agreement with Thomson whereby the Berry boys were to remain as directors with offices, secretaries, company cars and expense accounts – yet still had done nothing for his professional directors. Kemsley's nepotism had not stopped there, though. He had insisted that Lady Kemsley keep her Rolls. And Thomson, so close to unexpected realisation of a dream, gave in. He was now owner of the biggest newspaper group in Britain.

But was he? Towards the end of the hand-over Roy Thomson came into K's office and said, 'To think that all this is mine now, this whole group, and that I shall sit at that table,' looking admiringly at the huge, square, antique desk. Kemsley, who had already profited by some five million pounds from the sale, said, 'No you won't sit at that table. It's going to my house!' Furthermore, he announced he had one final request. 'Will you sign a cheque for me, Mr Thomson, a personal cheque?' Out of his drawer Kemsley produced the cheque, all ready – and Thomson had to sign it. It was an ex-gratia payment to Lord Kemsley's secretary – not his office secretary, but his social secretary, and for several thousand pounds, payable by the company. Fuming, but seeing once again that there was nothing else to be done, as the deal was now through, Roy paid up.

For me it was all, I suppose, the shattering of an illusion. For still Kemsley had been like a father to me; the more so as my own father had died in 1951. I therefore commissioned a valedictory tribute to Kemsley from his old editor, W.W. Hadley, to be published in the final issue of the *Sunday Times* under Kemsley's ownership, and took a proof of it to him.

Kemsley read it through and said, 'I detect some of your phrases in this.' I replied, 'Well, you know how I feel about our relationship, Lord Kemsley. You've been very kind to me and my family. I shall miss you very much. Lady Kemsley has been a great friend to my wife, you've lent us your flat in Paris many times, you've paid for many of my holidays when I've never asked for it. You've given me unlimited opportunity to meet your friends, and given me a wonderful start to life. I do hope there will be some way in which we can keep in touch because I have felt that we've been very close to each other.'

Kemsley coughed and said, 'In many ways you've been closer to me than some of my family. I've always been able to rely on your word, and know that my leg wasn't being pulled or that you had any ulterior motive in anything you said.' He stopped, and then went on: 'I'd like you to have a souvenir' – and I could see a cheque in front of him. I thought I was going to get some sort of final pay-off and I remember thinking, 'That'll pay the Westminster and Oundle school bills.' However, the cheque read: 'To Viscount Kemsley, three-and-a-half million pounds.' He said, 'That is the first instalment that Roy Thomson has paid me for acquiring the group and I thought you'd like this as a souvenir.' It was not even the cheque itself, but a photocopy he'd had made.

I looked at this thing and I looked at Lord Kemsley, and I said, 'Well thank you very much, it's a very interesting souvenir.' Then he said, 'Well, that's that,' and stood up and shook my hand. 'Yes,' he went on, 'I would like to see you again, but perhaps Mr Thomson won't like it if you keep contact with me, he may feel you're spilling things.' I said, 'Well, that's very understanding of you, Lord Kemsley, but I don't know how I'm going to get on with Mr Thomson; despite the contract, he can always pay me off . . . .' We shook hands. It was the last time I was ever to speak to Kemsley. Soon afterwards Hadley wrote to me: 'After the decision to sell had become known I wrote to Lord Kemsley, and left him in no doubt as to my surprise and shock. I scarcely expected him to say anything about the sale of the newspapers, and he didn't – not a word! But the letter was longer than his usually are, and his silence about the papers was more expressive than words, and I knew without words what he feels.'

Hadley died the following year. No member of the Berry families attended his funeral, yet without his perception of the qualities of the two brothers their journalistic and commercial dynasty might never have been – for it was Hadley who had given Gomer's brother William Berry his first job on the *Merthyr Times*.

All the millions that Kemsley made did him no good. His mistake was the same as that of 1937 – to imagine that without the *Sunday Times* he would be a figure of importance. His wife Edith had once saved him from that error; now she was too ravaged by her *tic douloureux* to care. Thus Kemsley, in a matter of days, sold off a lifetime's respect as the owner of a great national newspaper. He never hosted another important luncheon or dinner and was dropped by cronies, courtiers and politicians alike. From being a Lord of the Press, he became Lord Nobody, dying an old man, forgotten by the greater world, in a Monte Carlo hotel eight years later.

# CHAPTER SIXTEEN

※

# INNOVATING WITH ROY

ROY THOMSON'S CONQUEST OF FLEET STREET HAS BEEN RECOUNTED MANY times and I shall not retell it. But over the years, with Gordon Brunton, I came as close to Roy as anyone did. Roy and I were complete opposites in every respect – perhaps that was the secret. He trusted me; I became the instrument whereby he got his longed-for (and deserved) peerage, as well as the newspaper of his dreams – the *Times*. I persuaded him to diversify when it became apparent that further newspaper ownership would pose problems with the Monopolies Commission. We moved into book publishing, travel and most fruitful of all, North Sea oil. Of course, Roy had much better financial or business advisers than I could ever be, but he had reached the age when he cared about his public standing, and needed a figure, a man with a position in public affairs, upon whom he could lean and who would at all times tell him the truth. Our relationship deepened, and when he died I felt I'd lost a true friend.

Perhaps there will never be another Roy Thomson, a man with an insatiable appetite for ownership but without interest in exercising power. Behind his absurdly thick spectacles lurked neither envy nor spiteful ambition. He wasn't in any way religious, and yet his character was open and sincere. I never met a man less trumped-up, or simpler in his tastes and joys. He radiated a sort of goodwill, a confident courage, an almost childlike enjoyment of challenge. Beside the Maxwells and Murdochs of this world he was like an innocent. And unlike Kemsley, he knew how to delegate.

In time Roy told me the whole saga of being summoned by Kemsley to London, and the offer of the group. It was barely a year since Kemsley had made it plain he did not even wish to sell his Aberdeen newspaper, the *Press and Journal*, yet suddenly he was prepared to hand over his whole empire, even the jewel in the crown, the *Sunday Times*. Roy was flabbergasted. 'I can't believe it – you'd sell the *Sunday Times* – the whole lot, everything to me – you won't split it up?' He was utterly dazed, because he couldn't see how, on the relatively small profits of Scottish Television and the overall loss he was making on his Scottish newspapers, he could afford it. 'Denis,' he said to me, 'I saw the opportunity of a lifetime just disappearing because it came too early, before I was ready.'

The banker Henry Grunfeld's reverse takeover had solved all that – putting Thomson overnight in the heart of Fleet Street. He was made to pay twice the market price for the shares, but Kemsley's instinct had been right. Roy Thomson didn't quibble or insist on a minute examination of the books. It was a chance in a lifetime – and Roy seized it.

The following two years went so rapidly and were so eventful that it is difficult to unpick all the threads – for in that period he got rid of all the Berrys (soon deciding they were not what he wanted), faced eviction of the *Sunday Times* from the presses of the *Daily Telegraph*, closed down loss- making papers like the *Sunday Graphic*, invented Fleet Street's first colour magazine for distribution with a national newspaper, and retired the stalwart but in his view anachronistic editor of the *Sunday Times*, Harry Hodson.

In all this, Roy's courage I remember with most admiration. He was almost sixty years old, had never owned a newspaper nearer to London than the *Scotsman*; yet he not only took an instant grip on this, the still largest press group in Britain, but showed all Fleet Street where the future of quality newspapers lay. For an uneducated Canadian reputed only to be interested in the 'bottom-line', this was no mean achievement.

My own relationship with Roy began warily. My faith in Kemsley had been shattered, my interview with Roy explosive. Roy had brought to London his canny Scottish director, Jim Coltart; but where and how should we begin? Very quickly it became clear we had been living in a fools' paradise. Since Kemsley was so secretive about the finances of the company and had packed the board with his kith and kin, non-family directors had no idea where the company really stood. In that sense, Roy had bought a pig in a poke. If he wanted to get the organisation on to a proper footing with proper accounts and budgets he would have to sweep away the dead wood. 'How can we get to work without the Berrys?' Coltart asked me. I said, 'Well, I'd just have meetings without the Berry boys. Call it an executive committee or something.'

This was done. I still have the minutes. Thomson had assumed control on 23 August 1959; the first meeting of the executive committee of non-family directors was on Tuesday, 15 September. The first thing we did was sack Kemsley's great-nephew in Sheffield, whose appointment I had so bitterly protested against. 'It was evident from all that was said that Sheffield is suffering from considerable lack of direction,' the minutes ran. Fortunately, I had an excellent replacement as general manager: John Goulden, editor of the *Evening Chronicle*, Manchester, whom I'd groomed for many years – an editor with a keen understanding of business. 'Much discussion took place on a suitable position for Mr Berry within the organisation but it was unanimous that it would be unwise to retain him anywhere.'

Ironically, our committee – Eric Cheadle, Micky Renshaw, Angus Burnett-Stuart and myself – comprised the very directors, apart from Cheadle, whom Roy Thomson had wished to drop. When in November Lionel Berry protested against the way we were running the organisation Coltart looked at him with his canny Scottish smile. 'Of course you're *all* directors, I don't deny that,' said Jim, 'but I haven't put you on my executive committee because you are all too senior for that.' That afternoon the Berry boys all met, and that night resigned en bloc, even handing in their cars. It was the end of the Kemsley dynasty. Kemsley's nepotistic paternalism had left them ill-equipped for the real tasks of journalism. They left newspapers for ever – with a million pounds each to comfort them, and a safe Tory seat bought (I witnessed the payment) for the youngest, who wished to go into politics.

A new spirit now ran through Gray's Inn Road. That autumn we were going to serialise the second volume of the Alanbrooke story in the *Sunday Times*. The paper was, the more one looked at the organisation, the most potentially profitable of all our newspapers, since quality advertising was growing, and so was our readership. Inexorably, we were moving towards a 48-page paper – and with the *Sunday Graphic* losing money despite its popularity, we discussed at our 15 September meeting whether we ought to print the *Sunday Times* at Gray's Inn Road instead of the presses of the *Daily Telegraph* in Fleet Street.

Three months later the decision was taken for us, for Roy Thomson, in his innocence, invited Michael Berry, the late Lord Camrose's son, to his office, and asked to buy the *Daily Telegraph*. This was one of Roy's standard questions when meeting a fellow newspaper-owner – it might be irritating, even insulting, but it often sowed the idea, as it had with Lord Kemsley. Berry, however, was not only insulted but alarmed by Roy Thomson's alternative proposal: to print the *Daily Telegraph* at Gray's Inn Road once we had installed new machines. Berry – later Lord Hartwell – had fallen out with his uncle Kemsley over a share deal and was miffed that his family had not had first option to buy the *Sunday Times*. (They learned of the sale not from Kemsley, but in a phone call from Neville Berry, though in fact Michael Berry would have been unlikely to be able to buy the Kemsley organisation as, like Kemsley, he had eschewed going into television.)

As Berry later told me, Thomson asked not just once, but 'point blank three times would I sell the *Telegraph*, the third time [saying] "I would give you a very good price indeed".' For Roy to press Berry in this way, in those circumstances, was counter-productive, to say the least. This tactlessness was to cost Roy dear – for Berry now knew that Roy would eventually terminate the printing contract for the *Sunday Times*. Only an unwritten agreement between Kemsley and Camrose had stopped the *Telegraph* from bringing out its own edition on a Sunday. Now no such constraint need be felt. If the *Sunday Times* was going to move its printing away, the *Telegraph* would be free to print its own Sunday edition. It was war – and so, three days after Roy Thomson's misguided remarks, we received the first salvo: a letter from the *Telegraph* giving Roy six months' notice. As Michael Berry later put it: 'I decided there and then we would go in our time rather than his.'

It was clear that Roy's 'big mouth' had lost us the first round – for I knew the moment that fateful letter arrived that Berry was now intending to launch a Sunday newspaper in competition with us and the *Observer*. We had trounced the *Observer* with our 'Big Read' weapon. Could we trounce this new competitor whose weekday sales were in excess of one million? I confess I was distinctly worried, for I did not underestimate the editorial skills of the Camroses. In fact, the *Daily Telegraph* was in some ways the greatest editorial achievement of the twentieth century in quality journalism, a monument to Lord Camrose's flair and judgment – qualities his son Michael Berry had evidently inherited. It would be a tough fight – with only six months to prepare for the opening battle. How I cursed Roy's tactless bungling!

Where would we print the *Sunday Times*? New presses could not be installed in Gray's Inn Road in six months, nor could the *Sunday Graphic* tabloid machines be converted in time to cope with even a proportion of the edition – especially since extra sales had accrued with the Alanbrooke serial. Our second Black Monday in three years, however, was lightened when our company secretary told us that Michael Berry had erred. His notice had been based on a 1931 agreement, but in the company correspondence ledger was a letter of 1937, when the brothers parted, extending the period of notice to twelve months. This would give us just enough time to convert the *Sunday Graphic* machines and divert new ones destined for our Cardiff office.

Scarcely believing our luck, we attempted to delay the reissuing of the notice-to-quit for as long as possible – and in the event Berry finally issued it only on 25 January 1960. There was then a mad scamper akin to the preparations for D-day as we enlarged the Gray's Inn Road press room, strengthened the foundations and got the machinery ready. By 25 January 1961, when we moved out of the *Telegraph*'s printroom, we were able to boast not only our own printing facilities for the *Sunday Times* in Gray's Inn Road, but machines capable of printing a 72- or even 80-page paper – if there was enough advertising to carry it. The question was, with a third quality Sunday about to enter the field, would our advertising hold up, let alone increase – not to speak of our circulation?

To be honest, I was very worried. The *Sunday Times* was still not right as a newspaper, I felt – still retained its staid, stuffy predictability, was rather pompous and heavy-handed. Moreover, Harry Hodson had been in the editor's chair almost twelve years and was tiring. At his wife's insistence, so he explained to me, he had even renegotiated his contract in the last days of Lord Kemsley's ownership so that he did not have to stay at the office on Saturday evenings – the very night the paper was put to bed.

I felt he had always resented my connection with the *Sunday Times*. When W.W. Hadley received a farewell gift of a silver tray, Hodson would not permit my name to go on it with the rest of the *Sunday Times* team, saying I was not a member of the newspaper's staff. If Lord Kemsley did not attend the *Sunday Times* meeting on a Tuesday, Hodson refused to countenance my presence; I, therefore, only attended as the chairman's right-hand man. Despite all the boost I'd given the paper in its 'Big Read' serials and in bringing new staff – Frank Giles, William Rees-Mogg, the managing editor Pat Murphy and others – I had never once had so much as a verbal or written expression of thanks from Hodson. It didn't worry me at the time; I had responsibilities for a vast organisation beyond the *Sunday Times* and I certainly recognised Hodson's intellectual distinction, which gave quality and firmness to the paper. Once Michael Berry sent his warning shot across our bows, however, we had to put our thinking caps on – and an editor who didn't feel it necessary to watch over his paper on the night it went to press might be something of a liability.

Roy Thomson was all for a new editor. Whether Kemsley had renewed Hodson's contract for a further three years in order to placate the Prime Minister when the sell-out to Thomson became public, I do not know – others claimed so, Hodson denied it. Quite apart from the legal problem of terminating it, I felt we shouldn't risk upsetting the *Sunday Times* team at this stage. There was, still, a tremendous loyalty to the newspaper, despite Thomson's takeover; not a single journalist had left. Better, I felt, for Hodson to edit the paper while the directors looked after the transfer of printing to Gray's Inn Road and formulated a long-term strategy for the paper – including two new developments: a business section and a colour supplement.

The colour supplement was Roy's brainwave. His marketing men had worked out that, with a million-copy sale, the *Sunday Times* would be just the right size and readership to command expensive colour advertising. It had never been done in Fleet Street, but that didn't trouble Roy. He asked me – and I was enthusiastic. I knew the stuffier members of the *Sunday Times* staff would probably object, feeling it to be infra dig. But our readership profile remained an anxiety to me. We needed more younger readers, particularly if Berry's new Sunday paper were to steal a large number of die-hard conservatives, used to reading the *Telegraph* on a weekday. But a colour supplement needed time to set up (the printing would have to be done elsewhere, with the newsagents marrying the separate parts together) – and, in the meantime, Michael Berry launched his dreaded rival, the *Sunday Telegraph*.

Since the early 1950s I had argued against putting more news into the *Sunday Times*, as its size increased. There wasn't enough happening on a Saturday to interest a Sunday readership, other than sport; besides, as I'd proved with my serialisation policy, the public wanted something different on a Sunday. With the cost of serialisation escalating, my worst fear was that Michael Berry would outbid us for good serials, as well as packing the paper with features and news analysis. To my intense relief, Berry completely misjudged the problem. I almost cried with joy when I saw his first issue in February, 1961. It was filled with news! Twenty-five years later he admitted his mistake:

> Our idea was to follow roughly the same formula for the *Sunday Telegraph* as had been so successful with the *Daily Telegraph* – in short, to produce something of a seventh-day *Daily Telegraph* . . . . We even maintained the same order of pages so that *Daily* readers would find themselves instantly at home. Alas, we couldn't have been more wrong. British readers, I can say now, do not want the same thing on Sundays. The misapprehension proved very costly and it was a year or so before we really got the paper on the move after a disappointing launch. Moreover, we forgot the truism that competition is galvanic. No sooner had we started than a new editor, Mr Denis Hamilton, was appointed to the *Sunday Times*. It vastly improved.

Berry's tribute, two-and-a-half decades later, both surprised and touched me. I don't think he, or anyone else, can have known how worried I was by the *Telegraph*'s declaration of war, or the diffidence with

which I took on the editorship of the *Sunday Times* in 1961. Apart from
the interruption of army life, my whole career had, of course, been spent
in journalism, from the age of eighteen. By 1961 I was 43 years old; but
my experience in Fleet Street was as a director of the company – a War
Office general so to speak, not front-line command. Were I to take on
the editorship myself from Hodson, would the journalists themselves
accept me? Hodson was a brilliant, donnish writer, a master of the
instant leader on almost any topic, whereas my own writing since
Newcastle had been confined to the drafting of Kemsley's speeches and
memoranda. I didn't fit the mould of a writing editor, the traditional
tousle-haired, shirt-sleeved word-wrestler.

But then, perhaps the time for that kind of editor was over. Perhaps a
new kind of editor was needed – the sort of C.O. who knew how to
choose and encourage good staff, and could delegate authority as the
newspaper breached its million-copy sales target. It was, as the figures
showed, big business – and with a colour supplement and the business
section I envisaged, would become bigger business still. Tentatively,
and with considerable qualms, I let Roy talk me into it. I knew Ian
Fleming was behind the conspiracy – when he gave up as foreign
manager in 1959 Ian wrote to me saying, 'I only pray that you will soon
get a commanding grip on the *Sunday Times*. I regard that as essential.'
As the months went by under Roy Thomson, Ian fretted about Hodson,
casting him as a blinkered Oxbridge don jealous of the talent
abounding around him. Ian even took to sending telegrams of
congratulations to *Sunday Times* writers whose pieces he'd enjoyed, so
irritated was he that Hodson never gave praise where it was due.

Eventually it was Ian who, after one of our Tuesday conferences,
begged Thomson to change editors. Roy asked whom he would put in.
Ian replied: 'The answer's staring you in the face.' Roy asked Micky
Renshaw if he agreed – and it was Renshaw who assured him the whole
building would welcome the appointment. When I remonstrated that I
was editorial director of the group, with responsibility for a whole chain
of newspapers, Roy simply brushed my protestations aside. 'You can
get a deputy to take over those other responsibilities. With the colour
supplement coming and five million pounds invested in our basement
[printing plant] I want an editor I can trust to see it through. I
shouldn't rest happy otherwise,' he said.

Hodson was away at this time, on a world trip including Australia.
When he came back, Roy's mind was made up. He summoned Hodson,
and paid off his remaining contract as editor, as well as offering him an
annual retainer as a special contributor to the paper on certain
subjects. Fortunately, Hodson was being wooed by a new trust formed

to promote Anglo-American relations. A director was wanted for its proposed Centre for Anglo-American Studies at Ditchley, and Hodson was perceived to be the outstanding candidate for the job – if he would agree to go. Margaret, his wife, was consulted. At her suggestion, I learned, his proposed title was altered to Provost of Ditchley – perhaps more suitable for a Fellow of All Souls. Harry Hodson departed. Ian Fleming was cock-a-hoop. I'm not so sure about the staff – perhaps there was a slight fear that Hamilton, as a director, might kick a few backsides. Anyhow, on 29 October 1961 the announcement was made. For good or bad I was taking over the editorship of the Sunday Times, in addition to my other duties.

I can honestly say that I was both frightened and exhilarated. I'd made it quite clear to Roy that if I took it on, I would be my own boss, answerable neither to him nor to anyone else over the editorial policy of the paper. I'd worked in and studied the ways of Fleet Street since 1946 – a period of 15 years. I'd learned a lot. Above all, through our training scheme and the very size of our organisation I knew either in person or by repute every good journalist in the kingdom. I had had unusual experience in commanding men in battle, in large numbers – officers and men. I looked forward to the challenge.

Looking back, so many years later, I can only say that those heady years in the 1960s, with the chance to make the *Sunday Times* into a newspaper of world importance, were to be the most stimulating and rewarding of my whole life.

# CHAPTER SEVENTEEN

✳️

# COLOURFUL YEARS

UNDER ROY THOMSON'S OWNERSHIP THE *SUNDAY TIMES* BECAME immensely profitable and editorially the most innovative newspaper of the 1960s, winning award after award. The story has already been well told by Leonard Russell, with others, in *The Pearl of Days*, published in 1972 to mark the paper's 150th anniversary. I still receive letters from journalists referring nostalgically to those halcyon days in Gray's Inn Road, when their journalistic skills and creativity were backed by an editor who cared; and I *did* care intensely for every one of my team, just as I had done in the Army. But as I look back at Fleet Street before and after the Thomson years, I am more than ever amazed at Roy Thomson's greatness of spirit, his ceaseless courage in backing his acquisitions financially, while refusing to meddle editorially. He even had a printed card which he gave to each of his editors, assuring them that they were free to edit their newspaper as they saw fit. When one thinks of the Maxwells, the Murdochs and the Rowlands of this world, it is an extraordinary tribute to Roy. Without demeaning his papers by the introduction of sex or bingo, he was able to increase his circulation and advertising revenues. It was capitalism of the best kind – which perhaps explained why he was so well received by communist leaders from Kruschev to Chou En-lai.

Let no one imagine, however, that it was easy for him. He was, at first, an unpopular press baron, treated with great suspicion both as a foreigner and as a declared empire-builder. One of the things I had had to do at the start was to try to curb his tongue, for to everyone he met he would openly announce his intention of acquiring more and more newspapers – an ambition which naturally worried politicians and those who believed in a free press thriving on fair competition. There was, for example, his attempt in 1960 to buy Odhams Press, owners of the Labour newspaper, the *Daily Herald*. I don't think Roy had thought it out; in fact it frightened me that he was indulging in a fit of newspaper-greed, without considering the consequences. 'Oh Denis, you'll sort it out, m'boy!' he'd say, shooting down my objections.

How he imagined I could cope with the *Sunday Times*, the rest of the old Kemsley group, and an ailing *Daily Herald* with a commitment to the Labour Party, I do not know. It proves, of course, his genuine belief in diversity of stance among his newspapers; but it was naive inasmuch as an ailing newspaper needs more than finance to put it on its feet. As in war, so in peace there is always a shortage of outstanding leaders. With our plans to make the *Sunday Times* a still greater force in Fleet Street, I had my hands full already – and no one was more relieved than I was when Cecil King stepped in with a higher offer and Odhams went to IPC (the *Daily Mirror* group). Under King the *Daily Herald* duly died a miserable death.

The *Sunday Times* had its own trials to face, however. Almost everything we did in the early 1960s was bitterly denounced by the rest of Fleet Street – whether it was our new Colour Magazine or Business News, or Insight, or the hiring of Lord Snowdon. Fleet Street needed a good shake-up, but was as resentful as the old lags in 1942 when Monty arrived in the desert.

The paper's team was a different matter. I promoted William Rees-Mogg (aged 33) to political and economic editor the day I assumed the editorial seat – a fateful decision, for it was Rees-Mogg's feel for the moral pulse of the nation that gave the 'new' *Sunday Times* its intellectual cutting edge. My choice of Mark Boxer, aged only 30, as editor of our forthcoming colour magazine was as controversial as the launch of the magazine itself, for I'd had to remove the man Harry Hodson had provisionally selected: John Anstey. His early dummies didn't impress me at all; they seemed wonderfully safe but lacked the punch that I wanted. I was determined that the magazine would not be another *Illustrated London News*, that is, a rather nice, cheerful but slow-moving record of the events of the world. I wanted to make it attractive to people below the age of 35, who were building houses or furnishing homes for the first time, bringing up young children with all the attendant problems; people who wanted to extend their range of interests, their knowledge of living; who wanted to learn more about the world and, if possible, get to see it in an age of interesting travel. Mark Boxer – who had been sent down from Cambridge for carrying a coffin around the streets of the city – seemed the right sort of journalist for the job: he had edited *Queen* magazine and I felt he had the necessary kind of iconoclastic attitude, a chap I'd have to restrain rather than ginger up. Boxer's appointment was really the end of an era. Hodson warned me against the change, that it would be upon my own head, and so on, but as he himself was going, there was nothing he could do. Anstey himself burst into tears when I told him. But I was determined to clear out the dead wood, and even Hodson at the age of 55 seemed suddenly to belong to an eclipsed generation.

Of course, there was much snorting in the clubs and watering holes of the press – but Mark Boxer's appointment was only a foretaste of what I intended. The old-timers might scoff, as they did when Jack Kennedy swept away Eisenhower's antique administration; but I was sure I knew what I was doing. We had commissioned some market research which had confirmed my fears about the elderliness of our readership. If we were to keep up the momentum of our circulation growth, 'big reads' were not enough. We had to provide a paper that would attract younger readers; a younger generation of professional people, from business executives to civil servants. Not only did we need them as new readers of the editorial matter, we needed them as readers of our advertising, whence came our funds. I felt confident I could hold the balance between the old-fashioned qualities for which the *Sunday Times* was respected and the more radical approach to journalism inspiring my young turks. And the magazine, I was certain, could bring us a further 200,000 readers. There were two problems, though: the print unions and the advertising agencies.

Given the complexity of colour printing we had to contract out the printing of the magazine itself (a contract won by Sun Printers of Watford). The printers ought then to have been able to send the copies to the big W.H. Smith depots to await combination with the newspaper when it arrived. This, however, was too much for Sogat, the union in control of distribution and handling. They saw a splendid chance to squeeze more money out of the management, even if it killed the idea. They thus insisted that the colour copies be transported from Watford to Gray's Inn Road, then re-distributed (at vast cost in extra payments) to the wholesalers. It was utter nonsense that the copies could not be sent direct, but another sad example of the irresponsible attitude of trade union leaders to progress, a blackmail that pervaded every single corner of Fleet Street. Such demands could only be met if we got enough revenue from the magazine's advertisers to pay the extortioners, and for some time this looked extremely doubtful.

The first issue of the supplement was in many ways a disaster. With hindsight, I realised I should have taken editorial control of the first attempt; on the other hand it was my line always with editors to give them their heads as much as possible until it was time either to chop them off or give them a good haircut. I therefore let the boys get on with it, and it emerged as a bit of a hotchpotch, with an altogether too-clever cover. Roy Thomson came up to Watford specially to see the first copies off the machines, and was appalled. 'This is awful, absolutely awful,' he said, turning to me, 'how could you allow it? This is a disaster, we'll be a laughing stock.' I said, 'It doesn't really matter, people will look at it because of its novelty. It's what's coming ahead that matters.' 'Well,' he said, 'you've given too many of those young lads you engaged their heads. You should have done it yourself.' This was all shouted over the noise of the machines, with all those nearby listening.

I had to suffer more humiliation during the next two or three days, with people blaming me, and Roy doing nothing to protect my feelings, but agreeing what a shambles it was. Of all the commentators, the only one who had anything good to say was Francis Williams, in his *New Statesman* column on the Press. He remarked that while a lot of derogatory statements were being made, the rest of Fleet Street was missing the point: that here was something which in time would prove a stunning success. He'd shown it to his daughter, aged 21, and she was thrilled by it.

I wasn't worried myself, because I knew what we had up our sleeve for future issues. I felt we needed a better art editor than we had, and before long we landed the gifted Michael Rand, who raised the standard of layout and photographic presentation into a class of its own. And when Roy asked if I was satisfied with the staff I'd hired, I was able to say with complete confidence: 'Leave it to me, Roy, you're going to find very soon that you've got 200,000 copies per issue more, permanently, on the paper. That'll enable you to increase the advertising rate and will put us so far ahead of the opposition that we'll never be caught up. We're going to make everybody eat their words. You'll be very proud of it – but it's going to be a long struggle to get the advertising agencies behind it. You'll have to get them in for lunch, one by one, and let them criticise it as much as they wish. I'll always be there – they can throw as much mud as they like at me, but I'll answer them. I'm sure one lot will suddenly go for it, and the rest will all follow like sheep.'

And that was exactly what happened. Roy's courage and belief in the magazine subsequently never wavered, even as its losses rose above £500,000 and kept on rising. Like Monty at Alamein, he went on fighting, knowing that in the end the enemy would crack. And eventually, after a whole year of gigantic losses, the agencies caved in. As we forecast, they were like sheep: once space had been booked for a few major accounts, the rest followed suit. All of a sudden we found we couldn't accommodate the rush for colour advertising, and there were panic decisions on how we could reorganise the machinery at Watford to print more copies. From near-rout we had a landslide victory on our hands – perhaps the most successful single innovation in post-war quality journalism. One by one our competitors, having scorned our ambitions and early issues, and having claimed they would never themselves go in for such supplements, began to imitate us.

It was an immensely exciting and encouraging moment in British newspaper history. I got a deputy to help Mark Boxer: Clive Irving, and it was he who in due course spearheaded my new Insight team. Based on the analytical team efforts of *Time* and *Newsweek*, Insight was the first British effort to 'crack' a current theme or story in the news. It needed enthusiastic professional journalists, able to work under pressure and with a sense of team-mission. The journalists themselves needed to have courage – and so did the editor. Ian Fleming, commenting on the new *Sunday Telegraph*, had called it a 'drab sheet . . . . Above all, there are no GUTS anywhere in the paper.' This was certainly not a criticism that could be levelled against the new *Sunday Times*, which suddenly seemed to pull together like an Olympic rowing crew. We had collected, over the years, some of the best reporters, commentators, reviewers and columnists in the business. Our foreign news reporting under Frank Giles (pinched from the *Times*), was second to none. I don't think any editor can have been as proud as I was to lead such a team. Strangely, I was helped by the fact that I no longer had aspirations as a writing-editor – I had an array of journalists far more talented than I was to do the writing. What they needed was a C.O. with nerve and foresight, interested in exposing the truth and not afraid of political or even financial pressure from outside.

Any newspaper worth its salt will upset the establishment – at least the established order of things. All organisations become complacent and often it is only to the Press that a man or woman can turn in seeking to fight injustice. It is not the duty of the Press to be the mouthpiece of a political party or the government – therein lay Kemsley's mistake. But to stand up to the government or to vested interests – as we did in exposing the antique dealers' rings or the Thalidomide scandal – requires editorial resilience and dedication. As in battle, it is the C.O.'s face that is all important. To his officers and men he must radiate determination and confidence, whatever inner anxieties he harbours. Running a new *Sunday Times* was in many ways like being in battle again – sometimes in sad reality, with fatal casualties, as when David Holden and Nicholas Tomalin were killed on foreign assignments.

As far as possible I tried to concentrate on future planning rather than watching every dot and comma of the current issue. This latter task could be safely delegated, but on planning I agreed with Monty;

you cannot expect your staff to dream up the battle plan. This can only
be done by the commander – for only he has the instinct and experience
necessary to succeed. Once he has decided on his plan, then the staff
can take over, under his overall guidance. I therefore continued my
policy of buying serial rights years in advance of publication, as well as
commissioning articles well ahead. For instance, I asked Alan Moorehead, who was easily the best writer of his generation, to go up the Nile
with a colour photographer and produce a story which, ultimately, he
built up into his famous books on the Blue and the White Nile. This was
first published as a feature article in an early issue of the magazine, with
a dozen or more magnificent pictures of the Nile and Pharaonic objects
and temples, and set quite new standards in photojournalism.

Colour journalism of this kind was in its infancy. I could always put
my hand on writers, either from the paper itself or outside, but I felt
sure we should build up our own corps of photographers, and in due
course, we did, with names like Don McCullin, Roy Green, Philip
Jones-Griffiths – and Lord Snowdon. Tony Snowdon was an old
associate of Mark Boxer. Once again, the rest of Fleet Street protested
windily – but their motive, as so often, was jealousy that they had not
themselves thought of the appointment. In fact, Snowdon proved to be
one of the ablest of photographers, producing portraits of the famous
and the unknown, rich and poor, sane and insane that haunt the
memory.

At the same time, we began to cover the big exhibitions in London in
colour. Very swiftly we established a name for this, getting sole rights
ahead of other papers and helping to put certain exhibitions so much in
the public eye that readers who had rarely if ever been inside a museum
would be queuing up to get in. I suppose this all answered some
personal drive towards self-education. Inside me there still beat the
simple heart of a Sunday School teacher and Scout leader – as Mark
Boxer observed in an article on the 25th anniversary of the magazine:

> He ran a pro-consul system on the *Sunday Times*, recruiting brilliantly
> and effectively. Rugged under attack, he was in some ways of the old
> school and though he would deceive those who knew him slightly by
> his use of military phraseology, he was happy to describe himself as a
> Boy Scout. This attitude seemed to me to be the essence of his success
> in creating the modern *Sunday Times*. He believed the British longed
> to educate themselves in the broadest sense.

I did. However sentimental it may sound, it made me proud to see
museum visitors with a copy of the *Sunday Times* colour magazine under
their arm on a Monday or Tuesday. Certainly it was the inspiration for

my decision to start backing certain great national exhibition events such as Tutankhamun and the Chinese Exhibition, to which I shall come in due course. Those with elite educations who knew it all – perhaps had been to Egypt and seen it all – might scoff, but as time would show, there were literally millions more who were grateful for the chance to see such treasures in London, and the origin of this was Roy Thomson's intuition that there was money to be made in Britain with colour.

# CHAPTER EIGHTEEN

# THE BARBER'S SON

RELATIONSHIPS DEEPEN IN ADVERSITY. THE BUSINESS WITH MICHAEL Berry and the trials and tribulations of getting Fleet Street's first colour magazine successfully started drew the directors of Thomson Newspapers together. Jim Coltart set up a budgetary control system in place of Kemsley's secretive accountancy; Micky Renshaw produced the vital advertising; Eric Cheadle masterminded our circulation drives, and pioneered a new lightweight Finnish newsprint for the main paper that enabled us to run 72-page papers weighing a little more than 48 – and very much faster. After years of slow pressure-cooking, the lid was off. It was a tremendous advantage to me, as editor, also to be a director of the whole organisation, for it gave me the confidence and backing to introduce radical new ideas in the newspaper, financially as well as editorially; equally, I think, it gave my fellow-directors a sense of intimate involvement which might otherwise have been lacking. And at the centre of our cabal was Roy Thomson, whose money we were spending.

There can be no doubt that Roy changed in certain respects once he became a Fleet Street proprietor. Hitherto, he'd been content to be cast as a hillbilly outsider, in dress and in manner. With the move to London, however, he began to recognise that he was operating in a different world. It was as if he had finally reached Rome.

To begin with, there was the business of the Rolls. When Roy first arrived in London it was by overnight train - he had no car. It was part of his shoe-shiner approach to life that he ate at workmen's cafés to save money, and travelled the world with only a small suitcase containing two shirts and a pair of pyjamas. Even though the Berry boys had handed in their Rolls Royces, he could not be persuaded to use one. Instead, he acquired a very modest salesman's car from the company garage, with a driver. We were all invited by the Archbishop of Canterbury to lunch with him at the Reform Club, and Roy insisted on going in this tiny car. Jim Coltart, as an ardent MRA man, was anxious to go, and Thomson asked me to come as well: 'You understand about handling Archbishops,' he said, 'you'll be able to get some conversation going and keep me OK.'

Lunch went very well. But as we came out on to the steps of the Reform his grace said, 'Oh, Mr Thomson, we archbishops don't have cars, will you give me a lift?' So the large, rotund Roy Thomson, the Primate of All England, James Coltart and Denis Hamilton all started to get into this inadequate vehicle. After two of them had squeezed into the back I said to Coltart, 'Come on, we'll get a taxi.' As Roy and the Archbishop were driven off I remember saying: 'Well, if I was a betting man, Jim, Roy will be using one of the Rolls Royces after this afternoon.' And that was precisely what happened. He realised he was going to look foolish – that people in London ask for lifts. When it suited me to talk to somebody I often accepted them – in royal cars, prime ministers' cars, in all sorts of situations, with my own car following on behind. In the world of journalism, if someone wants to give you a lift and you want some information, what better place than the back of a car? In Roy's case the conversion was immediate and total: not long afterwards we noticed a proud new registration number on his Rolls, RHT 1.

Then there was his office. Roy had quickly decided to rebuild the half-finished Kemsley building, and gradually, new floors of offices were being built. By this time I was editing the *Sunday Times*. I knew Tony Snowdon was a designer as well as a photographer, so I asked Tony if he would do my new office.

Rumours of Tony's radical new design, as well as its escalating cost, soon travelled the corridors of Gray's Inn Road and naturally enough came to Roy Thomson's ears. Somehow, people who are in the ordinary course of things friendly and honest and trustworthy suddenly see a chance of gaining an influence with the new owner. As Roy was known to be stingy, certain persons whispered to him that my office was costing the earth, and Roy kept on ringing me up to ask, 'When can I see your office?' My answer was always, 'When it's finished' – I knew he was getting more and more worried about the cost, even though everything was bought off the peg. Finally he saw it. Immediately he asked if Tony Snowdon would do his!

Tony duly agreed, and when Roy's new office was finished, Tony, myself and John Russell (then art critic of the *Sunday Times*) all gathered there. One wall was bare, and fearing that Roy would fill it with some ghastly reproduction of 'The Monarch of the Glen', or something similar, I suggested we get Roy a real painting. This was no sooner said than done. John Russell took us to see Sydney Nolan in his studio, where he had a superb painting that to me suggested an elephant drinking at a waterhole. Because Nolan was a friend of John's, he said he wouldn't use his agent, he'd let us have it for £3,000. We put it straight into the car, took it to Gray's Inn Road and hung it.

Next morning Roy saw it, and frankly, didn't understand it at all. It demanded some imagination, and artistic imagination was not Roy's forte. Then the rats got in. 'You know, Denis has paid £5,000 for the picture,' they whispered. Then £10,000, £20,000 . . . . Roy became more and more obsessively worried about how much I'd paid, but he lacked the courage to ask me outright because he thought I'd take offence, and also that it would leak to Tony.

Some weeks later a prominent art dealer came to see Roy. He was about four steps into Roy's new office when he burst out: 'Roy! That's a Nolan! Where did you get it? It's never been through the galleries or I'd have bought it. Whatever you paid for it, I'll write out a cheque for double.' An hour later Roy rang me in my office. 'You know I've rather changed my mind about this Nolan, Denis,' he said. 'Do you think you can get me some more?'

Roy enjoyed bargaining, and making little gifts. On his death literally hundreds of cheap rings, trinkets and the like were found in a clothes wardrobe, but he hated to spend too much on any item. For some months he was nearly crippled and could hardly walk. Eventually I persuaded him to see an orthopaedic surgeon. When he returned he told me that this celebrated consultant had said, 'You wear your shoes too tight.' I said I would go with Roy to a really good specialist shoe maker in St James's Street. 'Not likely', he replied, 'these ones aren't worn out yet.' On another occasion Cyril Lord gave him some yards of Northern Irish poplin, and Eric Cheadle then took him to be measured at Moss Bros. for some new shirts. Having ordered three, Roy returned to his Rolls. Shortly, though, he stopped the car and rushed back to the shop – where he reduced his order to two.

Inevitably, the sycophants, those who wanted something from him, collected around Roy. I think this made my relationship with him a rather important one. He knew I would never take advantage of him, either financially or in terms of power. I was no longer merely one of his directors: as editor of the *Sunday Times* I held a position in public affairs, in which I was my own man. At one point in 1964 Roy asked me to accompany him to Russia. He had already taken a party of advertisers to Moscow on the magazine's first anniversary in 1962 – and to his surprise Kruschev had given him an audience. So well did the two get on that Kruschev invited Roy to return in 1964, when he would show him something of the rest of the Soviet Union. I declined Roy's

The Hamiltons' wedding in December 1939: the Durham Light Infantry subaltern was already in training before embarking for France.

2nd-Lieutenant Hamilton conducts Colonel Collins, honorary colonel of the 11th Battalion, Durham Light Infantry, on his inspection before departure for France in 1939.

Patrol Leader and King's Scout: Denis Hamilton (centre, back row) with his Scout patrol, Middlesbrough, 1934.

Hamilton the roving feature-writer in 1939 on his first assignment after joining the Newcastle papers from Middlesbrough.

Lieutenant-Colonel OD Hamilton DSO in Holland in 1944, on the day before the liberation of Arnhem, when he acquired his only "loot" of the war – a pocketful of tickets from the railway station.

Lord and Lady Kemsley leave Southampton on the *Athlone Castle* for Capetown, South Africa, on Christmas eve, 1947: Denis Hamilton was to meet Field-Marshal Smuts – and also to have to swear never to reveal Lady Kemsley's age.

Lord Kemsley in full fig: however, his ambitions to proceed to an earldom ("I want to be a peer of the realm" the Viscount told "CD") were not to be fulfilled.

The now ex-colonel Hamilton (the badges of rank gone from his officer's greatcoat) with Field-Marshal Montgomery at a Normandy reunion in the 1950s.

HV Hodson addresses his *Sunday Times* colleagues for the last time as editor, alongside his successor and the proprietor, Roy Thomson.

Roy Thomson's eagerness to employ Eric Cheadle (right) exposed Lord Kemsley's cavalier disregard of his professional directors, who became key figures in Thomson's subsequent success.

Denis Hamilton at his desk on taking over the editorship of the *Sunday Times*.

With Montgomery at Gstaad, Switzerland, 1957, while planning the serialisation of the field-marshal's memoirs in the *Sunday Times*. The "big read", of which they were an outstanding example, was one of the autnor's key contributions to the paper's success in the 1960s and later.

With Lord Snowdon and Princess Margaret: because of his connections, Tony Snowdon's appointment as a *Sunday Times* photographer caused a furore in Fleet Street, but led to some outstanding photo-reportage on subjects far from the royal scene.

With Roy Thomson: their association began with an argument, thanks to Lord Kemsley, but then became one of the most fruitful and innovative, as well as closest, in modern newspaper history.

Sir Denis and Lady Hamilton.

Three prime ministers at the party for publication of Macmillan's memoirs: the historian Hugh Trevor-Roper (Lord Dacre) is at the left; then Edward Heath, Macmillan, Harold Wilson and CD Hamilton.

President Johnson's signed memento of their Oval Office meeting provided the lasting evidence of something that surprised his visitor – the hole in the sole of LBJ's shoe. Lady Bird Johnson later told Sir Denis it was his "lucky" pair.

Boarding the aircraft which was to take Field-Marshal Viscount Montgomery and the author to the ceremonies observing the 25th anniversary of the battle of El Alamein.

Editor-in-chief: with William Rees-Mogg, the new editor of *The Times* (left), and Harold Evans, who took over the Hamilton chair at the *Sunday Times*.

With the Queen at the opening of the Tutenkhamun Exhibition in 1972: this was one of the most successful events of its kind ever staged, with more than one-and-three-quarter million visitors.

Prince Charles visits Times Newspapers in Gray's Inn Road, to be met by the editor-in-chief and, on the left, Marmaduke Hussey, architect of the ill-fated "closedown" plan in the battle with the print unions and later BBC Chairman.

Margaret Thatcher greeted by the author when she visited the exhibition of Montgomery's command caravans at the Imperial War Museum.

Journalist of the year, 1965: Denis Hamilton receives his award from Sir Lynton Andrews, the distinguished editor of the *Yorkshire Post*, who was himself a great admirer of Hamilton's achievement in establishing a system of proper journalistic training in Britain's newspapers.

With Reuters chief executive Glen Renfrew above the floor of the Stock Exchange: the successful flotation of Reuters was achieved under Sir Denis's chairmanship.

Denis Hamilton, by Snowdon.

invitation to join them, however, much to Roy's surprise. Roy clearly thought, like Monty in 1959, that having made a hit with Kruschev he could actually influence détente. I was all for Roy going as a private citizen, but he didn't realise that such trips were not new; that newspaper proprietors have always gone round the world, meeting the great and the not always good. Kemsley had met Hitler before the war, specifically to further appeasement or peace – a pathetically fruitless endeavour. After all, if a world leader pays court to a newspaper magnate, it is in the express hope that he will get a good press from it. I did not wish to be leant on. I was the editor of an internationally respected and independent newspaper, and I intended to remain free to criticise Khrushchev if I wished.

Roy accepted this. He will go down in history, I think, as one of the rare newspaper proprietors who encouraged his editors to form and formulate their own political and social stances in complete freedom. He himself, having failed to win a Conservative seat in Toronto, had abandoned politics. He always used to laugh and say, 'Thank God I lost' – because it was then that he thought of coming to Scotland and buying a newspaper here. People would often say to me: 'Roy claims that he gives you total control of the contents of all his newspapers in Britain – surely that's just a piece of play-acting? Surely a man who's invested so much of his money is not going to leave it to one man to do the supreme act which is necessary to get the contents of the paper right?' Yet that was Roy Thomson's achievement: that he accepted that his genius was in the business of newspapers, not in the content – a lesson so very few proprietors ever learn.

He was an indefatigable raconteur. He once had to speak at a lunch given by the US Ambassador for a crowd of visiting American business men. I worked with William Rees-Mogg and Peter Jay (then on the *Times*) on the speech. Its subject was the Common Market, of which Roy was a committed supporter. Our text was tailored to his style of speaking, and he rehearsed it throughout the morning. By 4 pm I had not heard from him, which was most unusual, so at about half-past-four I went into his room and asked how the speech had gone down. 'Look, Denis,' he said, 'I've got to confess that I didn't give it.'

'Didn't give the speech? Well, what on earth did you talk about?' I asked. He explained: 'You know I've got three kinds of cards' – pulling a number of them from his pocket 'with notes on them. The blue card is for men only; the pink card is for mixed audiences with rather broadminded ladies; and I've another card where I've really got to behave myself. In my speech I said, "Before I start my talking about the Common Market I'll give you a couple of stories." I looked round and I thought they're all business men, they've made their way, so I gave them a couple of blue cards and they kept shouting for more. At half past three I was still telling stories, and they said could they all come back next year!'

He was such a natural, straightforward man that people rarely took offence – the more so because, in spite of his policy of non-interference he drew the line at smut in his newspapers. Not only were they as 'clean' as in Kemsley's day, he even extended this edict to his book publishing empire. Great was the agitation, I remember, when some unsuspecting soul sent him an advance copy of a paperback of the verses of rugby football songs. He ordered every copy to be withdrawn, saying, 'I do not wish to make my money from that sort of thing.' He would have been deeply upset if any of his papers had carried a picture he thought too revealing. There was a difference, he believed, in what was broadcast publicly and what was private. He wasn't stuffy about it – it was a simple matter of right or wrong. In his view, it was wrong to peddle sex, and he would, therefore, have nothing to do with that sort of publication.

In this respect we were very much of one mind; and although I would tolerate quite radical journalism in the *Sunday Times* and its magazine, I would not permit any cheapening of our image by deliberate titillation – leading to several heated interviews with Mark Boxer, who could be very mischievous at times. I knew I would be cast as a prude, but I was confident I would achieve a sale of one-and-a-half million copies for the *Sunday Times* without debasing the newspaper or the fairer sex, so why resort to such tactics? It was, of course, part of Mark Boxer's talent as an editor that he should tilt at windmills; but breaching the code on the sexual front was not something I was willing to permit. If I was mocked behind my back for my prudery, I didn't care. An editor has to be a leader and be prepared to stand by his talents and by his principles.

If Roy and I saw eye to eye over newspaper decency, we were poles apart over many social and political issues. For instance, he felt very strongly that anyone shooting a policeman should be hanged, as should those who committed rape and murder – that they should be got rid of because they were liable to do it again. He also felt we were spending far too much on defence, when we ought to have been modernising our industry, which was falling apart. Now he may have been right, but I didn't share his view, and Roy respected this, recognised that the editor *has* to be free to put his own stamp on a newspaper, and that no one else can do so. He may have shaken his head when he first saw my salary, but he came to see that it is the *content* of a national newspaper that determines its success, not printing machinery, or distribution, or even budgetary systems. Of course, the business side *has* to be got right; but in the end the public is buying a product, and if the product isn't right, no amount of efficiency or gimmicks will make it so.

Equally, experienced editors who know their product and the market can make very good business men, as Roy soon learned. In Canada he owned a large number of basically local newspapers, whereas in England he acquired a chain of quality newspapers with national or regional importance. In the early stages he wanted to replace the Berry family appointees with business men brought in from outside. It was a policy which worked well enough in Canada, but made no sense in Britain, at least to me. For years I'd trained and brought on editors of the highest calibre – men who really understood their market. I was convinced they would make excellent regional managing directors. One by one they were appointed, despite Roy's qualms, and to his surprise, all made their mark as outstanding business men as well as journalists – Robert Clough in Newcastle, Alastair Dunnett in Edinburgh, John Goulden in Sheffield among them.

In this sense, as in certain other respects, Roy matured as he reached the pinnacle of the newspaper world. Certainly those of us who got to know him well came to recognise the qualities which made him the greatest proprietor of his time. At an age when most men think of retirement his restless ambition was to expand. Indeed, the problem became very much how, as directors, we could channel Roy's business energies once it became clear that an extension of his newspaper empire, at least in Britain, would raise the spectre of the Monopolies Commission.

Though I was primarily an editorial executive I could see real difficulties ahead unless we diversified, and so suggested we hold a conference in the country to gaze into the crystal ball – a sort of Camp David meeting, held at Liphook in 1961. As Roy recorded in his autobiography *After I Was Sixty*, 'our first efforts were not entirely successful' – and almost everything we did initially, from publicity to printing and educational learning systems, we had to sell off or close down. Yet, as with the *Sunday Times* magazine, Roy never despaired, however much he may have wept at the losses we incurred. Where Kemsley had panicked over the size of investment needed to start in television, Roy was challenged by big stakes. He'd brought in Gordon Brunton to the Thomson Organisation to take charge of his diversification plans, and his faith in Gordon never wavered. We moved successfully into magazines and – after a shaky start – into travel, eventually becoming one of the largest package-tour operators in the world. Most significant of all, we went into North Sea oil – the biggest gamble Roy ever took. When he died, Roy owed something like $75 million, because of his oil commitments, but of course, it was all secured on geologists' reports that the oil was there under the sea; and it all paid off.

As in all Roy's gambles, the extraordinary – at least to me – truth was that he didn't actually have the money he was risking. 'You may have the greatest brain that ever was, but you must have a bank behind you,' he would say. It was his genius to get the banks and pension funds to support him when he diversified; but it was also his shrewdness that kept his feet on the ground. Other millionaires like Jack Cotton got the finance to build vast empires which then collapsed when there was an unexpected dip in the market and the finance company pulled the carpet from under them. Roy trusted his business lieutenants and let them get on with their jobs, but he watched the figures very carefully and knew just how much rope to give. Every week from Canada came the figures for all his newspapers there, and every year he'd go over and spend a month working on the next year's budget. He was laughed at because he had no great newspapers there – just a huge chain of small papers on which the number of pencils, even of toilet rolls, was rationed. But it meant that his foundations were secure, whereas Michael Berry's *Telegraph* eventually collapsed as a family-owned enterprise because of the traditional Berry reserve about figures and approach to questions of planning – with, yet again, a Canadian millionaire having to take over control.

I think the key to Roy's success was that he was a man who was uncorrupt, who stood by his word, and who was unspoiled by the trappings of wealth and power. He remained unashamed of his provenance or his eccentricities, in particular his constitutional stinginess. I convinced him that my serials-buying policy was an integral part of the success of the *Sunday Times* and that he must not worry about what I had to pay for them – that I knew what I was doing, in a very competitive battle against the *Observer* and the *Sunday Telegraph*. 'If I put 100,000 copies on the sale, you get the outlay back through your advertising rates – just leave it to me.' He drew a deep breath. 'Denis,' he said, 'do what you want – do anything, but never tell me the amount.' 'Is it true you paid £100,000 for Kruschev's memoirs?' he asked once, after some loudmouth had whispered in his ear. 'Yes, Roy,' I said. 'Jeez, Denis, thank God you didn't ask me! I don't care if you pay half-a-million if that's your best judgment – but on one condition only – don't ask me, just do it.' Even directors' salary increases he had to leave to Jim Coltart because he couldn't bring himself to make them.

Once in Malta Roy was sitting having his breakfast, reading the *Sunday Times*, when his son Kenneth came in with his own copy. 'Ken, take that back to the bookstall,' Roy ordered, 'you can have mine when I'm finished with it.' On another occasion we were involved in some tremendous deal, with lawyers and accountants huddled round a table when suddenly Roy looked at his watch and went out. He was away for nearly an hour, and I couldn't resist asking him about it. 'Oh,' he said, 'I'm on the board of the London regional branch of the Royal Bank of Canada and it meets every Tuesday. I get $75 paid out in dollars for attending and I never miss it.' It was incredible; we were involved in a deal worth tens of millions and he risked it all to go and collect $75 in cash. But that was Roy Thomson, barber's son from Toronto; the man who took Lord Kemsley's withering empire and restored it to life, with new roots and boundless confidence.

Behind all the wheeler-dealing, diversification and journeying around the world, though, Roy's heart was increasingly set on one thing, something that couldn't be measured in money terms. He wanted a peerage.

# CHAPTER NINETEEN

# EDITING THE
# *SUNDAY TIMES*

THERE CAN BE NO DOUBT THAT ROY THOMSON BECAME, IN THE AUTUMN OF 1963, absolutely obsessed by his desire for a title. He had a Rolls Royce and an ever-expanding international newspaper, television and business empire. He had assets worth hundreds of millions of pounds; but only one thing now counted in his mind – to become Lord Thomson. I had by then, of course, considerable experience of the machinery of getting people gongs and honours. I discussed it all at length with Roy; I explained that he would be unlikely to get a peerage unless he was seen to be more than an employer. By setting up a Thomson Foundation to help train senior newspaper and television staff in developing countries, with an endowment of £5 million, Roy would be seen to be paying his dues, so to speak. He would be not only a Fleet Street baron but a benefactor directly contributing to Britain's overseas aid programme on a massive scale. Such a benefaction would remove any possible controversy from his elevation to the peerage.

All went well, and in September 1963 I suggested an arrangement to the Prime Minister, Harold Macmillan, whereby the government would benefit if he gave Roy a title. To Roy himself I indicated that he had to be on his best behaviour for the next few months because there might be some good news for him. To his credit, Roy said not a word when we ran some articles in the *Sunday Times* attacking Macmillan. He wanted that peerage more than anything in the world, but not by 'angling' the contents of his newspaper. Nevertheless, when Macmillan became ill in October, at the time of the Conservative party conference, Roy really began to sweat. From the moment one night that the news was released that Macmillan's doctors had advised an operation and he ought therefore to resign, Roy was constantly on the phone to me – 'What are we going to do about the peerage?' All I could reply was, 'Leave it to me, Roy' – hoping for the best.

After he had been in the King Edward VII hospital for a few days, Macmillan's secretary rang saying the Prime Minister would like a little chat. I went over and we talked about various things. Finally Macmillan said, 'Incidentally, I've just had Alec Douglas-Home in and I gave him a letter saying that it was my wish that Roy Thomson should get a peerage and hoping he will honour that wish.' Apparently Douglas-Home had commented, 'Yes, I like Roy very much, he did a good job for the *Scotsman* and, of course, I'll honour it.'

This was still October, the normal time for making up the Honours List; I indicated to Roy that I had reason to believe – I didn't tell him the details in case he would go and blab them – that all would be well. The protocol normally runs that in December the Prime Minister's office writes to say that he has it in mind to recommend to the Queen that you should be made a baron or knight or whatever. The first of December came, and nothing had happened. Roy rang me every half-hour: 'Have you heard anything, Denis?' I said, 'Just be quiet . . . you know, if it doesn't come this time, it'll be the next time. These things take time.'

By about December 10 I had started to become a little anxious myself, thinking that perhaps Douglas-Home had thought it would look odd as one of his first honours, and was saving it for the next time. We were having a directors' lunch, and Roy was going off that night to Toronto. He said to me, 'Well it looks as though it's off, Denis, doesn't it?' I said, 'Never give up, Roy, never give up.' Five minutes later his secretary came with a message: 'Mr Thomson, there's an envelope for you at your home [Alderbourne Arches in Buckinghamshire] from 10 Downing Street.' Roy said, 'Tell Gunther [his chauffeur] to bring it up here and break every speed limit!' Gunther arrived within the hour. Roy looked at the letter and said to me, 'Come into the next room.' There he opened it. It was the expected announcement from Alec Douglas-Home. Roy just said, 'Thanks, Denis.' But I refused to let him go back into the dining room. Mercifully he caught his plane to Toronto and so couldn't 'open his big mouth' – over which, as he admitted himself, he had no control.

He came back on New Year's Eve and had dinner with us in London. Olive and I took him to a Chinese restaurant in Knightbridge, with Jim Coltart and his wife. Then we went back to our flat, where I'd arranged for all the newspapers to arrive before midnight. When they came, Roy was over the moon.

I later said to him: 'Roy, you've got the two things you most wanted in life, a peerage, and the *Times*. Which did you want the most?' 'Oh,' he said, 'I've no difficulty in answering that. I wanted the peerage.' I felt rather disappointed, really, that he had said that; I had thought perhaps he had wanted the *Times* more, but it was certainly a measure of how much the title meant to him. I remember too, that it had an amusing sequel.

Roy wanted to become Lord Thomson of Toronto or of Ontario, but the Canadian government wouldn't allow either. They said they would permit him to be Lord Thomson of Mississauga. This was the old Indian name of the village in which he lived outside Toronto, but he said he didn't like it as a title. Various other suggestions were turned down by the Garter King of Arms. Finally I said, 'Well if I were you, I'd call myself Lord Thomson of Fleet.' 'How could I?' he retorted, and I thereupon explained how the old course of the river Fleet ran under our building. (In 1947 and 1948, I recall, it had in fact flooded the building to a depth of six or seven feet; we'd spent a great deal of money getting the water out and putting in permanent pumps.) Roy was overjoyed. He lifted the telephone and rang the Garter King of Arms, who said, 'I can see nothing wrong with that' – as it proved, much to the chagrin of Lord Beaverbrook. 'You know you're the cheekiest fellow that ever lived,' said Beaverbrook at the 85th birthday dinner Roy gave him. 'You tell us how to run our businesses more efficiently and then, right in front of our noses, you take the title of Fleet – when we should all have thought of it before you.'

Ironically, it was the new Lord Thomson's *Sunday Times* which was to cause Douglas-Home's downfall as Prime Minister. I did not think he was an inspired choice of successor by Macmillan, who fell into the same trap as Monty, not liking to appoint a man who might outshine him. William Rees-Mogg, the paper's political editor, had always felt badly over the rejection of 'Rab' Butler, Macmillan's rightful heir, and though Douglas-Home was a nice man himself, his tenure of office bore out all our worst fears. The *Sunday Times*, which had for generations been an almost obsequiously loyal Conservative organ, now took an independent, even pro-Labour line. We were particularly impressed by Harold Wilson's declared aim of introducing 'white-hot technology' to Britain, which was falling woefully behind the advanced nations of the world. We had in James Margach, our political correspondent, perhaps the ablest Lobby journalist of the period, and a most gifted team of foreign correspondents, headed by the unique Henry Brandon in Washington and Anthony Terry in Bonn, as well as roving correspondents like Murray Sayle, Colin Simpson, David Leitch and Nicholas Tomalin.

Our arts coverage – art, books, theatre, cinema and music – couldn't have been better, but I had kept a weather eye for some time on the *Financial Times* under its brilliant editor, Gordon Newton. With more and more of our new readers coming from the ranks of industry and commerce, I was anxious to extend our business coverage. In 1964, therefore, I launched a separate pull-out section called Business News. It was an instant 'hit' (unlike the colour magazine) with advertisers queuing up to take space. By the turn of 1965 we were nudging a circulation figure of 1,300,000 copies, and to my embarrassment I was named Journalist of the Year in the annual Hannen Swaffer awards. What was significant was the citation, for the award was really given to the whole newspaper: 'One of the great newspapers of the world'.

This the *Sunday Times* had undoubtedly become, and it made me very proud to lead a team of such professional and dedicated journalists. Yet more embarrassing was the way in which the world – or certain of its leaders – even began to look upon the *Sunday Times* as an independent instrument of peace. Over the years I had met almost all visiting heads of state, as well as prime ministers and senior politicians. Some, like President Kennedy, I met while travelling abroad and it was through my Egyptian journalist friend, Mohamed Heikal, that I got to know President Nasser.

Possibly because we were both ex-colonels, Nasser trusted me. This, in itself, was surprising, since he was notoriously anti-British. Gradually, I learned that this dislike of the British was not merely the national anti-colonialism of an Egyptian zealot, but had been inflamed by Anthony Eden long before Seuz. At a meeting in Cairo Eden had treated Nasser with deplorable rudeness. Eden had given a party at the embassy; the guests were all in dinner jackets but no one had warned Nasser, who arrived in army fatigues. Then, at the party, Eden told Nasser he must sign the Baghdad Pact to keep the Russians out of the Middle East, and that he'd already warned Kruschev and Bulganin that Britain would fight if the Suez Canal was threatened.

According to Nasser, Eden had behaved towards him as if he were a small boy who had to be told the facts of life, and ordered what to do. (I later asked Lord Harding, the CIGS, and Selwyn Lloyd, the Foreign Secretary; both confirmed that Eden had not been at his best, treating Nasser like an ignorant soldier.)

Eden's behaviour made Nasser see red – and he determined to pay Eden out; every time I saw Nasser he repeated the story. He had tried to make Eden see that Britain's strategic problems, in ensuring the supply of Middle Eastern oil and free passage to the Far East, were not Egypt's; that Egypt could very well guard its own canal and that he, Nasser, wished to concentrate on the problems of his own people. Eden later claimed that in invading Egypt in 1956 he was seeking, among other things, to put paid to Nasser's Hitlerian ambitions in the Middle

East. This is debatable. Certainly Nasser became almost Messianic in his dreams of pan-Arab progress (though it is arguable how much of this was engendered by his humiliation by Eden) just as Hitler expressed the outrage of millions of Germans at the humiliating terms of the Versailles Peace Treaty. Had Nasser been respected as the lynchpin in the Middle East (as we later came to treat the oil sheikhs), our whole standing in the area might have been significantly altered, for Nasser was undoubtedly a leader with the whole Egyptian people behind him.

I was visiting Nasser on the morning when Egyptian troops invaded the Yemen. He declined to cancel the interview and I was with him for about three hours. I said, 'Mr President, I know nothing about the Yemen, but when you need every penny you've got for Egypt, why do you go and get embroiled in a far-off country?' He replied: 'It is my duty, my duty! I want to be President of all Arabs [already he'd made Egypt the United Arab Republic]. It is my duty to look after everyone. These people have no roads, nothing. If we act quickly we will conquer the whole of Yemen and it will be ours.'

I said, 'But from what I understand, this is some of the most hideous fighting country in the world, with very wild tribes. They have a king, whose tribesmen will fight. There are no roads; it'll be old-fashioned fighting, you can't use tanks or anything like that.' – 'My advisers have said that in three days we will win it,' he declared.

I could only shake my head. Returning to London that afternoon I wrote an article about our meeting. The war in fact went on for a further nine years.

One consequence of all this was that I allowed myself for the first and only time in my life to be inveigled into a diplomatic mission – something which an editor should constantly guard against. It happened in this way. On the Tuesday after my article appeared I had an unexpected caller. He refused to identify himself, but sufficiently impressed my secretary with the importance of his visit for me to agree, warily, to see him – though outside my office rather than alone in it, in case there were difficulties. I came out and to me he identified himself as Jacob Herzog, assistant to David Ben-Gurion, Prime Minister of Israel. 'I have come by special flight this morning to see you,' he declared. 'My Prime Minister has read your interview with Nasser and wishes you to fly out in our plane later tonight to talk to him about the interview.'

Herzog, I was to learn, was the son of a rabbi, a passionate Hebrew scholar who had taken every honour at Cambridge; he was later offered the position of Chief Rabbi in London but died of peritonitis in his early forties. To his plea that I should fly to Israel, however, I protested that I was a journalist, not a politician, and could not consider going. 'It will be a matter of great sorrow to Ben-Gurion,' he said, and departed. Two days later he was back again. This time he suggested that I go as an ordinary tourist, and to this I felt I could agree.

I went out on an El Al plane but, tourist or not, when I arrived in Tel Aviv all the other passengers were kept back while I was secretly disembarked and whisked away in darkness to a car which immediately took me to Ben-Gurion's house in the suburbs. His first words were: 'I have been waiting for you – the destiny of the world may be in your hands!'

I said I hadn't quite realised this. 'Will you spend all tomorrow with me?' he went on. 'You must be tired, but just before you go to bed, tell me what happened when you met President Nasser last week?' This I did, without revealing any secrets. 'How many times have you met President Nasser?' he wanted to know. I said five or six times. 'Have you ever met him alone?' I said yes, I had had a three-hour conversation with him totally alone. Ben-Gurion said, 'Everything tomorrow will be cancelled, we'll have breakfast together, lunch and dinner while we discuss the matter.' But discuss what? 'You'll find out in the morning,' he assured me.

Next morning he put forward a proposition. I should fly to Cairo carrying a secret letter from Ben-Gurion to Nasser in an attempt to arrange a meeting between them. As there were no relations at that time between the two countries he felt I was the only one who could bring them together.

By lunchtime I had to say, 'What you have suggested is totally and utterly impractical. Nasser will never buy it. You're suggesting he should lay himself open to assassination just to meet you? But if you put something on the table that I can take to Nasser, to his advantage, perhaps I can work a deal for you.'

He asked what did I suggest. I said, 'I'm convinced – I've been thinking it over during the morning – I could arrange from world Jewry something like a hundred million pounds in order to settle the Sinai question and wipe out all those relief camps. This would show you are in earnest, and are willing to re-settle the Sinai people on your borders, and that you've got sufficient money from world Jewry to do it.'

Ben-Gurion reacted furiously. 'No, no, I do the negotiating with Nasser, I meet Nasser. We'll meet on a cruiser or some ship in the Mediterranean, no one will know, and we'll decide it between us.' He said, 'You can be there and make the announcement!'

It was grotesque. I said, 'That's making me a politician, which I can't be. It would ruin my career. I'm a professional editor, not a political diplomat! But,' I continued, 'will you think in the next hour of giving me something to take to Nasser which he can then study. The thought of solving the Sinai problem, the possibility of him giving you something in return, surely that might hold a very great attraction?'

'Oh,' said Ben-Gurion, 'I would never get it through my Cabinet, or the Knesset. They wouldn't trust me, they wouldn't trust Nasser. No, no, the deal must be that I have got to meet Nasser at a neutral place, preferably on a ship.' When I explained he hadn't a hope of getting Nasser to do any such thing, he countered, 'Surely with your influence, you could get a British cruiser or warship from Malta to do it?'

Still the next day he declined to offer anything other than a meeting. I now said, 'I'm prepared to see Nasser and tell him some of what has transpired between us, but it's absolutely hopeless, and I'm very surprised. You are totally out of touch if you think I can sell this.'

I couldn't fly straight on to Egypt. I flew back to London that day. I had to get out the week's paper, and I didn't want any suspicion. Then on Sunday, once the paper was on the streets, I flew off to see Nasser. I was able to see him in Cairo at one hour's notice, alone, and I told him some of the story of what had happened. Nasser looked at me. 'I've trusted you all this time, you are a friend of Heikal's. Now what are you; are you a journalist, are you an editor, are you a diplomat, are you a secret service man, what are you?'

I said, 'I am just a man with young children, seeing this terrible problem which may produce a third world war. If I can be of any help I wish to be of such help, without exceeding my duties as an editor and a human being. I told Ben-Gurion I didn't feel there was any likelihood of your agreeing, unless he gave something.'

'You're quite right,' said Nasser. Then he lit one of his legendary cigarettes – it was a heart attack which eventually killed him, brought on partly by overwork and partly by his heavy smoking. They were 'Kent' brand cigarettes, and all the airline pilots on international runs had instructions to bring boxes of them back for him.

I flew back to London the following day. Jacob Herzog was waiting in London with the Israeli ambassador to hear how Nasser had reacted. So I told them: that exactly as I'd forecast, he had just laughed in my face, saying: 'This is a trap to have me killed. My people would kill me, my own Cabinet would kill me, my army would kill me if it was found out that I'd had a meeting with Ben-Gurion and I was not being offered anything. I might be assassinated, it might be a trick, anything. It is all so secret – and he offers nothing, nothing.'

And that was it. I kept in touch with Herzog till he died, and Ben-Gurion consented not to mention the incident in his memoirs, or say anything that would connect the matter back to me. I insisted on paying my own air fares, lest it ever be said I was in the pay of the Israeli government. Whether Ben-Gurion was sincere in wanting to make a deal with Nasser is difficult to say, but it illustrates how little he or his parliamentary colleagues understood of Nasser's position – or, indeed, the proper role of a newspaper editor.

I remained on friendly terms with Nasser, despite this hiccup, and in 1967 I took Monty to Egypt with a party of *Sunday Times* journalists in preparation for a 25th anniversary Alamein feature of the colour magazine. Nasser even permitted Monty to come in uniform. 'As a military man, I'm sure President Nasser will understand my wish,' was how Monty phrased his request. And Nasser did – a personal concession to the ageing field-marshal, who was eighty that year.

Within months Israel and Egypt were at war. In the *Sunday Times* I attempted to steer a neutral course between them – not an easy task, as anyone who has had dealings with either side will testify. Much later I was invited to 10 Downing Street by Edward Heath to meet Mrs Golda Meir when Israeli Premier. There were only Mr Heath, Alec Douglas-Home, then Foreign Secretary and myself. Mrs Meir arrived very late, having been held up in traffic and in a foul temper. Brushing the Prime Minister aside she strode up to me and began a blistering attack on the *Sunday Times* for its pro-Arab, anti-Israeli reporting. Poor Heath was amazed, and Douglas-Home turned to look out of the window in embarrassment while this large lady harangued me. 'Prime Minister,' I said to Mrs Meir, 'you know what your trouble is? Like almost all the Israelis I know, you consider that anyone who is not one hundred per cent for you is against you. It is really very sad, you have *no* idea how much sympathy you lose.'

I think she was a little taken aback by this, from an editor, and realised just how rude she had been in front of her host, the British Prime Minister. I said, 'The *Sunday Times* is *not* partisan, and if you feel that your position in the Middle East is not properly understood by British newspapers, I will gladly arrange a lunch where you can meet all the main Fleet Street editors and put your case to them. Will you let me arrange this?' She looked completely deflated, and the next time she came to London I did in fact arrange such a lunch, with the editors of a number of national newspapers and senior figures in television and radio present. Though never exactly friends, I think Mrs Meir and I came to a better understanding. She was undoubtedly a great leader, and tougher than any male prime minister I've ever met.

The extent to which an editor 'hobnobs' with politicians and leaders in his own country and abroad is a moot one. I know that in some quarters I was criticised for abjuring the traditional image of an editor who fusses over the detailed production of his newspaper. My conviction was that it was perfectly possible to find deputies who could carry out this task. I put first Pat Murphy – perhaps the most capable news editor of the day – on to the *Sunday Times*, then brought Harold Evans from the *Northern Echo* to undertake the responsibility. I was not a writing editor. My talent, if I had one, was for leading a team of journalists, many of whom could write and report brilliantly, but who often lacked judgment. The exercise of good judgment had in fact become my creed as a journalist – and knowing personally so many personalities on the national and international scene gave me an advantage over every other newspaper editor in the land, not only in story-leads but in judging whether our reporting was fair or lopsided. The *Sunday Times* did not graduate to the distinction of being 'one of the great newspapers of the world' (a distinction it has to some extent lost, I fear) by simply being innovative or by buying great memoirs; it won the title by harnessing the talents of a great team of journalists and exercising them with good judgment, whether in covering the political scene, or conducting investigations, or running serials.

Even serialisation demanded a quality of judgment not greatly in evidence in British journalism after the war. Often we became deeply unpopular in certain circles – as when we published the diaries of Churchill's doctor, Lord Moran. Both the medical profession and Churchill's acolytes protested; but we felt that the bounds of normal propriety could and should be breached in this instance, for the insight into the mind and health of our greatest political leader surely outweighed the lack of taste. Queen Victoria bitterly condemned Creevey, but his journals remain to this day the most important insight into his time. Similarly, Moran's record is and will remain an indispensable counter to Churchill's magnificent but often self-serving accounts of his own greatness. For the same reasons Richard Crossman started keeping a weekly record of his time as a Cabinet minister, and I later ensured that it was published in the *Sunday Times*, despite the threat of legal action.

Obviously, we did not always come out on top, or in the right. The faked Mussolini Diaries still cause me to blush (fortunately we realised our mistake before publication); but the moral to my mind is clear. Every independent newspaper must have the courage to take its own line, imprinting its own image on the newspaper world. In this way it will win the loyalty of its readers – and readers are, let it be said, an extraordinarily loyal breed. That image, however, cannot simply be sustained by technical journalistic expertise; the editor must have judgment if he is to survive and if his newspaper is to be taken seriously. As Smuts said of character, 'Judgment is not something that can be bought; it is ingrained in a man and grows through the trials of his life.'

Editing the *Sunday Times* for six years was, after the satisfaction of commanding my battalion, the most rewarding experience of my life. There was never a dull moment, and the skirmishes and battles, whether with politicians or rivals, made it all the more exciting. I was still a director of Thomson's main board and thus a party to other worlds of business, from book publishing to travel. I did not see how I could go higher – until Roy bought the *Times*.

# CHAPTER TWENTY

# BUYING THE *TIMES*

OFTEN, IN RELATIVE RETIREMENT, I HAVE ASKED MYSELF WHY WE GOT embroiled with the *Times*. I suppose the answer is, because, like Everest, it was there. Roy had failed to get Odhams Press and the *Daily Herald*, he'd failed to get the *Daily Telegraph* or to persuade Lord Rothermere to sell the *Daily Mail*. And all this time the circulation and prestige of the *Sunday Times* continued to escalate. In 1961, the year in which I took over the editorship, its average weekly sale was 994,450 copies. The following year it rose to 1,120,000. With the addition of the magazine it was up to 1,180,000 in 1963, one-and-a-quarter million by 1964, and in 1967 our sale reached a staggering one-and-a-half million copies. With some justice, Roy felt that we'd found the formula for success in quality journalism – a mixture of modern marketing skills and sustained editorial teamwork. The next step, he felt, was to buy the *Times*.

Unfortunately, however, Colonel Lord Astor, its owner, had always refused to sell the paper, to Roy or to anybody else. Directing the paper's fortunes (or misfortunes) from his tax-exile in France, Astor had allowed the greatest monument to British journalism to run down. Lacking investment and flair, the *Times* fell, so to speak, behind the times. I am quite sure that if I – or any reasonably active editor – had got hold of the newspaper in the late 1950s, under a go-ahead owner, I could have restored its fortunes. Instead, it was allowed to wither and dry up, permitting the *Financial Times* under Gordon Newton to steal its once predominant place as a purveyor of City and financial news. Year by year the rich fields of financial advertising were surrendered, while the *Times* concentrated on a 19th-century ideal of being the paper of the landed classes. Again and again I warned Gavin Astor, Colonel Astor's son and representative in London, that the *Times* would sink unless it did something; but each time I was rebuffed. By 1967, I now realise, it was too late.

The editor, Sir William Haley, was a man of the highest calibre. He had been an editor in Manchester and then director-general of the BBC and was extremely well read, if a bit cold on first acquaintance. Someone said, when coming out of his presence for the first time, 'I've met a chap with one glass eye before – but never a chap with two!' On the surface there was no warmth at all, but underneath, as I came to know, there was tremendous warmth, indeed passion. But even Haley couldn't get Colonel Astor to budge over news on the front page or other attempts at bringing the newspaper into the twentieth century, until it was too late. By 1966, when news finally hit the front page of the *Times*, both the *Financial Times* and the *Manchester Guardian* (retitled simply the *Guardian*) had been given head-starts, developing their own brands of journalism in tune with the times, well financed, and with loyal and growing readerships. Even at straight news reporting the *Daily Telegraph* knocked spots off the *Times*, with twice as many pages and a circulation exceeding a million copies. Circulation of the *Times* had shrivelled to fewer than 250,000 copies per day, with an advertising rate already so expensive that even the surge in circulation following the facelift on its front page failed to produce extra revenue. In fact, it only aggravated the financial losses, every extra copy sold adding a loss of sixpence.

In these circumstances, Gavin Astor finally relented. He'd spent a fortune building a new headquarters for the *Times* in Printing House Square instead of investing in the paper itself. Astor's father was still damned if he would sell to Roy Thomson, but with mounting losses he recognised he must sell to someone. And looking round, he found the bride he ought to have taken a decade before: the *Financial Times*. By merging the two newspapers, Lord Astor felt, they would re-create the best financial and political newspaper in the world.

Haley was all for the deal. He was not only editor of the *Times* but chief executive of its board of directors. He assumed he would be editor of the merged newspaper, or at least would get his way in the proposed merger. In this he was thoroughly mistaken; I don't think he recognised that Gordon Newton was the stronger character, and backed by a remarkable managing director in Lord Drogheda, for whom Gavin Astor was no match. The *Financial Times* had forty to fifty pages of business and financial news, and twelve of news and sport; with only twelve pages in their whole newspaper there was no way Haley and Astor could have kept control of the merged publication – the tail would have been wagging the dog.

This, however, was not the reason why the engagement was broken. Haley went on holiday in July 1966 under the impression that a deal had been worked out, and the papers would be wed. What stopped the

merger was Lord Cowdray's sense of thrift – for in the event, with
agreement on both sides as to the logic of the move, Cowdray (a noted
polo player and owner of the *Financial Times*) balked. His negotiator,
Lord Poole, announced to Kenneth Keith, who was acting on behalf of
the Astors, that Lord Cowdray felt he was paying too much. Cowdray's
tightness in business affairs was legendary, giving him a reputation the
opposite of Roy Thomson, who was mean with himself, didn't play
polo, but was lavish (at least in the case of the *Sunday Times*) in business.
Thus it was, with Lords Thomson and Astor both out of the country,
that Kenneth Keith approached me to ask if I was still interested in the
*Times*.

It was very much on the rebound. Bankruptcy was staring the *Times*
in the face, so a new bride who'd pay the price had to be found quickly.
The fact was that Roy and I, when approaching Gavin Astor the year
before, had already worked out a careful composition for a board of
directors of a new company that would own both the *Sunday Times* and
the *Times*, by which the Astor family would retain sufficient nominees to
ensure the integrity of the *Times*. Thus, although Roy was out of contact
in Canada for several vital days, I was able to put to Kenneth Keith a
'package' which would satisfy the Astors – and the Monopolies
Commission if, as seemed certain, the deal was referred.

As Roy later wrote, it was the 'oddest deal' he ever made; for by
putting the *Sunday Times* into a new company, together with the *Times*,
he not only surrendered its soaring profits (which would be swallowed
up in the new company by the losses of the daily, for the foreseeable
future) but had to agree to surrender his place on the board of the new
company (Haley was to be chairman for two years, followed by
Kenneth Thomson). Even this extraordinary act of self-abnegation was
not guaranteed to pass the scrutiny of the Monopolies Commission. I
persuaded Roy to remain in Canada during the preliminary negotiations. As Roy admitted in his autobiography, 'the main obstacle
was undoubtedly me. I don't think Lord Astor could stomach the idea
of giving control of his paper to a rough-neck Canadian. He would
never have considered the merger if it hadn't been that Denis Hamilton
was there . . . .'

Roy's problem, as always, was his mouth; and it was during the
critical passage through the narrow waterway of the Monopolies
Commission that I had my only real blazing row with him. Roy simply
could not resist a joke. Once when I introduced him to President
Nasser, he asked if Nasser would sell him *Al Ahram*. Nasser said no, but
that he would sell him the *Egyptian Gazette*. 'You certainly are a cunning
old Jew!' Roy commented. 'You know very well the *Gazette* is losing

money hand over fist, while *Al Ahram* is making great profits.'
Curiously, Nasser took the remark without batting an eyelid, but I was
staggered by Roy's indiscretion. Now Roy returned to England early in
September 1967, with the Commission due to take evidence at the end
of October. It was vital that Roy should raise no extra hackles, and I
made him promise to keep quiet. No sooner had he promised than we
were invited to spend the weekend at Chequers with Harold Wilson.
Somehow the *Daily Express* found out that Roy was going to see the
Prime Minister. They got an interview with Roy in which he explained
at length what he was going to do with the *Times* once he got hold of it –
before he'd even met the Commission.

This was giving a hostage to fortune – particularly as there was an
ex-assistant editor of the *Times* on the Commission's panel. I knew all
its members, and had appeared enough times before Royal Commis-
sions on the Press to take the exercise very seriously. The whole point of
the new combined board, without Roy, was to allay suspicion that he
might wilfully take control and destroy the traditions of two centuries.
Giving this brash interview seemed to me, after all I'd done to get us
this far, to risk the whole venture and was really just Roy showing off.
He himself had gone home, after we'd stayed up half Sunday night
talking about politics. When I saw the *Daily Express* at breakfast at
Chequers I rang him and told him very forcefully what I thought of his
behaviour.

Later that day at the office, Roy asked me to see him. He was
obviously upset. He said, 'Now look, Denis, I think you're the most
splendid, most loyal man, with tremendous wisdom. But I am not
going to be spoken to as you spoke to me on the phone.'

'Roy,' I said, 'I'm very sorry if I upset you. What I gave you was
what I felt someone ought to say to you because you have endangered
something you've set your heart on. But if you feel like that, I'm very
sorry, and if it has broken our relationship, then I wish to resign. I'll go
back to my office and clear out my things and be gone by this afternoon.
I can't have a relationship which isn't an honest one.'

Roy got out of his chair and put his arms round me. 'What a silly fool
I've been,' he said. 'I was upset that someone had spoken to me like
that. I've never in my life been spoken to with such force as you did, but
I plead with you to stay. I'll go down on my hands and knees, I'll
double your salary but you must stay.'

I said, 'I don't want more salary. All I want is an understanding
between us that I can tell you when I think you are wrong. You can take
no notice, but I must be able to say what I really think, otherwise I am
of no value to you.'

He asked, 'Will you forgive me?' I said, 'There is nothing to forgive, Roy, nothing.' I was told that after I had gone out of the office he was so upset by the whole incident that he would see no one for about an hour. We never referred to it again. There were, of course, other occasions where I spoke my mind, perhaps less forthrightly than I had that time, because he was getting older. But that was our only real difference.

If keeping Roy quiet before the convening of the Monopolies Commission was hard, steering him safely through the meeting itself threatened to be yet harder. In fact, of course, the Commission really had no alternative – a City consortium, organised by John Wyndham, Macmillan's ex-private secretary, was bidding for the *Times*, but they knew little about newspapers. All we had to do was reassure Parliament that Roy's ownership of the *Times* would not be against the public interest. Roy, Jim Coltart, Gordon Brunton and I went twice before the Commission, the second time in late November. It was clear then, from the questioning, that it was all over bar the shouting, for the questions were rather of the 'supposing, Lord Thomson, we were to flag you through, would you be able to assure us that . . .' kind – which was an indication that all was well and Wyndham's eccentric consortium had been laughed out of court.

Roy had said that I would be running the new show, editorially, as editor-in-chief of the two newspapers, so for a further two hours I was grilled on the sort of editors I would appoint under me, and foreign correspondents and so on. Finally, as we all filed out, Roy suddenly turned round and said to the chairman, 'Well, very nice to have been here this morning. Confidentially, I'll be back soon because I've bought another newspaper this week.' The chairman's face dropped, and mine did too. It was some tiny paper in Tottenham with a circulation of about 5,000, but Roy couldn't resist a joke. Outside, I said to him, 'Well, Roy, it was such a good joke that they're all laughing their heads off. But it was a hell of a risk to take!'

'It's taking risks that's got me where I am,' he retorted. 'And look where it's got you!' He could have been a stage comedian with his ready wit and comebacks, which got him into trouble all over the world. He'd make some witty remark to a group of journalists in Singapore and in three minutes his words would be in London – as when he made some disparaging remarks about the *Daily* and *Sunday Telegraph*. Within minutes Lord Hartwell was calling his solicitors. It was all rather naive really, but Roy's simplicity was part of his greatness.

Otherwise Roy had behaved impeccably in front of the Monopolies Commission, and the transcripts show how clearly he spoke. For a supposedly uneducated man it was quite a feat. He dealt confidently with the accountants on the Commission, and if he was considering buying a business he could hold his own with anyone. He could read a balance sheet quicker than anyone I've ever known. He'd left school at 14, but he'd gone to night school and had learned both book-keeping and shorthand. His shorthand was extraordinary. An American once tried to interest us in a new system, at a time when we were diversifying into education. Roy was vastly interested, and dictated something. 'Now read it back to me,' Roy ordered. The visitor did so – but not perfectly and with some hesitation. Roy then said, 'Now take anything you like and read it to me, and I'll take it down in my shorthand,' which was Pitman's. This he did – the first time for many years – and read it back fast and clear. I have always regretted not keeping that note, the outlines were so sculpturally clear. His handwriting too was well-rounded, schoolboyish and clear, like Monty's, so that you couldn't possibly misunderstand any word he wrote.

Except to cranks he answered every letter he received, and one could only admire the way he would deal with an enormous pile of correspondence on his desk when he came in at 9 am; most of it was disposed of by ten. Even telephone calls were put through direct to him – he didn't like calls going through his secretary, feeling this was proclaiming a grandeur he didn't possess. I thought it wasted a good deal of his time – in the early days our *Sunday Times* conferences would sometimes come to a standstill because of a phone call from a stranger; but Roy refused to raise a fence around himself. As he said, 'You never know if it's some guy who's going to offer me a newspaper' – and sometimes it was.

It was strange really, given his many talents, that Roy had such an exaggerated respect for editors, almost an awe, assuming they had an education and a knowledge of the world which he lacked – when in fact he could construct a speech, without waffling, quicker than any of us. This respect for editors was only exceeded by his admiration for the royal family, which knew no bounds. Fortunately, the *Sunday Times* was a pro-monarchist newspaper – he would have closed it down rather than see it attack the royal family. It was touching to see, in reverse, how fond the Queen Mother was of Roy – and what amusement she derived from the sight of him in a kilt as the Colonel of his Canadian regiment.

Buying the *Times*, as he later wrote, was for him 'the summit of a lifetime's work'. I thank God he did not live to see his great summit erupt, like a raging volcano, eventually driving his son to the point where Roy's noble, 21-year guarantee of financial support had to be torn up and thrown away. For the bitter, galling truth is that the purchase of the *Times* was, like Monty's great thrust at Arnhem, a terrible mistake, and doomed to failure. It was mounted too late, against rivals who had been allowed to entrench themselves. Moreover, our 'allies', the men and women who printed the newspaper, had no understanding of the dire financial predicament we were in. For them, the main task was not to beat the opposition but to continue crippling the newspaper. Theirs was a Fleet Street disease, yet in its way it was a symbol of the whole malaise affecting Britain – a last-ditch stand against modernity. Like the *Times*, Britain was in danger of becoming ungovernable.

# CHAPTER TWENTY-ONE

# EDITOR-IN-CHIEF

OUGHT I TO HAVE TAKEN THE EDITORSHIP OF THE *TIMES*? ROY THOMSON certainly thought so - 'I am satisfied that he would be the best editor for the *Times*,' he told the Monopolies Commission. Three of the eight members of the Commission also thought so – Noël Annan, Francis Williams and Donald Tyerman, who all phoned or wrote to me, asking me to take it on. But Roy was 73 years old; more and more he had handed over the running of his newspapers in Britain to me. I'd had to create a board of management for the *Sunday Times*, of which I was chairman, in charge of the financial side, production, newsprint, everything, in addition to editing the newspaper. Although the success of the *Times* was vital to the new company's very existence, the company itself was simply too large and involved too great an investment – perhaps £30-£40 million – for me to sit and edit just the one newspaper with a current circulation of 270,000 copies. Roy therefore asked me to take charge of the whole operation, as Chief Executive and Editor-in-Chief of the *Sunday Times*, the *Sunday Times* Colour Magazine, the *Times*, the *Times Literary Supplement* and the *Times Educational Supplement*. (The *Times Higher Education Supplement* was something I added later.)

But if I was not going to edit the *Times*, who would? Haley favoured his deputy Iverach McDonald. McDonald had a very dependable pair of hands and, to an extent, his judgment was peerless in that it was in his blood that the *Times* would stand up to anybody. But his attitudes were in my view cautious and I knew I only had a short time in which to raise the *Times* from the commercial quicksand that was dragging it down.

Meanwhile, I had had a letter from my deputy at the *Sunday Times*, William Rees-Mogg. He wasn't interested in editing the *Sunday Times* but, he made it perfectly clear, he wanted to edit the *Times*. In his long letter he said he thought my position would be rather like that on board HMS Victory; Hardy was the captain but he'd had on board Admiral

Nelson, sailing with him, in charge of the Fleet. It was a well argued letter. I had great trust in Rees-Mogg. I greatly admired his writing and, of course, he had outstanding political contacts. He had been brought up on the *Financial Times*, where he'd been an assistant editor and written the 'Lex' column as well as many leaders, so that even before his ten years on the *Sunday Times* he had proved himself a very accomplished daily journalist. At the *Sunday Times* he'd been a stalwart executive, acting as editor when I was away on holiday or business. As far as I was concerned he didn't put a foot wrong in my absence. Indeed, part of the menu that enabled the *Sunday Times* to expand in the Sixties was Rees-Mogg's signed articles, which were a great draw and extremely influential – as Alec Douglas-Home had found to his cost as leader of the Tory Party.

Rees-Mogg was a man who made up his mind quickly and there was enormous respect for him on the *Sunday Times*, but not great love. He didn't throw himself all round the paper but concentrated on the parts he liked, the literary side and the business and political side. In particular he'd made a first-class job of developing the Business section of the *Sunday Times*. All in all I felt that he had the right qualities to be editor of the *Times*. After all, what did the job demand – a great organiser, a man with an instinct for what readers want, or outstanding political judgment, with the ability to write the leaders that would be discussed all round the world that morning? And if I had not appointed Rees-Mogg editor of the *Times* after he had put himself forward for the job, he might have gone elsewhere – he would have made an outstanding editor of the *Financial Times* after Gordon Newton.

The only other person I had in mind was Charles Wintour, who was editing the London *Evening Standard* – and a high quality newspaper he'd made of it. He'd been a colonel on the staff at Supreme Headquarters during the latter part of the war, a civilised man, deeply interested in the arts. He also wrote to me asking to be considered. But with the many millions of pounds that were going to have to be poured into the venture the stakes were too risky. I felt I had to have somebody I knew well, much as I admired his work. Besides, Wintour was very anti-Common Market, in line with Beaverbrook's view, and it was impossible for him to change overnight.

I discussed all this with Haley, who accepted my choice of Rees-Mogg. Iverach McDonald became associate editor, and Oliver Woods, an assistant editor of the *Times*, my new chief editorial assistant, so that the staff would feel they had one of their own sitting in the office next door to me, and able to put in a word to stop me from doing anything too far from the *Times* tradition.

I had accepted that I could not myself take on the editorship of the *Times* or continue to edit the *Sunday Times*, that I must put the needs of the Thomson Organisation before my own wishes at this moment. And yet I agonised. Next to the two years in wartime command of my battalion, the six years I'd spent editing the *Sunday Times* were the happiest of my life. I would have loved to tackle the *Times*, to lift the paper out of the rut it was in. But it was not to be.

It remained only for me to appoint my successor at the *Sunday Times*. There, the obvious candidate was Frank Giles, the number three and once Rome correspondent of the *Times*. All his working life as a journalist his speciality had been foreign affairs; he had little interest in home news or politics, though was greatly interested in the cultural, arts side. He was a most cultivated man but as a newspaperman, though he had a safe pair of hands, he was not likely to run investigative journalism and take chances. He was not a natural leader, though unquestionably a man of integrity. On balance, despite my admiration for him, I felt he lacked the brio and sparkle that the *Sunday Times* needed to maintain the lead we'd sprung on the *Observer* and the *Sunday Telegraph*.

For that I felt, and Roy felt, Harold Evans would be our best bet. Harold could be wild and impulsive, but he had the sort of crusading energy a Sunday editor requires. Roy was no great admirer of Frank Giles whom he found a bit formal, whereas Harold's northcountry cheek matched Roy's own. In order to convince myself – and others – that Harold was the man, I asked him to set out his ideas of where, over the next few years, the *Sunday Times* should go. This paper, written over a weekend, was an impressive document and tipped the scales.

I put my nominations to the first Times Newspapers board meeting on 14 January 1967. Sir William Haley strongly approved my nomination of Evans, feeling that Giles was not the man to stand up to governments. Some of the outside directors who were friends of Giles pressed his case, but didn't wish to oppose my wishes. Evans was duly appointed. After the meeting I sent for Rees-Mogg and told him he would be the new editor of the *Times*, and then went to Gray's Inn Road from Printing House Square and sent for Giles. I told him he was probably expecting to be made editor, but that I had selected Harold Evans. I knew he would be disappointed but I was offering him the position of deputy; I felt sure I could count on his loyalty and that an important part of my decision to appoint Evans was the conviction that he, Giles, would pull Evans back if he got a bit too wild; and to see that our brilliant foreign coverage was maintained. He said, 'All right. That is your decision. It will be a massive disappointment to me and my wife, but there it is. I'll stay with the paper and will be loyal to Harold, whom I admire. I'm sure we'll get on well together' – which they did.

So Frank Giles left my room, nobody knowing what the decision was, but assuming it was him. Then I sent for Harold Evans and told him I was appointing him editor. He was rather surprised. Of course, he was enormously gratified, and I felt sure I could count on his wholehearted loyalty in the coming struggle to create a profitable company. Other appointments naturally led to the *Sunday Times* losing some very able men, like Anthony Vice and Michael Cudlipp, to the *Times*. I was so involved in the problems of getting the new company running that I gave Evans his head to recruit replacements – and there I found his weak spot: he was the world's worst recruiter. I am on record as saying that any editor must spend 25 per cent of his time in recruitment to get the right people, and I am afraid Harry spent nothing like enough time on recruiting. The result was that although he recruited some very able journalists some of his appointments disappointed me. In a couple of extreme cases I had contracts rescinded, which led to a showdown with him in which I said that recruitment above a certain salary had to have my permission.

I was also uncertain, in the beginning, what Evans's attitude might be to the magazine, and did not allow him to have it under his editorship for at least a year. I kept it in my own hands because, I told him, I'd taken so many of his staff to put on the *Times* that I wanted him to give all his time to the paper and not be sidetracked by it. But I confess that in my heart I was really worried stiff about his at times impulsive approach.

I suppose all three of us, Rees-Mogg, Evans and I, were cast in different moulds. I shunned publicity, never having liked it. Rees-Mogg was not adverse to a little personal publicity though he didn't particularly seek it. Harold Evans, by contrast, revelled in it and it got to the point where, without my permission, he started appearing on television chat shows, which I had to stop because I thought it totally improper for the editor of the *Sunday Times* to be seen there or on quiz programmes. This great weakness of his for self-projection continued even during his ill-fated one-year editorship of the *Times* – leading to his demise as editor.

Having said that, properly harnessed Harold had no peer as a crusading editor of the news, with enormous skill in the design and layout of the paper as well as an instinctive 'nose' for a good story. Luckily I'd managed to buy serial rights in William Manchester's *Death of a President* – and this proved an even greater spur to circulation growth than Monty's *Memoirs*, so that Harold Evans was given a flying start to an electric career as editor of the *Sunday Times*. Being emotional and highly-strung he needed, however, constant counsel and comfort – for instance, when we took on the law over the Thalidomide case (which was his idea) I controlled the whole campaign. No sentence appeared in the newspaper without my having seen it beforehand, and I ran the strategy – as I did the fight against the Cabinet Office over the Crossman Diaries.

Over the years I had amassed a fair amount of experience in dealing with the law and the government, and I was confident we would win, providing we kept to the agreed plan, decided at a meeting attended by Lord Goodman and Michael Foot, the literary executor of Crossman, and the publishers (Jonathan Cape and Hamish Hamilton): this was for the *Sunday Times* to face Sir John Hunt at the Cabinet Office and fight from strength, not the sidelines. In view of the possible penalties and the money involved, I decided that the *Sunday Times* would take the burden of it all, and in the end we won the right to publish the diaries – though in the book which Harold Evans later commissioned to record the case my name did not appear, to my great interest. I didn't object – I came to know, over the succeeding twelve years, Harold Evans's strengths and weaknesses better than any man in Fleet Street, and when I was asked whether he would make a good editor of the *Times* I was able to give a resounding negative – though my advice was ignored, with dramatic consequences. Harold's strength was his brilliance as a journalist; his weakness was his need always for a stronger figure behind him to see that his talents were not wrecked by his misjudgments.

When all was said and done, however, Harold proved himself an editor with immense flair, and in this respect he rather outshone his opposite number at the *Times*. I think William Rees-Mogg will go down in history as a most distinguished editor of the *Times*, a man who modernised the paper without in any way diminishing its authority. Yet the truth is that he didn't give the paper quite the kick up the pants which, certainly, Noël Annan and Francis Williams and Donald Tyerman were hoping for. He made Roy Thomson – who had assumed I could double the *Times* circulation from 270,000 copies in the same way as I'd done with the *Sunday Times* – hopping mad, particularly as our losses began to get not better but worse and worse. I think to some extent Roy regretted he hadn't insisted I take the editorship; but whether that would have made any difference, in all honesty I doubt. William undoubtedly lacked the sort of drive which would have made the *Times* take off, but I defended him before Roy and others because I admired him for the qualities he did have, and which gave the newspaper a solid, dependable feel.

Sometimes William did make errors of judgment, as we all do. I remember my intense anger when, going off to Switzerland with Roy Thomson very early in the day, and having to buy the paper at the airport, I opened it to find a large leading article saying that the country's future depended on the formation of a National Government. I did feel this was a matter on which the editor-in-chief ought to have been consulted, even if the editor would have the last word. I think a good many of the staff were inclined to disparage his manner, which was unfortunate. It was obvious he was most at home with those who had good degrees from Oxbridge or shared his interests in antiquarian books, for instance – and he didn't really put himself out to get to know the rest. This didn't adversely affect the paper – many reporters like to be left alone to get on with their job – but it didn't give the *Times* the sort of collective cutting edge it needed if it was to claw back readers from the *Guardian*, *Daily Telegraph* and *Financial Times*. His great strength was the leader page, especially when he was on form – you might not agree with what he said on economic affairs or the Common Market, but he had a wonderfully incisive pen and in his writing gave something to the *Times* which it didn't have before, and has lacked since. But he was largely uninterested in news and sport, which put a brake on what was and wasn't possible in pushing up the circulation.

However, one has to ask in retrospect whether our target of half-a-million copies per day was either realistic or even advisable. A report commissioned two years before we bought the *Times* had laid down this figure, which Roy accepted, as did Haley and the whole of the *Times* board – except the marketing director of the Thomson group, Harry Henry. He had been brought in when we decided to diversify and he had a brilliant mind, though quite often a grave lack of common sense. Harry Henry sent a paper both to Roy and to me saying that he felt the decision to go for 500,000 copies would only bring disaster; that the *Telegraph*, the *Financial Times* and the *Guardian* had gone so far ahead that there weren't enough AB readers (readers in the professions and higher income groups) left to be picked up. To succeed in achieving a sale of half-a-million copies, the extra readers would need to be won from existing readers of the other newspapers; and he very much doubted whether it would be worth the vast expenditure of money and effort.

Harry Henry's paper was discussed by the board but the consensus was against him, and he was the odd man out. Harry was in the habit of submitting extravagant papers, so it was not altogether surprising. But, in retrospect, I have to say I think he was right – he was all for increasing the sale but only getting it up by degrees, without too much expenditure, whereas Roy was never off the telephone to me from the minute I'd taken over, asking how many copies we'd put on – till the terrible year of 1969–70 when the British economy went haywire and the *Times*, instead of losing a million pounds or £2 million a year, which Roy assumed would be the case for about five years, exceeded £3 million and looked as if it would get worse. William Rees-Mogg's patient 'traditionalist' approach to the editorship of the *Times* would thus have suited Harry Henry's strategy – whereas, in my zeal to push up the circulation, I did rather press William to pull his weight. The result was a pull-out Business section which was frankly a disaster.

At the *Sunday Times* the advent of a pull-out business news section had proved a great success from the first issue, netting a welcome increase in advertising revenue. By transferring its editor, Tony Vice, from the *Sunday Times*, we hoped to give the *Times* a shot in the arm. Moreover, Rees-Mogg had been largely responsible for organising the *Sunday Times* section. Unfortunately, instead of going for quality, and recruiting the best commentators and analysts in the business world – not necessarily journalists but people in the City who could give leads – Rees-Mogg went for quantity, doubling the number of columns of business coverage. Gordon Newton astutely forestalled recruitment by putting all his best people at the *Financial Times* on contracts with large salary increases. In 1967 business journalism, which is now a major part of the make-up of a newspaper, hadn't really got going. It was almost symptomatic of the British economy; we had plenty of potential foreign correspondents and crime reporters and political commentators, but too few business journalists with good contacts among industrialists. At the same time, both industry and the City were in the hands of old-fashioned people who regarded journalists as people who could only be admitted through the servants' door, and not, therefore, to be given any great confidences. In the coverage of business, therefore, and the City, there was far too much guesswork, simply because company chairmen wouldn't talk. (Now, of course, the problem is to stop them talking and they ring up day and night.)

We launched the *Times* Business section one night with a spectacular dinner, with James Callaghan, then at the Treasury, and Harold Macmillan among the guests. Most of these, of course, were not industrialists but people involved in financial advertising, and my bright young marketing men said we ought to put on fifteen minutes of entertainment to amuse these lads. The most popular programme on TV at that time was *Till Death Us Do Part*, so we produced the actor who played Alf Garnett, Warren Mitchell. The script was a hilarious sequence about the *Times* going into business. Alf Garnett went off to the whole room cascading with laughter, but I shall never forget the look on Harold Macmillan's face as he sat beside me. He was utterly bewildered, obviously didn't watch TV and had never seen Alf Garnett.

Macmillan's reaction, unfortunately, was soon mirrored by our readers when they saw the new Business section. The rest of the press then jeered, as they had over the colour magazine, saying that every railway carriage bringing commuters to the City was full of discarded copies and the railways were using extra staff to clear them. It was par for the course, only this time there was some truth in it. The section did not have enough quality, there were too many errors, we offended companies because of failure to check everything, and we simply didn't have first-class columnists to hold the thing together.

I suppose the honest truth is that we took over the *Times* in 1967 on the crest of a wave. The *Sunday Times* was going from strength to strength and we thought nothing could stop us – whereas, in reality there was a great deal to stop us. The market, as Harry Henry pointed out, was already formed – the *Times* had had its chance to seize a growing quality market in the late Fifties and early Sixties, and had missed it. Now, in a period of recession, there were no new readers going spare – each one had to be prised from another paper; and whether in news, sport, features, women's pages or business coverage we failed to prise them.

There were other problems, too. Roy proposed that the two newspapers and their supplements be brought under the same roof, for he was certain there were large savings to be made on the administrative and printing side. He insisted that we sell the *Times* building and move the *Times* to purpose-built new quarters in Gray's Inn Road, next door to the *Sunday Times*. This was itself a nightmare and caused great jealousies among the staff, who began complaining vociferously about differences in pay and conditions; they came soon to resemble two warring tribes, something of which no one had warned me. The GLC meanwhile objected to the demolition of a row of Georgian terrace houses next door; we lost at the inquiry. Having re-designed the new building, we were assailed by the various union chapels who each demanded special payments for having to move. More and more, then, I became not Editor-in-Chief but a sort of glorified general manager. Eventually I had to take on someone to help me – I was being driven to distraction by the managerial problems of the new company. William Haley, the supposed chairman for the first two years, quit after one and Ken Thomson, who was supposed to succeed him, could also only stand a year of this front-line shelling, returning with his wife to Canada.

On top of all, deliberate sabotage in the various printing and distribution departments now surpassed all records. The *Sunday Times* never achieved a full run, and problems on the *Times* were as bad. The *Sunday Times* ought to have been climbing to the two million-sales mark; often it did not manage to get a million-and-a-quarter copies on to the streets, angering the editorial staff and devastating the morale of the advertising people. Even at that figure, however, it made money; whereas the *Times* was losing even more heavily.

Sad though this was, Roy was quite prepared to stomach the losses, as long as we eventually introduced the new printing technology into Fleet Street. It broke poor Roy's heart to see the progress being made in North America and yet watch the unions turn their backs on it in Britain. He was prepared to invest the bulk of his fortune in new technology in Britain – and we spurned him. The union business soured the last years of Roy's life, poisoning the pride he felt in owning two of the world's greatest newspapers and the growing excitement at the discovery of North Sea oil. He could not comprehend the viciousness and jealousy displayed by the leaders of the various unions who, far from concerting efforts to make the company succeed, seemed content with ultimate self-destruction, so long as, in the meantime, they could profit their members by clinging to their 'old Spanish customs', covert absenteeism and overmanning.

Over the years, as relations between the various union chapels, and between chapels and management, deteriorated, I did my best to defeat the 'them and us' spirit that was destroying Fleet Street – as it was British industry generally. If for reasons of history the unions would not amalgamate, then, I argued, why not at least negotiate via one main body, rather than undergo the remorseless, time-consuming and morale-breaking rivalry and leapfrogging of having so many different ones? In return for an agreement that there would be no unofficial stoppages – industrial sabotage – I was prepared to offer, immediately, a doubling of staff pensions. Wasn't it better, I argued, to cooperate with one another and with management to get better working conditions, cantcens, pensions, and so on, than to continue in anarchy, distrust and internecine rivalry?

A joint board of the national newspaper industry had been set up in 1964 to oversee all agreements with the various unions and chapels – but the chapels soon killed this effort, as they did the national newspaper steering group I helped set up at the Newspaper Proprietors' Association under Frank Rogers in 1970. My files bulged with correspondence and promises – but it was clear that the unions were themselves powerless to deliver since they were run by men of straw who had not the character or moral authority to discipline their chapels. These chapels, in turn, fell increasingly under the control of activists and wreckers – with the majority of their members too gutless or indifferent to halt the slide, especially when their pockets were lined by the profits made by chapel blackmail. Often I thought of my battalion soldiers in Germany the day compulsory Sunday services were abolished – the way grown men, fearless in battle against the Germans, were cowed and frightened into submission by the prospect of what their mates might say if they showed courage and loyalty to the padre who had seen them through the war. It was shaming.

From the early 1960s power had slipped from the general secretaries to the chapels – and because we, the management, allowed the chapels to recruit our casual employees, the bully-boys bred bully-boys. Roy used to say to me that he saw no hope for England so long as we had trade unions of the type we had then. For all that he venerated England – its old craftsmanship, its inventions, the warmth of its people, and its institutions – he could not see any future for us. Poor and weak management had handed over too much power to unions which were themselves held to ransom by their activists. Edward Heath attempted to tackle the problem and was voted out of office; Barbara Castle tried to face the issue with her White Paper *In Place of Strife*, but was defeated by Jim Callaghan. The nation was simply not prepared to confront the issue – and Roy Thomson could only watch helplessly as even his plans for new evening newspapers outside London were smashed by the unions.

I think that almost every day of his last five years Roy was on the phone to me saying, 'Have you made any progress on the new technology? I see no hope for the *Times* unless you can get it in, like my papers in America.' He said it on every occasion on radio, television, addressing public meetings, lunches, dinners. He would argue it with the trade union leaders – but he got nowhere. What upset him even more was the way people, instead of showing concern for the viability of the *Times* in these circumstances, would wilfully knock the paper, to his face. We went up together to Gleneagles, to a meeting of the Commonwealth Press Union, where I gave a speech about the history of newspapers with special relationship to the *Times*. Afterwards I found Roy in a very low state in his hotel suite, and asked why. 'Something has happened,' he answered, 'that really hurt me and has removed all sense of purpose in me.'

The conference had opened with a speech by Alec Douglas-Home, and the Duke of Edinburgh also said a few words. Roy had sat next to the Duke, who said to him: 'Roy, I simply have no idea why you pour all that money into the *Times*. I never read the newspaper myself, it's a rotten paper anyhow. In fact,' he went on, 'I don't like the press at all, they way they've treated the Queen and myself. But if I were you, I'd have second thoughts about pouring all that money into such a lousy newspaper.'

This had shattered something in Roy – who was a devoted monarchist. I too had been at the receiving end from the Duke of Edinburgh. 'This is the sad side of him,' I told Roy, 'he is a most gifted man, but he's got a heavy Germanic style of humour.' To comfort Roy I recalled taking the Duke to task for talking nonsense about the press. I had said that I took it as a personal insult: 'Some of us try. We have got to be commercially viable, we can't just produce papers for Sandringham and Balmoral.' He had accepted my offer to get a group of editors secretly to lunch at my flat, which was just around the corner from Buckingham Palace, so that he could tell them what he thought of them and they could answer back. We had had a good clearing of the air, and his points turned out really to be against the popular press, and not the *Times* and its competitors at all.

Roy was quietened and soon recovered his spirits, if not his faith in the commercial future of the *Times*. He had already been forced to move out of Gray's Inn Road because the unions had issued an edict that when he arrived, if he'd been travelling and had a suitcase, the non-union commissionaire was not allowed to carry it – a union man had to be sent for. I think Roy considered this the greatest humiliation of his life – after saving the *Times* and trebling the staff of the *Sunday Times*. For several years his legs had begun to let him down, for he had a form of diabetes and became very exhausted. I had shown him round the new building and he'd said, 'I can manage it for ten minutes.' After five minutes going round the *Times* newsroom he said, 'Denis, I'm going to collapse.' I opened the nearest door and put him into a chair. He looked up at the occupant and said, 'I'm not very well, who are you?' – 'I'm Colin Watson.' – 'Oh, Colin; what's your job?' And Colin Watson had said, 'I edit the obituaries.' 'Well,' said Roy, 'I bloody well hope you've got mine ready, because it may be needed tonight.'

In the end this modest man died after catching a cold on a free Thomson Travel tour to Tenerife, which he chose simply because there happened to be a seat available. The day he left we had a long talk. His last words to me were, 'Denis, do your utmost to get that new technology into the *Times*. The *Sunday Times* doesn't need it so much, but it's the only way we're going to save the *Times*.' Ten years later Roy's dream came true. But he never lived to see it. He came back from Tenerife with a cold, finally had a stroke and was unconscious for five weeks. Roy died on 4 August 1976 – in my view the most enlightened newspaper proprietor of modern times, and certainly the most warmhearted.

It was the end of an era. Within two years we were at open war with the unions. A year and a half after that we sold Times Newspapers. Thank God Roy Thomson didn't have to watch it happen.

# CHAPTER TWENTY-TWO

# THE GREAT
# EXHIBITIONS

ALTHOUGH MY TWELVE YEARS AS EDITOR-IN-CHIEF OF TIMES NEWSPAPERS were to end in tragedy, there were positive aspects of which I am still proud. The quality of the two newspapers and their supplements, editorially, did not deteriorate as did, for instance, the British economy under successive governments, both Labour and Conservative. We even added a successful new supplement, the *Times Higher Education Supplement* (covering universities and polytechnics), which crowned our coverage of education and the literary arts in Britain. Collectively, I employed by far the largest number of quality journalists in the country. We produced some excellent books, such as the *Times* Atlases; and when I became a trustee of the British Museum in 1969, I was able to use my connections with Egypt to help mount the most successful popular archaeological exhibition in a museum in British history: the Tutankhamun Exhibition of 1972.

As a non-graduate I'd been diffident about accepting the trusteeship when the Prime Minister, Harold Wilson, asked me in 1969. My twin sons had been to Oxford and Cambridge; I asked their advice. They, and others, urged me to accept on the grounds that the museum might in fact benefit from the advice of an 'outsider' who knew something about the worlds of newspapers, advertising, and commercial publishing, and had many influential political and international contacts at the highest level.

The Tutankhamun venture was my first opportunity to make a decisive contribution on behalf of Times Newspapers. I had already tried to do a deal with Nasser, before I'd become a trustee, but his death put an end to those preliminary negotiations and there were all sorts of difficulties with his successor, Sadat – who had worked as a spy for the Germans in Cairo in the second world war, and disliked the British even more than Nasser did. The Keeper of Egyptian Antiquities, Dr

I.E.S. Edwards, was obsessed by the idea, and profiting from our many contacts in Cairo we were able to work very smoothly together. He wanted to hold the exhibition in 1972, which would be the fiftieth anniversary of Lord Carnarvon's and Howard Carter's discovery of the tomb. After enormous efforts and guarantees, we got an agreement with the Egyptian government that the exhibition would go ahead then, to be held in the British Museum but sponsored by the *Sunday Times* and the *Times*. (The *Times*, of course, had contributed to the finances of Carnarvon's excavation in 1922 and had published the day-by-day story of the discovery.)

Carnarvon's death four months after entering the tomb gave rise to fears that it and its contents were somehow jinxed. Harold Macmilan certainly believed so – he rang me up and said, 'My dear boy, I see you're running the Tutankhamun Exhibition – please don't. You'll be dead.' I asked why. 'You've heard of the curse of Tutankhamun?' I said yes, I had, and that it was nonsense, got up by the *Daily Mail*. 'Well,' he said, 'I believe it, don't do it.' I told him it was too late and I would see it through. About five weeks after the opening of the exhibition, I got another call – to be told that the foreman carpenter who'd unpacked the exhibits had died. The question was, what would happen if the news got out? Would people feel the curse was true, and not come? I went bustling down to the Museum. There were worried faces everywhere. Their immediate question was, 'How do we keep this out of the press?'

I did feel there was something mysterious about a man having a fatal heart attack when only 50, even though he had worked desperately hard to get the exhibition ready in time. The museum staff found me the name of his doctor and I rang him up. I was quite frank and told him our problem. Had the foreman's death caught him by surprise? 'Oh no,' he answered, 'there's no problem there. It was his fourth heart attack – he was going to die some time very soon.' I thanked him, and went back to the staff to tell everybody to relax – and that if anyone leaked the story to the press, we'd tell the plain truth; proving it was nothing to do with any Egyptian curse.

We had other problems, though, particularly from the French. Despite elaborate organisation to escort the exhibition from the airport at night, with half London's police involved, the convoy arrived in Museum Street to find the gates blocked by a thirty-ton French lorry whose driver had gone off. No one knew where – or how to get this priceless convoy into the safety of the museum. A police hunt had to be mounted and after several hours the French driver was at last found. To the relief of Scotland Yard and ourselves, as guarantors of the treasure, the convoy passed through the gates.

Such obstruction by a French lorry was entirely coincidental – but there was nothing accidental in the French attempt to prevent our having fifty exhibits. Only once before had there been an exhibition of these treasures outside Egypt, at the Louvre in Paris, thanks to the cordial relations between the French and the Egyptians, particularly in the field of archaeology. The French had been allowed only thirty items, and they were most jealous. Dr Edwards wanted fifty, both to mark the fiftieth anniversary and in order to mount a more spectacular exhibition. However, Mme Desroches-Noblecourt, deputy director of the Louvre, happened also to be chairman of the UNESCO Committee on Pharaonic objects, and had blocked all Dr Edwards's attempts.

I suggested we invite Mme Noblecourt to London and give her a big reception. So she came over, a rotund lady archaeologist, with her husband, and I laid on a private room and dinner for them at the Savoy, with the director of the British Museum, John Wolfenden, and Dr Edwards. I put everything I could into trying to charm this imposing lady, but she saw straight through me from the start. 'I know exactly what you want: you want fifty objects. As chairman of the UNESCO committee I have to decide how many objects can safely be brought over here. The Louvre had thirty. For you too it will be thirty.'

I said, 'Well, you've made your decision, it's no use arguing any more about it. Let's enjoy our dinner and have a few drinks.' Then, to make conversation, I asked where she lived (Paris) and about her family home. 'We live in Normandy,' she told me, 'and go there every weekend if we can.' I pressed her for the name of the village, and when she told me, asked, 'Is your house in the main street – a big house?' She nodded. 'Has it got a huge farm attached to it?' Yes, it had; and I then described the building to her. 'How do you know?' she asked, wondering.

'Well,' I said, 'I liberated your house in 1944. In fact I used it as a battalion headquarters for about four hours before we moved on. The Germans were shelling us with everything they had. The house had very thick walls and saved our lives.' She spoke in French to her husband. Suddenly she burst into uncontrollable tears. 'If you want fifty, if you want a hundred, you can have them,' she announced.

She was as good as her word; we got fifty of the finest objects from the tomb. In due course more than a million-and-a-quarter people, from all over the world, came to see the exhibition  possibly the most successful of its kind ever mounted, not only in its impact on the general public, but because it raised over £750,000 for Unesco towards the restoration of the Temple of Philae, which was rescued from being swamped by the Aswan Dam. When we gave our closing dinner, I invited her again, and said, 'Thanks to you all this has been possible.' Once more tears started from this woman who was known to petrify her staff, and she flung her arms around me in front of everybody, including Olive, saying: 'People like you who restored the honour of my country . . . if there is *anything* I can ever do . . . .' It was an extraordinary moment.

The following year I was able to help put on another popular exhibition of archaeological finds – the Chinese Exhibition. Owing to lack of space it couldn't be held in the British Museum, so we put it on at the Royal Academy in Piccadilly, where in a matter of four months it drew about 800,000 visitors. I had visited China in 1972, and was determined that the *Times* and *Sunday Times* should sponsor such an exhibition. In the end, it proved in some ways more difficult than the Tutankhamun affair, for this time we were dealing with a Communist government largely ignorant of the ways of the West.

It was a travelling exhibition, exhibited in nine countries in all, but ours was the only country in which the exhibition was not government-sponsored. In every other country the Chinese government made themselves just about as difficult over the catalogue and name of the exhibition as it could. In the US they were such a nuisance in that the Americans withdrew their English-language catalogue altogether, leaving only the one printed in Peking. In Paris there was an all-night session with a crowd of about fifty people tearing out two offending pages of the French catalogue before it was reprinted.

I'd taken all the Tutankhamun catalogues and photographs with me when I went to see Chou En-lai in Peking in 1972. I was met at the airport by a Mr Kim, who announced that he did not wish to live without my forgiveness! He had been responsible, during the so-called Cultural Revolution, for locking the Reuters correspondent, Anthony Grey, in a tiny room for nine months. Mr Kim wanted me to understand that his own life had been at stake, and he had had to choose a scapegoat, but now that the worst excesses were over, he was consumed with remorse.

The Chinese are a strange people – at once intensely human, and yet intensely bureaucratic. Chou En-lai, of course, was in a league of his own, as sharp as an acupuncture needle, even though he was already 74. He was impressed by the dossier on Tutankhamun and recognised the goodwill and interest that a similar Chinese exhibition could arouse in the West. Not so his colleagues – the Chinese archaeologists were terrified of putting their prized treasures in an aircraft and we had all manner of difficulties getting the exhibits to London. Worse was to come on their arrival in London, however, for the Chinese Ambassador indicated to me that they wanted the exhibition to be called

'Exhibition of Archaeological Finds of the People's Republic of China'. How they imagined that this tedious title would fire the people of Britain to stand in long queues in Piccadilly I do not know. I simply ignored the Ambassador's request and told our team, under Professor William Watson and Robin Wade, the designer, to go ahead using the title, 'The Genius of China'.

The day before the opening, matters came to a head – in the president's room at the Royal Academy. The Chinese refused to allow the exhibition to open without their own title – even though I was paying for it. I simply said: 'I am the Chairman and Editor-in-Chief of the *Times* and you are not people from whom I take orders. This is the exhibition I arranged with Chou En-lai to mount. If you won't permit the exhibition to open except with your title and your version of the catalogue bearing your title, then there won't be an exhibition. We are not the government, we're the *Times* and *Sunday Times*, with 200 years of tradition and independence to think about.' Among those present were Sir Humphrey Trevelyan, the distinguished British ambassador, and a number of Foreign Office officials, all looking very white. I went on: 'The name of the exhibition is "The Genius of China"; it's on the buses, it's right across the entrance to the Royal Academy. Nor am I going to change a single word in our catalogue. Do you seriously think I'm going to state in the catalogue that those emperors who made these beautiful things were guilty of being obnoxious to their people? That's a *political* matter. I'm only concerned here with artistic matters – it's not a political exhibition. No, no, no!'

The Chinese Ambassador, Mr Sung, realised I wasn't going to budge. He asked if he could withdraw to another room with his advisers. After a while they came out, looking inscrutable. Hearts were beating as the ambassador announced his decision, through his interpreter. He said he recognised how much work had gone into the exhibition; they realised too that they were dealing with the *Times*, and with friends, not a foreign government; he would withdraw his objections.

We'd won – but I knew how much pride had been swallowed that night and a few weeks later, when the Queen came to visit the exhibition, with the Chinese ambassador again present, I made a special arrangement. At the bottom of the Academy stairs I had a huge board put up and painted across it, about twelve feet in length, 'Exhibition of Archeological Finds of the People's Republic of China'. When the Queen arrived I introduced her to each member of the Chinese delegation, saying, 'They are very important people in China,' and she slowly shook them by the hand. 'They are all good Communists,' I added, and we shared a smile. I then asked: 'Your Majesty, there *is* one thing you can do which would be a great help. Will you have your picture taken with the Chinese?' She agreed – 'Of course I will – here?' I said, 'No, I'd like you all to move to the bottom of the stairs.' No one knew what I was up to.

The Queen stood in the middle of the group, beneath the great board, while the cameramen – including Chinese photographers – snapped away. Afterwards the Queen said to me, 'What was all that about?' I explained it was for Chinese amour propre, and would very likely be on the front page of the next day's edition of the *People's Daily* – which it was. Honour was satisfied.

Over the years we sponsored a number of such exhibitions, including the Fishbourne Roman Palace excavation, the '1776' Exhibition in Greenwich, and the Viking Exhibition at the British Museum. Using our own designers we were, I think, able to blow some fresh air into the somewhat stuffy thinking and presentation of archaeology and history: an extension really of what I had tried to do while editing the *Sunday Times* in the 1960s.

Unfortunately, however, the country was going through a prolonged political and economic crisis, which was mirrored not only in the antics of the coal industry, but Fleet Street itself. Our national newspapers reported each day the scandals and dramas attached to government and economic life, but dared not expose the rot pervading our own industry. The excitement of producing a great national newspaper had turned into a nightmare of industrial disputes, of attacks on journalists' freedom by the Labour government, and betrayal of one another by the newspaper proprietors themselves. As a nation we seemed hell-bent on international suicide, destroying our industrial inheritance by a sort of collective greed and self-centredness. Pride in our own workmanship plummetted, and neither Conservative nor Labour governments seemed able to lead us out of our gathering misfortune.

The job of running Times Newspapers simply became too much for my strength, as industrial disruption reached new depths. In 1971, therefore, I had decided to hand over the administrative side of the business to a separate director, a man with a reputation as a fine administrator and able negotiator with the unions: Marmaduke Hussey. I had dropped my title of Chief Executive and become Chairman and Editor-in-Chief, in order to concentrate my efforts on the editorial side. I fought off Michael Foot's attempt to impose a virtual Communist-party style 'closed shop' for journalists in Fleet Street (masterminded by Anthony Wedgwood Benn, who acted as Foot's evil genius), helped by a sudden general election, and got the two newspapers settled cheek-by-jowl in Gray's Inn Road in 1974.

In 1975 the *Times* finally broke even financially. But we had had to abandon our attempts to raise the circulation to half-a-million, abandon our pull-out Business section, and resign ourselves to being a high-priced quality newspaper for the élite. Given the state of the British economy as reflected in lower advertising levels and the £2 million per annum losses since Roy Thomson bought the *Times* in 1967, we could only have fulfilled our dream of making the *Times* a high-circulation quality newspaper if we'd been able to reduce manning levels and introduce modern technology. In the climate of the 1970s this was not possible. Worse still, in the year the re-modelled *Times* broke even, the fragile unity of the Fleet Street proprietors was smashed by Victor Matthews, the new chief executive of *Express* newspapers.

Matthews represented an important change that was taking place in newspaper ownership. With the rise of television, most newspapers had been forced to diversify. The old newspaper barons like Lord Beaverbrook were departing, and the Newspaper Publishers' Association was now studded with men running big corporations of which newspapers were only a part. Matthews was one. He declared that if a rival newspaper failed to come out, he would print two million copies extra. This marked an end to the one collective weapon the employers still possessed which could halt the slide of Fleet Street into anarchy – for it was only the arrangement between the old proprietors not to print extra copies when a fellow-proprietor lost a night's edition which kept a semblance of order. Matthews belonged to a new breed of entrepreneurs, ambitious and competitive. Hoping to profit from other men's disputes, he did not see that the whole of Fleet Street stood to lose from his blinkered approach – since no management could effectively stand on its own against union or even unofficial industrial action if rival newspapers merely cashed in on its attempt to be firm.

To some extent, I think, Matthews was put up to it by his managing director at the *Express*, Jocelyn Stevens, who'd made a great name with *Queen* magazine, and had then been a successful managing director of the *Evening Standard*. Anyway, when the *Daily Mirror* had a strike, the *Express* attempted to print two million extra copies. There were protests from the other proprietors, but Matthews refused to back down and the *Mirror* was forced to act. It sought an injunction in the High Court to stop Sogat, the union involved in the *Mirror* strike, from bringing one newspaper to its knees in a dispute while deliberately printing extra copies for extra money around the corner. The application was contested, and heard by Lord Denning, Master of the Rolls. To our dismay Lord Denning's ruling was that there was nothing to stop them. 'I think,' he said, 'it is a very unpleasant thing, but in law I cannot see why any union should not print more copies if the management wishes them to do so.' He also said something like, 'far be it from me to condemn the management for taking advantage; I am here to interpret the law'.

That evening I went to dinner in Lincoln's Inn and the first person I met, at the top of the stairs, was Lord Denning, whom I liked very much. He was Treasurer of Lincoln's Inn and had several times asked me to their guest night. He put his arm round me and said, 'Dear Denis, thank God we've got you running the *Times* – the space you give to the law courts and the accuracy of your reports, everything you do – I simply don't know what we'd do without you.' I said, 'Well, you made a bloody awful decision this morning, Tom, you really made a muck of it.' He seemed surprised. I said, 'There's been an agreement among all the newspaper publishers that if one newspaper is in trouble, the others won't take advantage. You've busted it. It's going to be a free-for-all evermore.'

'Oh, my God,' he said, 'are newspaper proprietors as awful as that?' I said, 'My dear Tom, I think that newspaper proprietors will turn out to be worse than the unions.'

He was crestfallen. 'There's nothing I can do about it,' he explained. 'You can go to the Appeal Court against me and to the House of Lords, but I don't think there is any appeal to the reading of the law as I've seen it.' He shook his head. 'It's just so sad. I'm desperately sorry – the number of lectures I've given on the freedom of the press, supporting you; to be the means of giving support to the baddies now makes me very sad. I wish I could have seen you in advance about this.'

I said, 'It would have been improper of me to discuss the matter with the Master of the Rolls. Anyway, the law is the law – ass or not.'

This greatly distressed Denning at the time, and when it came to the long shutdown of the *Times* he once said to me: 'I suppose you think I am the cause of it all?' I answered that I didn't feel he was the cause of it; it was simply the law, and it happened that one company new to Fleet Street took advantage of it. From that moment, when any newspaper was in trouble with its chapels, those on other newspapers were able to extract appallingly extravagant blackmail money to print extra copies on standby machines, or to run the presses longer, even though they belonged to the same union. It became a sickening experience to go to meetings of the NPA, where everybody shook hands on what they were going to do with a great show of sincerity and then went back to their offices and give instructions to do the opposite. The behaviour of the proprietors became, collectively, as bad or worse than than of the unions.

Meanwhile, at Times Newspapers, things deteriorated still further. I have said that in battle a commander needs a modicum of luck, however professional he is. Even the most outstanding leadership will not withstand more than five or six things going wrong at the same time. So it was with the *Times*. 'Duke' Hussey was a strong-minded chief executive and we had two distinguished editors – but we were fighting a guerrilla war against a skilful enemy determined to exploit the economic and political situation to maximum advantage. We tried negotiation, Hussey managing to assemble the general secretaries of the various unions involved in Fleet Street and, with the sponsorship of the TUC, issuing in 1976 a *Programme for Action*. This noble document was to be as ill-fated as Barbara Castle's *In Place of Strife*. It outlined a constructive future for the newspaper industry in which large sums of money would be set aside by the employers in order to ensure an orderly transition to new technology and reasonable manning levels. Even today it reads like a religious charter. It was signed by the various union secretaries and utterly rejected by the union branches or 'chapels'. It was clear that the general secretaries had lost all authority over their members, and there never would be an orderly transition.

The *Times* and *Sunday Times* thus had a choice: to hunt with the herd, knowing that there was less and less vegetation; or to fight alone, hoping that the increased 'clout' of a now international Thomson oil, travel and communications empire could achieve what other newspapers could not. Our problem was that a large part of our revenue – like the British government's – was tied to the North Sea and its prospective oil. Mindful of the need to keep our drilling licences, Gordon Brunton urged us to observe the government's pay restraint policy, while the rest of the Fleet Street proprietors were ignoring it in order to buy industrial peace. Had we paid up, we might have saved the *Times* and *Sunday Times* as genuinely independent liberal newspapers of the highest standard – but at the risk of losing the very oil revenue with which to pay the enormous annual losses incurred by industrial disputes and the refusal of the unions to allow the phased introduction of new technology.

We therefore chose to fight.

# CHAPTER TWENTY-THREE

# THE POWDER KEG

THE DRAMA BEGAN EARLY IN 1978. AND IT WAS AS FOREDOOMED AS THE Battle of the Somme, a total and utter misjudgment. Industrial disruption had driven the Times Newspapers board to the point of despair. We could not go on losing tens of millions of copies, with readers never certain whether they were going to receive their newspaper, and advertisers in uproar. On three separate occasions the *Times* hadn't appeared for five days running, while our competitors simply printed more copies and took our sale.

So in March 1978 the whole board, including the 'independent' directors, whose very role was to help secure the paper's continuity, instructed 'Duke' Hussey to act. He decided to meet all the general secretaries of the unions once again, in Birmingham, with an ultimatum. He wanted to take all his management colleagues with him, and also asked permission to take the two editors – only I could give that permission – in order to show the general secretaries that it was truly a crisis, with morale near breaking-point in editorial as well as advertising and production departments because of the continual stoppages and sabotage.

Hussey of course knew that his *Programme for Action* – the most sensible of documents, with the imprimatur of the TUC – had been thrown out by the local branches of the unions involved. He was vice-chairman of the Newspaper Publishers' Association, and had been in Fleet Street for almost thirty years. How he imagined that a riot act read to the general secretaries would have any effect on the chapels is difficult to understand. It was obvious to the whole of Fleet Street that they, however loud their voices, had no power to deliver their members. At Times Newspapers, for instance, there were some 56 union chapels, and they behaved like separate regiments.

Nonetheless Hussey delivered his ultimatum – that if the unions didn't pull themselves together, our newspapers would shut down – and the message was received with all seriousness by the general secretaries and by Len Murray, the general secretary of the TUC. But instead of insisting simply and clearly on an end to industrial anarchy first, Hussey tried to add in the whole new technology deal as well. By the end of June it was obvious that it was a non-starter: the chapels were saying they would need at least two years to negotiate what we wanted – whereas Hussey had given them until November. The National Graphical Association – the printers – in particular said they would not even *discuss* new technology with us as it was years before its time and they hadn't yet discussed it with the Newspaper Society, the provincial owners. Hussey, nevertheless, continued to insist on the new technology as an integral part of the ultimatum, and began making plans for war, including provision for printing of the *Times* in Germany.

I got more and more worried about where this was all leading, and talked privately to the managing director of our Thomson Regional papers, David Cole, and Arthur Montgomery, his production director. Both said that Times Newspapers was collectively off its head in trying to put new technology into the package, when the employers had tried and failed in monopoly areas outside London, from Aberdeen to Cardiff. New technology, the printers knew, would halve their numbers, so they were going to play a long game.

I spoke to each editor, Evans and Rees-Mogg, separately and at length – I still have my notes – saying that I thought we were most unwise to include the new technology at this point, and that we should shelve the demand for another time. To my dismay, both of them supported Hussey. They were exhausted by the incessant stoppages, which had begun to warp their judgment of what was and was not practicable. In their view, the new technology issue would have to be fought one day; it might as well be a feature now, an aim to fight for in the coming, inevitable battle. In addition the owner, Kenneth Thomson, who had gone back to Canada, also wanted the new technology, knowing how close to his father's heart the issue had been.

I also had a long talk with Harvey Thompson, our production director, a brilliant man in his forties who was to die soon afterwards. I told him my doubts: that in my view we were, so to speak, trying to take on with one battalion the whole of the German army – and failure was inevitable. To my horror, I had found Thompson was behind Hussey, feeling that the general secretaries of the unions were with us on the issues, and would back us in a showdown.

The demand thus remained that the unions not only allow the phased introduction of new technology, but give formal and binding guarantees in return for considerable productivity payments and special payments for finishing print runs on time. At my suggestion we even offered to double their pensions if they would offer a new no-strikes agreement. But it was obvious to me that it would be hard even to get the new production agreements signed, let alone obeyed – for there was a group of 'fathers of chapels' (that is, their chairmen) who were either left-wingers or just plain anxious to get promotion within their unions, and were thus eager for battle honours.

I was now almost totally isolated, despite being still chairman of the company. There was a pause while we all went on holiday, then in September I rang Gordon Brunton, chief executive of the Thomson Organisation as well as a Times Newspapers director, and told him my fears – that the proposals were a monumental nonsense which we ought to stop while we could. We had lunch, and he agreed with me completely.

That afternoon the Times Newspapers executive board and the editors met, and the fateful decision was taken. We'd lost millions more copies over the past eight weeks, there seemed no end to the disruption, no hint on the part of the unions of compromise or willingness to talk seriously. Hussey's 'package' and his ultimatum had been completely ignored by the chapels. One by one we went down the line of those present – Hussey himself, Michael Mander, Derek Jewell, Dugal Nisbet-Smith, Donald Cruickshank (responsible for the new technology deal), Harold Evans and William Rees-Mogg. All were in favour of declaring war – of carrying out our threat to shut down in November. Brunton and I, who favoured calling off the whole thing, or postponing the ultimatum, were in a minority. The others pleaded to be given their heads, claiming they were certain to win.

And so the decision was made. Both Brunton and I knew we had been weak and foolish to bow to the majority. In the face of a universal line-up that they should be allowed to go ahead, we had given in.

Brunton himself now went to the general secretaries, to get a private view. They all told him that the ultimatum and, if necessary, a shutdown of the papers would enable them to re-assert their authority and bring the chapels to heel. But this alas, was sheer bravado, because they did not exercise any control whatever over the chapels. The place was riddled with 'Spanish customs' of every sort – I could fill another book with them, from people signing the wage book as 'Gordon Richards of Tattenham Corner', to others' absence for a whole week being covered up by someone else. The chapel fathers (FOCs) kept their hold because they had the right to hand out the casual work cheques. Payments were high, and so were expectations and commitments – the men were not villains, but often the nicest possible people, with mortgages, cars, and in some cases expensive hobbies or little side-businesses of their own. But they depended on the FOCs for their huge wages and therefore went along with everything the FOCs said. They had to. It was very sad, it did the long-term interests of Fleet Street no good, it did the country no good – but that we at Times Newspapers seriously imagined we could reverse the rot of decades on our own seems in retrospect incredible.

Brunton and I were the two most guilty parties, I think, because we were the ones with enough common sense to see the disaster we were heading for, and ought to have stamped on the scheme and killed it. With its colossal lead over its rivals, the *Sunday Times* was capable of surviving the guerrilla warfare however wearing on the management. The *Times*, true, was in a different position. It was locked in deadly combat with the *Guardian*, the *Financial Times* and the *Telegraph*. Its cumulative losses could not have been borne if we hadn't struck lucky with North Sea oil. As long as there was light at the end of the tunnel, Ken Thomson had been willing to tolerate the financial burden, but now his patience had been sapped. We'd carried the *Times* flag for eleven years: something, he felt, *had* to be done.

But what? One answer was to produce the *Times* on a green-field site – if we'd had the money to set up a new plant – away from London, free of the crushing anarchy of the chapels. But a newspaper has to be printed and distributed, and the other unions involved would clearly have come out in sympathy with their Fleet Street colleagues if we had moved the paper away. A further alternative was to sell the *Times*, merging it with one of its rivals – a possibility that was eventually addressed when the shutdown proved fatuous.

As chairman of Times Newspapers I was, I suppose, like Eisenhower before D-day, sandwiched between the Thomson group –which would have to finance a shutdown – and the TNL management team, which would have to fight the battle, under 'Duke' Hussey. It was for me a tormenting situation. All my adult life, save in the war, I had been a journalist. I'd never seen myself as a tycoon, or as a tough managing director, let alone production director. My forte had been that of an editor, handling news issues of the day, politics, economics, the arts .... The exercise of editorial judgment, and the forming of journalist teams, with trained reporters and good writers working under good editors: it was to these areas I had devoted my life. If I had been in any way useful on the boards of great organisations, whether Kemsley, Thomson or the *Times*, it was not as an administrator, or manager or accountant, but a simple man of Fleet Street, with a journalist's feeling for topicality, for originality, for creative ideas and their presentation, whether in books, magazines or newspapers, with a sense of what readers really wanted.

While I felt naturally frustrated when years of effort in getting some serial was ruined by the non-appearance or sabotage of one of our papers, I also had a certain sympathy with the men in the print or despatch rooms. I had commanded such men in battle when their loyalty and courage came to the fore. I'd given gold watches on their retirement and had made an effort to understand the nature of their grievances and fears about the new technology. From the Thomson point of view, the attitude of such men, as exemplified in the actions and practices of the various chapels, was 'bloody minded'. But the Thomson group, given its need to keep its oil-drilling licences, its aviation permits for its Thomson travel aircraft, and government assistance in restructuring the company so that a great deal of the profits could go direct to Canada, was itself partly to blame in that it had refused to breach the Government's pay restraint policy as all the other newspaper owners had done. James Callaghan, the prime minister at the time, had said in public he would show no mercy to those companies that got round different wage controls or wage restraints – which put the wind up Ken Thomson and Gordon Brunton as they contemplated the next oil drilling licences.

But how could our printers, clerical and manual workers appreciate this? Fleet Street was a web of almost incestuous employment. Giving a gold watch to a man on retirement I'd often find he had five brothers all working on different newspapers as their fathers and uncles had done before them. Wages in some of our departments – compositors, machine minders, despatch room – were lower than at the *Express* or the *Telegraph*, which had found their own ways of getting round the Government's policy. To these men, such differentials were iniquitous and socially divisive, a matter of recriminations over a drink or at home. At the weekend whole families would become embroiled as the question was asked: why are payments lower in Gray's Inn Road?

I tried my best, informally, to meet the FOCs and the men, and to explain the difficulties. However, with the losses mounting and the guerrilla warfare escalating, words were becoming redundant. Hussey had issued the ultimatum: it would soon be time to act. Whatever qualms I and Gordon Brunton had, there was a *chance* that a shutdown of the two newspapers and the supplements would bring the union chapels to their senses.

But if so, what was our plan of campaign? Were we to plan for a three-week campaign, a three-month campaign – or a three-year campaign? I have to record that, so far as I was aware, Hussey had only a plan of attack, not of campaign. We thus went to war with the chapels with no estimate of how much the war would cost us – no idea that within a year we would be facing losses of between forty and sixty *million pounds*. In fact it was in some ways like the start of the first world war – with everybody believing it would all be over by Christmas. Hussey predicted that the shutdown would be a short one because the men would be out of work. This proved to be a severe miscalculation, for within days our rivals were printing millions of extra copies to exploit our absence, and needed extra clerical and manual staff to do so. The result was that, except for a minority of highly skilled compositors and printers, almost all the staff we locked out were soon in employment elsewhere.

By busting the agreement between newspaper proprietors, Victor Matthews had put us all at the mercy of the union chapels. But Hussey knew this as well as I did – and it struck steel through my heart, when I asked him what agreement he'd made with the NPA, and he made the sensational reply that he was not going to consult the NPA, that it was pointless to do so, that they would not give any support because most of them were not ready themselves to contemplate new technology on their papers. I said, 'Can't we get a statement at least from the NPA that, as we are going to fight their battles, they will not take advantage of the situation?' Hussey replied that it was impossible – that everyone would grab what they could, but that it would only be for a short time – a fortnight at most. 'After a fortnight,' he said, 'the TUC will have been brought in and there'll be pressure on the fathers of the chapels to bring them to heel.'

Had Roy Thomson been alive I might have been able to halt this business, for Roy trusted my instinct and our relationship was one of confidence and closeness. But with Ken Thomson in Toronto there was inevitably a lack of clear direction. It was war with the supreme commander far from the front. We had appointed Hussey to manage the newspapers and deal with the unions. Either he or I should have resigned, I suppose. Instead we went into battle with the same long-term aims, but with dramatically opposed views on the advisability of war, let alone how we should wage it or how long it would last.

# CHAPTER TWENTY-FOUR

# THE SHUTDOWN

TIMES NEWSPAPERS LOCKED ITS DOORS ON 30 NOVEMBER 1978, HAVING made no alliances, or even provision for a prolonged struggle. Pickets appeared – and every rival newspaper in Fleet Street added pages to its next issue. This meant all our advertising had gone to the other papers, which together put an extra quarter-of-a-million copies on their daily sale. Far from bringing the saboteurs to their knees, the outcome was that a great proportion of our staff were not only getting strike pay from the union, but casual employment from our rivals. Hussey's much-vaunted ultimatum thus proved a hollow threat. By giving him his head, Brunton and I effectively silenced the country's two greatest liberal newspapers.

Could Hussey have won his war if we had immediately locked *everyone* out of Gray's Inn Road – not just the printers but the management, staff, journalists and those chapels which had made meaningful agreements in response to Hussey's threat?

The answer must be no – that we were doomed to defeat from the start. Gradually more and more staff *were* dismissed, as their contractual notices expired. It made no difference. Locking more men (and women) out at the start would not have forced a collective surrender and would only have lost us goodwill among the moderates – upon whom our only chance of an eventual settlement rested. As for locking out the journalists themselves, the answer must be even more emphatically negative, for the journalists' unions had never had any truck with the print unions and could never have forced them to the negotiating table. Had Hussey put pressure on Toronto to sack the journalists as well – journalists whose unions had in fact made binding agreements with the management over working practices and new technology – I would have resigned. The journalists *were*, after all, the *Times* and the *Sunday Times*. By inheritance and recruitment we had built up the finest editorial teams in Great Britain and I, their editor-in-chief, was not going to watch them broken up in a cause which, however noble in intention, was utterly misguided at that moment of Fleet Street and British trade union history.

The shutdown bore out all my worst fears. It fuelled the ambitions of chapel leaders with eyes on union advancement, while driving normally sane management executives to silly acts of bravado. Instead of 'being over by Christmas' the war had continued into 1979. Far from showing signs of collapse, the chapels were rejoicing at their ability to find alternative employment for their locked-out troops. Far from helping the general secretaries to impose discipline over their chapels, we had merely exposed their impotence: an impotence symbolised in the gathering demise of the Labour government itself as it tottered to its final performance in power. Great efforts were made by the TUC general secretary, Len Murray, and the Minister of Labour, Albert Booth, to break the deadlock, but in vain. Booth himself had been a strong trade unionist, yet he and Murray both deplored the sabotage and intransigence of the chapels.

'We're totally helpless,' Murray confessed to me. 'The general secretaries come to our meetings and promise this and that, but the fact is you've got more communists, Marxists, and more Militant Tendency types in your industry than any other. I know the names, I can recite them to you. You're in a hopeless position.'

Strangest of all, he said this to me at a dinner at Windsor Castle, where the Queen put on a revival of Gilbert and Sullivan's *HMS Pinafore*, to mark the 75th anniversary of its being first sung and played before the monarch. Poor Len Murray was too depressed about the business of the *Times* to enjoy it.

Albert Booth made a public attempt to bring all the sides together in March, which failed – and this had the effect of shutting down Murray, who said that Booth had tried to do something which was the TUC's job and that had spoiled efforts which the TUC were about to attempt. So Booth failed, and we lost Murray.

April came, and our losses amounted to a staggering £30 million. Hussey and his team were now being driven to the edge of sanity, for everything they tried, however near it came to success, would always be wrecked at the last moment by one or other of the unions. It was in this situation that they arranged for the printing of an issue of the *Times* at Frankfurt. Hussey was instructed by Brunton not to do it, but Hussey said they'd gone too far with it and Rees Mogg was by now almost frantically determined to try some way of bringing out his paper. Once again, although Brunton and I thought it was crazy, it was decided to let Hussey have his head. Mike Mander was put in charge of the operation to search Europe for somewhere with people who would set the paper and print it. Frankfurt was historically a centre with many printing shops, and Mander hit upon one that had mostly Turkish workers. So in great secrecy a copy of the *Times* was set by Turkish girl operators who hadn't a word of English – and set incidentally, without a single literal error, which ought at least to have raised a blush on a few NGA faces.

Before long, however, the non-union German staff were being attacked, and then one of our own staff who was representing us was savagely assaulted. Brunton and I said then that the operation must stop, that if the German trade unions – who never sabotaged their own country's newspapers – were going to make an issue of supporting their British brothers, and incite the worst violence we'd seen until then, then we must in all conscience call it off. Those who had wanted to show us the way could only say, 'Well, we don't want anyone killed', and agree – for someone *could* have been killed. It was a pretty frightening turn – and all to resist a code of working practice that would enable liberal and by no means anti-labour newspapers to survive, as well as bring in technology already introduced in most other advanced countries.

In the May general election Labour was toppled and the Conservatives got in – on a manifesto that included trade union reform. Unfortunately the new Minister of Labour, James Prior, was as powerless to help us as his Labour predecessor. Tory sights were at that stage on bigger fish than the print unions, and it would take time to pass the sort of legislation that would allow an employer to tackle his own work force without outside unions muscling in on a dispute. I went to have a long talk with Prior, but he said, 'I can't see what we can do. Fundamentally we want to keep out of it, we don't want to be a fire brigade rushing round every trade union dispute. It just seems to widen the dispute. Instead, we're going to look much more at the law.'

This was a considerable blow. With Len Murray helpless and Jim Prior unwilling, it was now clear that the shutdown could go on for years. Again it was like the first world war, with our management team under Hussey behaving like Haig and his staff, resentful of criticism from above about casualties. Hussey had been a junior officer in Italy in the second world war, where he'd lost a leg. He was a born fighter, but even his best friends would not have said he was a man of great intellect. He fought hard and with great energy; moreover he inspired loyalty among his team and among a number of the journalists, like Bernard Levin. Their fighting view was that we should sit tight, refusing to compromise, for as long as it took to bring the chapels to heel.

Unfortunately, by sitting it out, Thomson, the parent company, was going to get itself into grave financial difficulties. Although the Thomson family owned more than 70 per cent of the shares, there were some 55,000 non-family shareholders. If the shutdown were allowed to go into a second year, there would have to be a reduction in their dividend – and the Thomson board of directors (of which I was a member) would have faced considerable criticism. The first year's loss looked like being £40 million; a second year would amount to £80 million – while all the time our rivals the *Observer*, the *Sunday Telegraph*, the *Guardian*, the *Daily Telegraph* and the *Financial Times* were making hay at our expense. They did not, like the tabloids, go all out, but the damage to our balance sheet was still appalling.

Worst of all, in my view, was that a second year of shutdown would inevitably have meant the dismissal of the journalists, who were still on full pay. I had been told privately that the moment was soon coming when such a decision would have to be made. But it made no sense to me to destroy the work of a lifetime in building up those teams, just to prove a point – no sense at all. Besides, it would need years of trouble-free production and new technology to recover the £80 million or more squandered in a two-year shutdown. It was in this knowledge, then, that the hardliners and the wets began to divide: those who wished to fight to the bitter end (on full salary and at monumental expense to the company), and those willing to settle for a compromise peace.

A number of the journalists themselves began looking for a way out, with plots for an 'alternative' *Sunday Times* and *Times* being hatched with Jocelyn Stevens (irony of ironies, considering Victor Matthews's breaking of the proprietors' collective weapon) and even Lord Rothermere. For myself, I attempted to get to the heart of the union problem by inviting various leaders of the militant chapels to my London flat for off-the-record, private discussions. I learned much about their backgrounds and psychology, and encouraged them to see me not as an ogre but as a genuinely caring employer. The pickets were always most civil to me at the office doors and, undoubtedly, they felt that I was their only chance of breaking the solid front of the directors. Yet at the end of the day we were still at war, and like the troops fraternising with the enemy on Christmas Day 1914, there was no hope of a breakthrough as long as we maintained the same hardline war aims.

'Duke' Hussey had chosen to establish a high public profile. He was on television and radio whenever possible, putting the management case against a panoply of print-union leaders. He was determined and bullish, and we had many letters of support from retired colonels in the shires. But the truth was, the union leaders had come increasingly to dislike Hussey and his belligerent attitude in a war he couldn't win.

The Times Newspapers board was thus faced with an unhappy situation where our field commander, so to speak, who had promised a quick victory, had failed to produce it. Now, as it became more and more apparent that we would have to arrange a compromise settlement, his presence as the high-profile leader of our management executive was becoming an obstacle to peace.

There were a number of initiatives, which had now necessarily to come from other parties. I had become chairman of Reuters in 1979 and at the annual lunch I placed the guests deliberately – putting Harold Evans next to Joe Wade of the NGA. Harold, despite his initial support for the ultimatum, completely disagreed with Rees-Mogg over possible printing abroad, and would not consider a Frankfurt edition of the *Sunday Times*. More and more he accepted that the shutdown was a mistake and a hostage to fortune – a free gift to the *Observer*. Born the son of a railwayman, Harold had no 'hang-ups' like Rees-Mogg in talking to trade unionists. Although Rees-Mogg had helped shift the ultra-Conservative *Sunday Times* of Lord Kemsley's day to a more centrist, liberal stance in the 1960s, his heart was and always remained that of a Conservative, undeterred by wealth and with some of the attitudes of a country squire. Just as his staff admired his talents but often thought of him as a bit out of touch with the rank and file, so the trade unions could find no point of contact or understanding – whereas with Harold Evans they were, in a sense, talking to one of their own. Harold and Joe Wade got on extremely well – with the result that within twenty-four hours Evans went up to Bedford, the headquarters of the NGA, and between them they drew up an outline of what might be considered as a basis for a return to work.

I think subsequent events proved that the NGA were not sincere with him or in the follow-up with Brunton and myself; I don't think they ever intended to give anything on new technology. But it did start a threefold momentum. I spoke to all the chapels in a series of meetings, to the fury of my management colleagues. A piece of paper was signed by Ken Thomson, Gordon Brunton and myself about a return to work by the NGA. And Bill Keys, the secretary of Sogat (and also chairman of the TUC print committee) came in on the act with Owen O'Brien, secretary of Natsopa. This momentum slowly built up, but I don't believe the NGA, in the agreement they signed that they would investigate methods of moving towards new technology, ever really intended to do anything. It was really 'kidology': they recognised we were desperate for a return to work, and were anxious themselves to get kudos for arranging it.

Hussey and his management team, meanwhile, were adamant that we should fight on to the bitter end. More and more they were seen to be out on a limb, supported neither by the government, nor the TUC, nor fellow-proprietors – and therefore the initiative, in a compromise peace, had to come from Brunton, myself and Ken Thomson, who was bearing the financial burden. Certainly there was no visionary leader among the chapel leaders, no one who could inspire a change of heart, no collective will to end the dispute and put all our best efforts into producing a profitable *Times*. To them, I suppose, the *Times* was still the spokesman of right-wing political, social and economic views; they simply did not see it as a jewel in Britain's crown, a Thunderer which for generations had stood up against governments of the day. Not a single chapel officer had changed his views on working practices or the new technology. I confess that with all my sympathies for them, I did feel they were narrow-minded and bigoted. A note of despair now began to creep into proceedings. We had deliberately engineered a war in order to solve fundamental differences – the most common cause of war. The result had been not solution but stalemate, at which our rivals had merely laughed.

Rees-Mogg, meanwhile, was pursuing his own solution – the idea of moving the *Times* to a green-field site outside London. In vain I reasoned with him: 'How, William, are you going to distribute it?' There was still no law that would make it possible. William's answer was that he would get the paper sold at street corners and delivered directly to small newsagents not fed by the big wholesalers like W.H. Smith and John Menzies, who would face refusal by the distribution unions. But without a change in the law it was pie in the sky. The *Times* would have become a news-sheet, unable to pay even the wages of its journalists, let alone the cost of production.

It was quite clear that the divisions between some of the chapels were so basic and so deep (as also the divisions between the chapels and their own union general secretaries), that we were as far from the start line as ever. I suppose Reg Brady, FOC of Natsopa's *Sunday Times* machine-room chapel, was the worst offender. He'd already caused more trouble in the machine room than any other man in the history of the newspaper, discovering all manner of disputes and grievances; he became known as 'Whose finger on the button?' – in reference to a dispute between the NGA and Sogat that was literally about which should push one, as we shall see. During the stoppage he grew a beard and wore a fur hat with a Natsopa badge on it, managing to look like a Russian politbureau member watching the May Day parade in Moscow. He had been born into a poor family in the street next to the office, and had natural intelligence and leadership qualities which could have been harnessed to a constructive cause; with the benefit of education he would have made a fine manager – indeed at one point he did apply in writing to be Director of the Newspaper Publishers' Association. He was ambitious, but he had an enormous chip on his shoulder and revelled in his publicity – for if you put a minor trade unionist in front of TV cameras, he becomes a star, and develops star-like habits. Later, under Rupert Murdoch, he was shut up in an office as part of the management and disarmed. He and Barry Fitzpatrick, also a Natsopa FOC at the *Sunday Times*, in charge of about 800 clerical members, were in my view our most implacable opponents. Both had ambitions to become general secretary of their union. While Brady was a leader, the brainier Fitzpatrick had phenomenal staying power as a negotiator. He could drag out a meeting on some trivial issue for about ten hours until the management side were weak with exhaustion, and then still insist on every last detail. Whatever his union's general secretary might agree, he himself was determined, at chapel level, to extract the highest payment for everything.

Gradually, by a process of attrition, agreements were signed with all fifty-six chapels on a return to work. At last, in November 1979, almost twelve months after the shutdown had begun, the great day came for the *Times* to reappear. Suddenly, in the afternoon, with the paper well on the way to being set and an enormous publicity campaign organised, with the world waiting for the paper, there came yet another inter-chapel row, on who was going to press a certain button operating the string-tyer – the NGA or Natsopa?

As chairman of Reuters I had had to go to Stockholm and Helsinki, leading the Reuters board for important discussions with the whole Nordic press and to sign agreements. In each capital there was a banquet given by the Prime Minister and Cabinet, and there was no way I could absent myself without giving offence. I left London as late as possible, arriving in Stockholm at 5 pm, and went to the first banquet at 7 pm, having organised an open line to London in the room next door. Luckily, the Scandinavian practice is for the first speech to follow the soup, and the reply to come with the dessert. Sweden's Prime Minister made the speech, and said that they were all looking forward to reading the *Times* the next day. I alone knew that, at that moment, there was very little prospect of that. I kept nipping in and out of the next room, on the line to Dugal Nisbet-Smith, the general manager, who was keeping me briefed. At 9 o'clock, when the presses were due to start, they were still idle. It was by then 10 o'clock in Stockholm. I was due to speak at 10.15 – not about the TNL dispute, but relations between Scandinavia and England, and the role of Reuters – but my mind was entirely on London, as was that of the audience, since the newsprint manufacturers and salesmen from all over Scandinavia wanted to know if the *Times* was ever going to be printed again.

At about ten minutes past ten the waiter tapped me on the shoulder, saying I was needed on the telephone. I was told that Bill Keys and 'Duke' Hussey had patched up some agreement, the presses had started rolling, and 10,000 copies were going to be put on a special chartered flight for distribution round Scandinavia. At 10.15, at the end of the dessert course, I was thus able to rise and say, 'Prime Minister, ladies and gentlemen, I have news for you. The *Times* is now printing.'

# CHAPTER TWENTY-FIVE

# SELLING TIMES
# NEWSPAPERS

FROM STOCKHOLM I WENT TO HELSINKI, WHERE I MET THE FINNISH President. Everyone was full of congratulations and relief that the *Times* and *Sunday Times* were back. But by the time I had returned to my office in London on Monday and had had the first meeting with my staff, it was clear that every agreement with the unions had already been broken. In fact I don't think we even finished the first run of the first return edition of the *Sunday Times*. All had gone sour again. No new technology had been achieved, and no one was prepared to honour the agreements which had been made regarding productivity, manning and phased redundancy, which would have made operating costs more sensible. The shutdown had been a fiasco.

For Hussey it was a personal defeat. He was exhausted, and of course disqualified as a negotiator, for he had no further standing with the unions. During the final discussions before the return to work, his role had already been taken by Dugal Nisbet-Smith, who became managing director. Hussey took it all greatly to heart. He had made the running in terms of publicity, there had been profiles on him on radio and television as the great strong man of Fleet Street who was going to bring about a new era and stand up to the unions: even Joyce Grenfell had been heard singing his praises, that if there was any man in England who could lead the troops over the top, he was the man. But he had put himself in a position from which there was no personal retreat.

From that time Hussey never corresponded with me, feeling presumably that he ought to have been supported to the bitter end in his hopeless fight for victory. He quickly faded from the *Times* picture to become chairman of the governors of the Royal Marsden Hospital, whence, years later, he was plucked to become chairman of the governors of the BBC. Meanwhile, at the *Times*, I threw myself in at the side of James Evans, who came in from Thomsons as executive chairman of the management board, as we tried to reforge a long-term dialogue with the unions. This was far from easy. Instead of concentrating on getting the newspapers out after the year-long shutdown, the NGA seemed obsessed by the need to 'get even' with the few members of the union who had had to cross the picket line in order to keep the machines ready for a resumption of work throughout the strike: the printing overseers.

There were some fifteen of these – including the *Times* head printer, George Vowles – who ought not to have been ordinary union members, and I had often pleaded with the NGA to release them, as their tasks were to all intents and purposes managerial. But the union steadfastly refused. The overseers had already begun to worry, even before the return, about losing their union cards, and thus being forced out of printing work. I assured them personally that if the NGA behaved outrageously, I would consider it a direct affront to me and would resign, making the whole issue public. This relieved their minds, but though on 21 October 1979 I received written assurances from Les Dixon, the president of the NGA, that there would be no victimisation the union behaved abominably, forcing the overseers to wait throughout the autumn and winter before their cases were heard by an NGA tribunal – at which they were, in effect, 'tried' for their loyalty to the newspaper and its production plant. Most were subjected to savage fines, well in excess of £1,000, before their application for re-membership could be granted – and this on top of months of uncertainty and outright vilification at work.

It was heartbreaking to see grown men behaving in such a spiteful, vindictive manner towards their workplace superiors, while all the time breaking the very agreements which had been made in obtaining a settlement; agreements which the unions, or their chapels, now actually began to claim did not exist, such as the NGA's agreement to discuss the eventual introduction of new technology. By March 1980 I was having to write to Joe Wade, general secretary of the NGA, of my 'incredulity' that the written agreement we had arrived at on 29 June 1979 was now being denied by the union altogether – and on 10 April I wrote to him saying, 'We know each other well enough now for me to say that I find this breach of agreement the most depressing event in my 40 years in newspapers.'

One by one, every agreement made in getting a resumption of work was broken or repudiated; production sabotage resumed with the same irresponsibility, even anarchic fervour, as before. At one point the head printer had to write to the combined chapels demanding an apology for deliberate defiance of his authority, as well as intoxication and abuse to his staff. In spite of this, the management did everything possible to build bridges, hoping to inspire a common goal. In mid-May I organised a conference of FOCs and overseers at Gatwick Park under the independent chairmanship of Lord McCarthy. Impassioned speeches were made about a better, even a glorious future. But the fine words belied an ever-deteriorating situation at Gray's Inn Road, where it seemed impossible to produce a single night's uninterrupted or unsabotaged paper.

The lockout had achieved none of our objectives. It had merely proved our impotence in the eyes of the wreckers. From November 1979 to the summer of 1980 we did everything possible to formulate a financial and 'social' strategy for Times Newspapers. We brought in consultants, we produced a great deal of paper, lots of speeches were made about everybody wanting harmony and a constructive future – but all the time it came down to how much we would pay the chapels to shore up the *Times* and how many more men we would go on paying, despite the losses.

I remained at least proud that I'd kept the journalists together, on full pay, hardly losing a man. However galling our defeat and bleak the current outlook in terms of progress, this was something – it was as though we had been forced to retreat, but were, as an army, still intact. But were we? The long shutdown had evidently worn the patience and loyalty of the journalists to breaking point, or else they had become indifferent to the fate of newspapers whose survival had been on-off, on-off, for an entire year of their professional lives.

They had all been given, on the return to work, increases of between 30 and 40 per cent, but now claimed, as part of some national negotiation, that they should get a *further* immediate rise of 22 per cent from August. ACAS became involved and our management agreed there should be separate and very quick arbitration. Before leaving for a holiday in Italy in August, I asked James Evans and the management what would settle the claim. They felt that 14 per cent was all they could do, but when I asked if 18 per cent was acceptable, they said yes. In my absence arbitration went ahead, and awarded 22 per cent.

This was very awkward, and the management rang me in Italy to suggest that I come back and speak personally to the journalist chapels, because Rees-Mogg was in America, and it was felt I might be able to convince them that this was not the moment to press the company till the pips squeaked, given that it had kept them on full pay throughout the shutdown and had already given enormous salary increases: that they were thus playing with fire.

It was known the *Sunday Times* journalists were happy to settle for 18 per cent, but would not make a public statement to that effect in case their *Times* colleagues secured more. It was at this juncture that Jacob Ecclestone, the FOC of the *Times* journalists' chapel (now deputy general secretary of the National Union of Journalists, a post on which he was known to have fixed his ambitions) called a sudden chapel meeting. It was a Friday, a day when traditionally office attendance is thin because Saturday's newspaper is mostly features. Ecclestone, whose left-wing views were well known, sought and gained a mandate to call a strike. By the time I got from the airport to the office, it was too late. The editorial department had shut down.

For me it was the last straw. I had *personally* protected them and their families all through the shutdown; I could not but feel personally attacked and humiliated. Hussey's long battle had worn me out, mentally and physically; I simply did not see how I could explain to the proprietor why he should throw more good money after bad. Without the journalists' loyalty we had nothing left to fight for.

On the Saturday I therefore rang Ken Thomson in Toronto to say that in my view we should take steps quickly to sell the newspapers for whatever we could get: that we couldn't possibly run them any longer, the costs were too great, our credit too low, and we were too exhausted. Though I didn't say it, I could well have added that, in the climate of hara-kiri among the journalists, an absentee owner living in Toronto, was not calculated to make things easier. From all angles selling now seemed the only recourse.

I rang Gordon Brunton and said the same thing. I dined with him that night and the directors of the Thomson Organisation on Sunday. It was agreed we should discuss with Warburgs whom we might approach, in great secrecy, in order to sell the newspapers.

Unfortunately, all through September and October, as we tried to find a buyer, production disputes broke out with even greater ferocity, the *Sunday Times* losing at one point *half-a-million* copies through industrial disruption. It was a farce – and made selling the newspapers an almost insuperable problem. In 1967 the government of the day had appointed a whole body of distinguished men to judge whether a great newspaper like the *Times* should be sold to a Canadian; now, twelve years later, it did not look as if anyone wanted it. Matters came to such a pass that we were forced finally to issue a warning to the unions that unless they honoured the working-practice agreements we had made with them, we would simply close the papers down for good in February 1980. In the meantime they were for sale.

The truth was, once the *Times* journalists had pulled the plug on a newspaper losing £10 million a year, I'd no fight left. Ecclestone had won his union spurs, but in doing so he had signed the death warrant of the *Times*, at least in its Thomson format, and the journalists who supported, or did not oppose, him were equally to blame. Their reward was Rupert Murdoch.

We announced that anyone who could establish a genuine interest in buying the newspapers could apply to Warburgs and receive confidential information which we'd prepared for them – two bound volumes which they could study, and then make an offer. Of course, we had half-expected that somebody would come to us before we made the sale public, but no one did. I suppose everyone was so frightened at the losses being made and the militants we had, that no one really fancied it – and this didn't alter when the news was made public.

However, as chairman of Reuters, I had to fly to Bahrain for an overseas board meeting with colleagues from the board in England. On the plane, Rupert Murdoch sat next to me. He believed, I think, that he was quietly extracting what he could from me. In fact I had known I would be travelling with him and had come prepared, hoping to plant as much of a seed as possible – for my fellow-directors felt that only a really strong owner who would be prepared to take savage measures, and of whose determination the unions could have no doubt, had any hope.

At this stage neither Harold Evans nor Rees-Mogg knew that Murdoch was in the running. When I informed them that he was seriously interested, their immediate reaction was to see, independently, if they could organise a management buy-out. My own position was that of the company's directors: I would have nothing to do with such a plan. Of course, you might get enough money in the City to finance a management buy-out of the *Sunday Times*, which was basically a very profitable newspaper. But I felt I hadn't spent all those years running the *Times* just to see it sink, while the *Sunday Times* survived. If it were possible to preserve the company, owning the two newspapers and their supplements, Peter could at least help pay for Paul until the day new technology *did* come, and the newspaper became profitable. A management buy-out of the *Times* never would make it profitable, any more than the vague indications of interest we received from people like James Sherwood of Sea Containers. Though Rees-Mogg told me privately that he didn't wish to go on editing the *Times* after the sale, he did explore the prospect of a buy-out, without success. Harold Evans, though he made a great show of leading a cavalry charge of *Sunday Times* journalists intent on buying out the owners, soon threw his hat in with the Murdoch camp.

Murdoch was certainly the first serious outsider to put his head over the parapet, substantially based on the conversation we'd had on the plane to Bahrain. Whatever people said of him, he was a professional newspaperman, prepared – perhaps too prepared – to take off his jacket and go in and sub a story or do the negotiating with a union himself. The other potential purchaser who was attracted by the light was Lord Rothermere, but to my surprise he wouldn't have any discussions himself with Warburgs or with Gordon Brunton, who was acting on behalf of Kenneth Thomson. He would only send messages via his managing director, Mick Shields. This made it hard to assess what Rothermere really intended in making an offer for the company.

Broadly speaking, Murdoch was prepared to put around £15 million on the table. Rothermere was talking about £20 million, so it could be viewed as a better financial deal. But we found that what he really wanted was the *Sunday Times* and its printing plant in Gray's Inn Road, leaving him to sell his Bouverie Street site, and that he didn't entertain much hope for the *Times*. Rothermere did offer me a personal meeting, so long as no one knew, but I saw no point in one.

Rupert Murdoch wanted both the *Sunday Times* and the *Times* with its Supplements. I had no option but to recommend Murdoch's bid to the board. Only Murdoch had the will and expertise to carry the newspapers through the last, final death-throes of an old printing technology with old union structures – the commitment to take on the papers and fight through the necessary reforms. With the national directors of Times Newspapers and the two editors I put Murdoch through a third-degree interrogation. He came through it very well. He'd prepared himself very carefully and I don't think we had any difficulty in making up our minds that, although not a perfect purchaser, he was the best available.

I had made it a condition that there should be no foreign owner of the *Times* – a British Commonwealth one yes, but not a foreign one. I had been under enormous pressure from the Middle East; Philip de Zulueta, a merchant banker, rang me regularly for almost three weeks, wanting to buy the *Times* – but would never disclose on whose behalf, whether a purchaser from Taiwan, Hong Kong or Switzerland. It was even rumoured that the Aga Khan was interested. But there was no point in selling the company as an entity in order to preserve the future of the *Times* in particular, unless the journalists themselves were likely to work for the purchaser – a fact which de Zulueta, as a banker, found very hard to understand. Moreover, we had come to grief partly because of the absence of a committed owner, on the spot, willing to face the problems of the paper and Fleet Street head-on – something which even the other rumoured parties interested, the *Sydney Morning Herald* Group, could not have done.

Rupert Murdoch had emerged as the first serious contender, and he remained so over the next critical weeks. He wanted the newspapers; they presented to him, as they had to Roy Thomson, a personal challenge. For good or bad, then, the decision was made to sell to Murdoch. The industrial anarchists were now to meet their match.

# CHAPTER TWENTY-SIX

※

# MURDOCH'S *TIMES*

PERHAPS I MADE A MISTAKE BY NOT LEAVING THE *TIMES*, LIKE REES-MOGG, after the sale of the papers to Murdoch. But Murdoch wanted me to stay, and after the traumas of the past years, I felt it might give a certain amount of confidence to the outside world that I was staying for a while, as well as to the journalists, even though they had brought upon themselves such a fate. But I didn't accept any payment from Murdoch; my salary continued from the Thomson Organisation. I therefore remained chairman of the *Times* board, with Murdoch as vice-chairman. Once more in my newspaper life, it was clear that an era had passed.

For all his instincts as a newspaperman, Murdoch was a poor picker of men. He had no judgment of what makes a good editor, only gossip about who was good or bad, and our first disagreement came immediately, when William Rees-Mogg had to be replaced at the *Times*. Both Rees-Mogg and I felt Murdoch had an excellent replacement at hand in Charles Douglas-Home, who was young but highly experienced, and popular with the *Times* journalists. Instead, Murdoch proposed Harold Evans, my own protégé from the *Sunday Times*. Harold was keen, and the two men fixed it up between themselves before the first board meeting. I told Murdoch it would turn out disastrously, and it did. Harold failed to make the right kind of appointments, or to win over the existing staff, and in addition to taking over the duties of his leader-writers, leaving them unemployed, he busied himself with the minutiae of sub-editorial detail when he should have been reflecting on the issues of the day, so that the paper's editorial views did not oscillate all round the clock. Evans also fell foul of Murdoch's new general manager, Gerald Long, because he was constantly (as he had done with me) overspending, or temporarily disguising expenditure. Everything I thought would happen, did happen. He no longer had guidance from me – I was now not his employer and editor-in-chief, merely the titular chairman of the company during the transitional phase. Evans was, it would be fair to say, one of the best Sunday newspaper editors in our newspaper history; but as a daily newspaper editor he could not repeat his previous success, his reign at the *Times* ending ingloriously after a single year. But it was Murdoch's fault, from start to finish: a grave error of proprietorial judgment for which Murdoch would have only himself to blame.

Another of Murdoch's mistakes had taken place before the sale even went through. I had already been chairman of Reuters for several years and the managing director there was Gerry Long. Long had been a news agency man all his life. He had a first-class brain, but he was not a leader. This didn't matter so much in a news agency of those days, and his Reuters record was a distinguished one. Suddenly, on Christmas Day 1980, he rang me to say he was resigning to join Rupert Murdoch's organisation, at the age of 58, as prospective managing director of Times Newspapers. If, for any reason, the sale of the *Times* did not go through, however, he wished to keep his job at Reuters.

I was flabbergasted. It was obvious that Murdoch, in his astute way, had thought it would be a clever move to impress the world that he, Rupert Murdoch, could get the managing director of Reuters to work for him in a key position. After consultation, I told Long that the Reuters board could not accept a provisional resignation. He must either stay or go. He chose to go. I later heard that his departure from Reuters was not mourned.

Long found himself out of his element in Gray's Inn Road. His flair as a news agency man was wasted in an environment of competitive newspapers, requiring rapid decisions, and with great union problems. He had no knowledge of newspaper production, editing or advertising. Moreover, having departed from Reuters under my chairmanship, he was again under my chairmanship at the *Times* – and our relations became most uneasy. He knew I was a man of principle, that I would accept no short cuts that were unworthy of the newspaper's prestige and name. We were on a collision course, and later that year we collided, leading to my resignation.

Murdoch's other choice, at his first board meeting, was the new editor of the *Sunday Times*. Again, Murdoch turned down my suggestion that Hugo Young, the political editor, take the post – possibly because Young was favoured also by Rees-Mogg, whom Murdoch disliked. He deliberately chose a caretaker editor in Frank Giles, whom I had rejected in favour of Harold Evans in 1967, and the chance to start off the Murdoch-owned *Sunday Times* on a bold new footing was thus missed. Frank's hands remained safe, but he was soon retired. Gradually the *Sunday Times* lost credence as a great newspaper, its sales declined and its prestige diminished, both nationally and internationally.

My own position was increasingly invidious. After one very difficult talk with Gerry Long, I told Murdoch that I would chair the December 1981 meeting, the next one, but would announce to the board that it was my last, and that I would be leaving the building that afternoon – which I did.

Murdoch's right-hand man was Richard Searby, a brilliant Australian lawyer who might have been a judge. He and Murdoch had been together at the same college at Oxford, but it was clear to me that, like Long, Searby deeply resented the fact that it was not possible to manoeuvre me in any way – that I had made them sign various conditions in purchasing the newspapers from which they could not easily back away. They were now having second thoughts, and they realised that as long as I was chairman I would never agree to any modification of the conditions of sale. I suppose I could have just stayed there and been a damned nuisance but, as the board was packed out with Murdoch's representatives, if it came to a question of counting heads, I'd have got very little support.

I had half-expected Murdoch's cronies to try to get round the conditions of sale, which were then enshrined in the Articles of Association of the company – for it was my intention, from the beginning, to put a great fence around Times Newspapers so that in no way could it be mixed up with the operational or financial side of News International. Obviously, this was to Murdoch's financial disadvantage, but to me he had always been a man of his word, whatever he might say behind my back, and I expected him to stand by his sworn promises. When Long and Searby tried, in Murdoch's absence, to modify the conditions and transfer the *Times* and *Sunday Times* into News International, I therefore resigned. They tried nevertheless to put through the proposal via the smaller executive board, but this backfired. The national directors had not been consulted, there was a public outcry, Rees-Mogg made a public protest and, together with my resignation, this put Murdoch in a very bad light, forcing him to reconsider. To his embarrassment and shame, his executive board's decision had to be rescinded, leading ultimately to Gerry Long's own departure.

I found Murdoch's style of proprietorship cowboyish – but then, I had not chosen him, from among the potential purchasers, to be nice. Ken Thomson is the most charming of individuals, but ownership of a great Fleet Street newspaper demands enormous qualities from a proprietor, just as it does from an editor. Murdoch might wriggle and squirm to avoid the onerous undertakings he had made in order to get

hold of Times Newspapers – but he was the only man in the
Commonwealth with the guts and tenacity to ensure the papers
remained in business, something which the Thomson Organisation,
with all our international experience and expertise, could not. His
desire to put the *Times* into the same stable as the *News of the World* was
not pernicious; it was designed to give him certain commercial and tax
advantages which would help the newspapers stay alive. I objected
because Murdoch had signed specific undertakings on the matter – but
I sympathised with his predicament, still faced by the same anarchic
structure of trade unions and chapels in Gray's Inn Road.

It was obvious that the war with the unions was not over, and
would get dirtier. I had tried to provide a calming influence during
the hand-over, but clearly the gloves were being put on and there
would eventually be a punch-up. In due course Mrs Thatcher grasped
the nettle which all her predecessors had balked at: trade-union
reform. Her new laws on picketing, though forgotten in the jingoism of
the Falklands War, probably did more for the renaissance of British
industry and working practices than any measure since the previous
century. By taking advantage of Eddie Shah's revolutionary example
in printing *Today* with only a single union (the electricians), Murdoch,
backed by Mrs Thatcher's new laws, took the union bull by its horns
and left it kicking and bellowing on its back.

The speed with which Murdoch assembled his plant in Wapping,
together with his own road transport company for distribution, and
the way in which he masterminded the move, must surely rank as one
of the great newspaper achievements of the century. Like all battles in
all wars, it was bloody and demanded a certain degree of bloody-
mindedness to succeed. But succeed it did, and Fleet Street will never
be the same again – indeed Fleet Street is no more. By holding on to
their privileges, Spanish practices, and internecine, anarchic ways the
chapels gave away the rights of their children to a union place in
modern newspaper printing. All the picketing and violence outside
Murdoch's plant in Wapping could not conceal the plain fact that for
more than three decades they had acted as laws unto themselves,
defying all attempts by their own union general secretaries to impose
reasonable order or prepare, gradually, for the inevitable introduction
of new technology. As a result they were redundant, beaten by an
Australian at their own game: bloody-mindedness. They had made a
mockery of British ideas of fairness and common sense, preferring
greed, bullying, and disloyalty. They had truly met their match and,
as the pickets finally melted away in Wapping, had to admit as much.

# CHAPTER TWENTY SEVEN

# THE REUTERS
# FLOTATION

FORTUNATELY I COULD WITNESS MURDOCH'S STRUGGLE FROM AFAR. BUT IF I thought I had at last freed myself from the 'unacceptable face' of modern newspapers and their proprietors, I was very much mistaken – for Reuters now entered an historic phase in its own 131-year existence as an independent world news agency.

To run an international news agency of any quality is a very expensive exercise. It became, at Reuters, more and more expensive, until it looked as if the reporting service would in fact fall apart. The main shareholders in the agency were notoriously unwilling to invest in a better service, as the Trust Agreement of 1941 (in which the bankrupt service was bailed out by the Newspaper Publishers' Association in return for a 41 per cent shareholding) laid down that the shareholders should consider their holding to be 'in the nature of a trust rather than an investment'. Nevertheless, in the 1960s and 70s there was the first attempt to widen the base of Reuters by developing Reuter Monitor.

For it had become increasingly clear to all of us at Reuters that we had to go for the huge financial markets if we wished to expand further. In a sense it was going back to our 19th-century origins, for the Reuters News Agency had been started on the basis of Stock Exchange reports. Our plan had been to develop our economic, financial and commodity communication services and thus make substantial profits from people who were very prosperous in the banking and financial community, instead of hard-pressed newspaper and media people – who would quarrel like chimpanzees if you asked them to pay one per cent more per year for the Reuter news service. In other words, our financial services would subsidise independent news gathering. Within ten years Reuter Monitor was in fact providing almost 90 per cent of our revenues.

When Gerry Long resigned, I appointed Glen Renfrew chief

executive. Under him, Reuters grew in leaps and bounds. Meanwhile, as the revenues soared, I insisted we plough back a high proportion into research. In this way we were able to develop our Dealing services and to crash through all sorts of technical and technological barriers in our communications systems round the world.

Soon after I left the *Times*, it became clear to both Renfrew and myself that we were going to need a lot more money than our normal banking facilities. Everything so far had been done by bank borrowing – we hadn't had to ask permission of the Press Association and Newspaper Publishers' Association, who owned all the shares on behalf of their constituent newspaper members. We'd had three- and five-year loans, and had leased our equipment and shared satellites where necessary, in order to avoid having to ask our shareholders for help. But by 1982 the scale of the operation had become so immense that I arranged with Renfrew that we should begin to canvass our members on the need for greater investment, and possibly the issuing of special non-voting private shares if this would help raise the money. I arranged for Renfrew to speak to all the newspaper publishers on 14 July 1982, and in the same week to all the members of the Press Association (which had about fifty or sixty members). The idea was that the company would remain private and unlimited but issue new *private* shares which would be taken up by underwriters and banks if the existing Reuter members would not invest in them.

Unfortunately, it was at this rather nerve-wracking juncture, with Renfrew pleading with the Reuters members to back an accelerated expansion programme because of the enormous opportunities in financial communications, that I had to go into hospital for a prostate operation. Although straightforward, it was found that I had cancer – and there now began a life of semi-invalidism, punctuated by surgery, radium-treatment, and hormone therapy which made me prone to tears and depths of emotion I had never previously known. On the one hand, the business at Reuters wearied me; on the other it was a vital ingredient in fighting the cancer – for it was an infinitely more fascinating challenge.

The rewards, for Reuters, were almost mind-boggling, given the coming financial revolution on London's Stock Exchange (the 'Big Bang') and around the world. In Glen Renfrew, Reuters was blessed with a chief executive of quite extraordinary calibre, but the compli- cated structure of Reuters meant that the chairman, although in a part-time role, was the only man who could sign documents and take full legal responsibility for the conduct of the agency. Above all, only the chairman, in the end, could bang the heads of the directors and trustees together and get a constructive, collective decision on Reuters' somewhat radical future.

It was after Renfrew's 14 July meeting with the members of the NPA that Lord Matthews – the man who had already smashed the newspaper publishers' only weapon in dealing with union anarchy – got a notion in his head. If they are thinking of raising money by issuing these sort of private shares, he reasoned, why shouldn't Reuters go public? He didn't speak to Renfrew or to me. He didn't consider the consequences of such a move or the danger a public flotation might pose to Reuter's traditional independence as a world news-gathering agency. He merely waited until his own company's annual general meeting when, in reply to a question, he announced that he'd been chivvying the Reuter news agency towards a stock-market quotation. Asked how long it would take for this to happen, Matthews invented a figure, right out of his head: twelve months.

Although a trustee (one of the members of the NPA charged with overseeing the 1941 Trust agreement) Matthews was not a director of Reuters. He had never in fact shown the remotest interest in Reuters, but his newspaper empire was collapsing, the shares of Fleet Holdings were rock-bottom, and he was clutching at straws. In front of his Fleet Holdings shareholders he declared that Reuters' profits were rising (we'd given a £1·9 million dividend, the first for forty years) and that for many years he'd been helping to prop up Reuters – a surprising claim, considering that he had never lent Reuters a penny and in fact had forced us to look elsewhere owing to the meanness of his and other newspapers. 'Suddenly there's a new look about Reuters,' he said, 'in the end it will lead to a market quotation and we are certainly urging them to go public. I'd imagine there'd be two classes of shares; they'd still have to be controlled. It could happen this year; we'll have to wait and see.' Later, Matthews told me that he had never intended to blurt out all this at the meeting; in fact his only knowledge about Reuters came from Murdoch, who was one of the ten directors.

Renfrew and I were shaken. We didn't *need* to go public, we had excellent relations with the merchant banks, we were making excellent profits, and by issuing further private shares we could have avoided any problems over our charter, so to speak – the 1941 Trust document. By going public we not only opened a can of legal worms relating to the Trust, which might need parliamentary approval to be altered, but we defeated the whole object of Reuters: to remain as a truly independent news-gathering and communicating company, subject to no national or political bias whatsoever. If suddenly the majority of our newspaper shareholders sold off their shares after a public flotation, we could find ourselves owned by any group of individuals who might wish to tamper with the flow of news in the world.

To begin with, the Press Association was totally against a public flotation, but such was the greed of certain proprietors, and the need for 'free' equity amongst ailing newspapers, that Matthews began a momentum that was hard to stop. It soon became obvious that a second gold rush had started. I think Matthews – who owned a large number of shares in Fleet Holdings – must have benefitted to the tune of some millions. I don't suppose this really made his retirement to the Channel Islands any happier, since wealth cannot buy that precious commodity, but it did make my life as chairman of Reuters just about as difficult as possible.

Somehow I had to keep the board of Reuters together and to chair innumerable committees which had to look into the matter. I didn't feel that, in view of the shareholders' eagerness and the enormous interest now being shown in the markets of New York and London, there was really any way of getting out of a public flotation. As at the *Times*, I could have put a temporary spanner in the works, for as chairman I had considerable authority, not only within the company, but in public affairs. But eventually I could have been outvoted and forced to resign, which would have damaged Reuters' standing. In the circumstances I felt we should allow a public flotation, but only by issuing non-voting shares which would enable control of the company to remain, as before, completely independent. It would not be easy to get the warring press barons to co-operate, or to persuade the big financial institutions to accept a two-tier system of public shares, but I was convinced it could be done, and I made clear that I would not myself take any shares at all in the flotation, lest it be said that I favoured the move for reasons of personal gain.

Gradually, then, I managed to persuade the owner-members of Reuters that there was a way in which they would retain control of the news agency, and yet benefit from this windfall – a windfall created in fact by the brilliance and foresight of the Reuters management team under Glen Renfrew. One of my worst difficulties was to get Lord Matthews and Lord Rothermere to attend a meeting together. Matthews was using the *Daily Express* to attack the *Daily Mail*, and they didn't get on. Rothermere regarded himself as an aristocrat, and I felt objected to Matthews because he'd been a Brixton bricklayer. So if I wanted to move the Board of Trustees in a certain direction, I had to give lunch to Victor Matthews one day and Rothermere the next – but never together.

Somehow, over the months, Renfrew and I had to mastermind a

public flotation that would strengthen the Reuters Trust Deed, not weaken it – and that is where we spent most of our time: devising a formula and selling it. Eventually, having finally convinced the proprietors of Reuters that we were on the right lines, I had to convince the City. This – particularly in view of the fact that we would be the first company in history to float on both the New York and London stock markets simultaneously – proved a hair-raising business. The London Shareholders' Association met Warburgs, our advisers, and in vain insisted on one share, one vote. They then led a tremendous campaign to try to spoil the flotation, forcing the insurance companies and many of the investment trusts to boycott the sale of shares. However, I refused to budge. I sent out a memorandum, explaining that there have to be exceptions in life, and that Reuters was one. I asked, 'Is it your wish that the greatest news agency in the world should be put in the hands of Arabs, Israelis, Taiwanese or Far Eastern interests, or even America, merely because of your "one for one"?' But it didn't help – we got a message back saying that the ownership was no business of theirs, only the money. They boycotted us, and this had the effect of lowering the opening price. The chairman of the Prudential, Lord Carr, for instance, told me he was mortified, but he was in the hands of his investment and pension fund managers, handling millions of pounds every week, and he had to go along with what they said.

It was a tribute to Renfrew's management that these narrow-minded souls did not ruin the flotation. The issue was taken up by the underwriters, there were enough small investors and others to buy them, and it became perfectly clear that as soon as the shares went on the market, they were bought by the Prudential and other people through stockbrokers, at an increased price. So much for their 'one to one' boycott.

The American flotation was even more complicated. I had plane-loads of American lawyers and advisers coming to see me, I had to sign hundreds of pages of undertakings and documents, and really had to work very hard to make sense of so much mumbo-jumbo which for legal reasons only the chairman could do – while all the time preventing splits on my Reuters board.

Naturally there was an attempt in Parliament to stop the sale. Jim Callaghan made two speeches in the Commons. In the end I had to write to him personally, saying, 'We have known each other for a very long time and I am very distressed you think I could involve myself, as chairman of Reuters, in putting forward anything that would leave Reuters open for anyone to walk through the door and take control. Someone is giving you the wrong story.' He rang me up and said, 'I suddenly realised I'd been taken for a sucker on this – and I should have realised you would never stand for it yourself.' He withdrew his objections.

The flotation thus went ahead. The barons were pleased (as pleased as millionaires can ever be) and the financial basis for Reuters' world-wide expansion was secured, without affecting the control and independence of the news agency. As my final contribution to the world of journalism, it was something to be proud of.

# CHAPTER TWENTY-EIGHT

# In Which
# I Drop Names

THE SUCCESSFUL FLOTATION OF REUTERS WAS, I SUPPOSE, THE CROWNING act of my journalistic career. I retired in 1985, having managed to persuade Christopher Hogg, the chairman of Courtaulds, to take my place – and having enshrined, within the Articles of Association of the new company, the ethos and aims which I felt should guide Reuters over the coming years. It remains a world leader in its field of communications, while setting the highest standards of reporting around the globe – objective and immune to political or financial pressure.

I was now, to all intents and purposes, retired, though I held directorships of several companies and sat on the boards of trustees of a number of institutions, including the Independent Broadcasting Authority, the British Museum, the British Library, and the Henry Moore Foundation. I can confirm that lust for money or glory are not confined to newspaper proprietors, and that some of the strangest people are generous benefactors to our national institutions, while others are mean beyond all understanding. I have seen great treasures of art lost to the nation out of blundering bureaucracy or overweening family greed; but the challenge of helping to secure for the nation important milestones in artistic history has been constantly invigorating and I count myself lucky to have 'pulled together' with distinguished men and women from many walks of life.

We have had signal successes as well as failures, and for the most part I have enjoyed the struggles, knowing they were in a good cause. To have detached, for instance, the publications and retailing department of the British Museum from the stifling grasp of the Treasury was worth every hour of our long-drawn out battle – for what rapidly emerged, under the managing director we recruited, was a completely new British publishing house, able to sell to the public the fruits of a great museum's dedication to archaeology and our cultural heritage, as well as making it possible for the museum's expert staff to transmit their knowledge to a wider audience. The success of the British Museum, in this respect, became a model for its sister institutions, almost all of which have now cast off the Treasury's chains.

As a journalist I had, from the very start of my career, been aware of the importance of good contacts – the value of getting to know the sources of good information. Perhaps unsurprisingly, I found it to be very much the same in the spheres of museum work. I do not mean an 'old boy' network. I mean facing the fact that in all walks of life it is the individual that counts; that despite the acceleration of communication, nothing will ever substitute for personal knowledge and contact. Whether one is appealing for funds or seeking advice, it will always pay to make personal contact. It may mean extra effort: but it will, in the end, repay handsomely.

During my career I have had the privilege of getting to know a huge number of talented people, from politicians and industrialists to artists and writers. Their time, companionship and often friendship I count as perhaps the greatest blessing of a long life spent in newspapers, and in my way I hope I have been able to reward them. I remember going to see Field-Marshal Earl Alexander of Tunis to offer him a substantial sum for his *Memoirs*, if he would write them. 'Bless me!' he said, when he heard the sum I proposed, 'I'll be able to afford a boy to help mow the lawn!' In fact, I had to pay for someone else – the historian John North – to do the writing. Alexander turned out to be a man of surprising vacuousness considering that he had commanded great armies; but integrity and devotion to duty are also important factors in command, and I never begrudged Lord Alexander the amount we paid.

He certainly was an unassuming person – something one could not say of Field-Marshal Lord Wavell's widow, 'Queenie'. After Wavell died, there arose the question: who should write his biography? I was summoned by Lady Wavell. 'I want Arthur Bryant to do the book,' she announced. I shook my head. 'Arthur has at least six books already signed up,' I explained. 'Well, who do you suggest?' she asked. The answer was obvious. 'Lady Wavell,' I said, 'you have the very best possible biographer at your right hand, and I happen to know that he would love to do the book.' 'Who?' 'Why, Bernard Fergusson of course.' 'Fergusson? Fergusson? Do you believe, Mr Hamilton, that I would permit my husband's life to be told by his ADC?'

She told me how angry she had once been with her husband while he was Viceroy of India. At her request he gave a banquet, at the end of the war, to thank the women of India who had helped contribute to the

Allied victory – and then did not speak to anyone at the table throughout the proceedings. Afterwards, Lady Wavell remonstrated with him – that he had not even opened his mouth to the head of the Red Cross, which had done so much. 'What were you thinking about, Archie?' she demanded. Wavell lifted his eyes to hers. 'I was thinking,' he said, with a very faint smile, 'of how I would play the seventh hole at St Andrews.'

I met all the post-war American Presidents, from Truman and Eisenhower, to Kennedy, Lyndon Johnson, Carter and Reagan. Usually this was fixed for me by our resourceful *Sunday Times* Washington correspondent, Henry Brandon – the man with the best contacts in the United States. When Henry arranged for me to go to the White House to meet Jack Kennedy, I found the president rooted to his rocking chair. We were the same age, and we hit it off from the start. 'My back is giving me hell today,' he said, 'but remember – if you ever suffer from back trouble, a rocking chair can be a great help.' As he said that, a mysterious telephone bell sounded. I couldn't understand where it was coming from. Finally I realised it was under the rocking chair. His daughter Caroline was calling to say that he hadn't said 'good morning' properly and would he kindly go up and see her? Kennedy had a little chat with her and smoothed her down. He explained, 'Well, Daddy's got something to do, but he'll come up straight away.' She must have interrupted him, for he was soon protesting: 'I may have said that before – but this time I *mean* it!'

After the somewhat senile last years of Eisenhower, Kennedy's style and humanity were refreshing – though one was well aware he had enemies, and that there were many unresolved tensions in American life. Bobby Kennedy I saw many times. Once, when I arrived, he grabbed and put on a tin hat – as the Sheriff of Washington DC – to amuse me. I shall never forget his saying he was quite certain, after his brother's death, that he too would be killed in due course, and there was no way out of it; that those responsible for his brother's assassination would go for him and get him.

I also had a most extraordinary meeting with Lyndon Johnson when he was President, just after the bombing of Haiphong harbour and a diplomatic crisis with the Russians. His cabinet sat late, so I sent in a message saying that I had to go back to London and would not detain him, as it seemed unfair to take any of his time. A message came out saying, 'You would be doing me a very great favour if you would stay over, because I want to talk to you.' This was hardly something I could refuse. Eventually Johnson came out – he was a giant of a man, nearly 6ft 6in I think, massively built, and he immediately asked me to excuse him if he lay down on the sofa while we talked. He revealed that he'd spent the whole afternoon with General Eisenhower. I was a bit nonplussed. 'What can you have discussed for such a long time?' I asked – Eisenhower was by then a very, very old man. 'I was talking about what it is like to the morale of your troops if you sack the commander-in-chief in the field.'

Eisenhower had advised caution to Johnson, who was then thinking of sacking General Westmoreland in Vietnam, and had given his reasons for sympathising with Westmoreland: 'There was a stage in the [second world] war, Mr President, when nearly four million soldiers were under my command in Europe, of all nationalities. All my sympathies are with General Westmoreland. It's an impossible war, you don't know whether the man to your left is Vietnamese or Viet Cong – certainly the ordinary American soldier doesn't know. It must be extremely difficult to operate in those conditions.' I was rivetted by this conversation – and my attention was doubly held because, as Johnson talked, I could see two huge holes in the soles of his shoes!

Johnson then went on to talk about Churchill. 'There's another thing I want to discuss,' he said: 'that speech of Churchill's – "We shall fight them on the beaches, etc." – it's the greatest thing that's ever been said beyond the Bible!' I thought this was putting it a bit high, but he then asked about the reaction in Britain to the speech. I explained that it was still available on a gramophone record, and that I would get a copy of it sent to him if he wished, 'But,' I said, 'don't forget that Dover is only twenty-six miles from Calais, while Vietnam is thousands of miles away. I do implore you not to waste your time writing a speech about fighting on the beaches.'

'But I've got the best speech writers in the country!' he countered.

'Well,' I said. 'Many people believe that Churchill's speeches were his greatest contribution to winning the war – but I honestly feel you're on the wrong track here.'

He looked rather downcast. I felt sorry for him in his predicament – and amazed at his two old worn-out shoes.

When Johnson died his widow, Ladybird Johnson, paid a visit to Britain, and I was put next to her at a dinner given by Fleur Cowles. As the meal progressed I could see that Mrs Johnson had a sense of humour – she was a very astute lady in fact – so I said, 'If I may say so, Mrs Johnson, why didn't you ever get the President's shoes mended? It seemed very strange to see that the most powerful man in the world had to greet foreign visitors in shoes with holes in them.'

'What an extraordinary thing to say!' she cried – and burst out laughing. 'Well, you've found out the secret,' she confided. 'If we had a crisis on, he would not attend any meeting, or do *anything*, without his lucky shoes on. What you saw were his lucky shoes!'

It was easier to get on with American presidents, I have to say, than with oriental potentates. I must have paid half-a-dozen visits to the Shah of Iran, each time seeing him in his palace audience chamber that was larger than Mussolini's. I remember questioning him on his handling of the religious factions in Iran. As a journalist I had my own sources – in particular Mohamed Heikal in Cairo, who had interviewed about 200 religious and political figures. I'd also talked, in Tehran, with a retired general who sought me out to warn me that the whole régime was likely to crumble because the Shah was ignoring religious feelings. In my audience I therefore attempted to discuss the matter – but the Shah tried to brush it aside. 'I have four members of our staff here,' I protested, 'and they have exceptionally good contacts – I'm quite certain you are playing it wrong.' The Shah looked disdainful: 'I never play anything wrong.' When I asked why he didn't at least throw a sop to the religious fundamentalists, lest they topple him, he snorted: 'I am not prepared to – I am the Shah.'

He was a most obstinate man. He even tried to hang on to some priceless objects on loan from the British Museum, until I warned him we would make a major issue of the matter. He felt he was invulnerable because the West wanted his oil – and the attention paid to him even by the Queen in an effort to get industrial and military orders went to his head. 'I spent one whole day discussing with your Queen how her son should be educated,' he boasted to me. 'It's obvious - he should go to Eton,' he had told the Queen 'the best school in England.' Apparently the Queen had replied: 'My dear Shah, I do not want Charles in my back garden. Besides, he would get into bad company. He will go to Gordonstoun.'

Indira Gandhi was not a very pleasant person either. She was stubborn and very tough – very much the determined daughter of her father Jawaharlal Nehru, who was much more gracious. I recall one trip I made to India, under United Nations auspices, with the Secretary General, when Mrs Ghandi made a blistering and unexpected attack on the West and our attitude towards Asia. Everyone was abashed, save for Shirley Williams, then an official of Unesco. She took up the argument and won the day. It was quite a sight, watching those two fight it out verbally. Afterwards, Mrs Gandhi showed me the gardens. I still didn't form any liking for her, but she did agree to let Tony Snowdon have the freedom of the country so that we could produce a whole *Sunday Times* magazine issue devoted to India. She berated me for the way the British press had covered her failure at the polls, when she lost the election to Mr Desai. To defend myself, I said I would organise a lunch for her when she came to London for the Commonwealth Prime Ministers' meeting, to meet the London editors she so despised. I also said a number of complimentary things about the arts of her country, to show we were not one-sided. To my consternation I found, the next day, that she had had secret microphones in her room, that our conversation had been tape-recorded, and all my laudatory and flattering remarks – made in self-defence – had been 'leaked' to the Indian Press!

Not all such meetings were conducted in animosity, though. In Japan, the Prime Minister, Mr Sato, insisted on meeting me. I had been chairing a big conference, and got a telephone call asking me to call on him. For a long time we just waffled, via the interpreter, so that I began to wonder why he'd summoned me. Finally, he got to the point. 'Tomorrow,' he announced, 'is my weekly audience with the Emperor –and I don't want to be caught out. I think you can understand, there is no one in this city I can ask, but Providence has sent me you. I want you to advise me.' Puzzled, I asked how.

'The Crown Prince is going to Europe, like the Emperor did in 1923,' he explained. 'What reception would he get, do you think? We haven't fully committed ourselves to the trip.'

'I don't think you'd have any trouble,' I said, 'but I would advise him to keep away from Northumberland and the North of England – there were a lot of Northumbrian soldiers taken prisoner in the war and savagely treated.' Sato seemed grateful for this advice, which he promised to follow. 'But I have one further request for help', he added, 'before I see the Emperor.' I waited.

'This morning, in the newspapers, I read that the firm of Rolls Royce has gone bankrupt. The Emperor, I know, will be greatly distressed – and worried.' 'Why?' 'Because the Emperor will only travel by Rolls Royce. Where will he now get spare parts for his sixteen cars?' I had to laugh – and assured him that immediately I got back to England, I would ensure that five years' worth of spare parts were put aside. Sato promised eternal gratitude. 'I will be in especial favour when the Emperor hears this!' he declared – telling me that the Emperor so loved his Rolls Royces that he was delighted when, one day, the representatives of Mercedes Benz brought a demonstration model of their finest limousine to the Imperial Palace – and the car wouldn't start!

In closed societies like the Soviet Union, on the other hand, a Western newspaper editor is a rather threatening figure – as I found when I tried to pay an informal visit to Leningrad and Moscow, with a Thomson tour, over Christmas 1977. Olive and I took two friends with us. Our intention was to visit the great museums and monuments, as private citizens. It was bitterly cold but we saw everything and were delighted with our visit – until a so-called Russian 'lunatic' burst into our hotel bedroom one night, almost naked. I jumped out of bed and chased the fellow out. I then bellowed on the landing, for the Rossiya Hotel, like all Russian hotels at that time, had a huge, fat lady in charge of each floor, sitting all day and night with a vast bunch of keys and a list of hotel guests. She didn't speak English but pretended the man was a lunatic, and that we should take no notice.

I thought no more of the matter, we went to the ballet the following evening – and again, in the middle of the night, an almost naked man burst into our room. Once more, furious at the intrusion, I chased him out. The concierge, poker-faced as ever, again indicated that he must be a lunatic – but for a lunatic to get past her, two nights running, and gain access, naked, to our room seemed a bit far-fetched – especially when, meeting our friends and other members of the tour party the next morning, we found we had been the only ones so singled out.

I didn't wish to make a fuss in Moscow lest it spoil the tour for the others, but on our return to London I had to attend, the very first night, the annual dinner of the Indian Press Corps. Jim Callaghan, then Prime Minister, was there, and I told him the story before dinner. He started to laugh just as the Russian Ambassador, Mr Lunkov, came up to us. 'Ah, Sir Denis, I hope you enjoyed your visit to our country – I gave instructions that you should be dealt with specially.' 'Well, I hope you don't treat me the same way you treated Denis, when I go!', said Callaghan, and at that moment the toastmaster ordered us to our seats.

Next day, outside my office, I saw the Ambassador's car. My secretary explained we had a visitor – a minister from the Russian Embassy who insisted on seeing me. In he came, saying, 'Sir Denis, we understand strange things happened in Moscow. I want to find out if you are pulling our leg or we are pulling yours!' I told him exactly what had happened, and he looked most embarrassed. I assured him I wasn't upset about it, it wasn't going to cause the third world war, in fact my wife and I had very much enjoyed our visit. Nevertheless, he would have to admit, there were strange goings-on at the Hotel Rossiya.

He looked at me. 'The trouble is, Sir Denis, we have a lot of hooligans in Russia. Some hooligan must somehow have got the key to your door and found his way in.' There was silence for a moment. 'That's quite a good theory,' I said, 'but not really good enough. Though on the spur of the moment, off the cuff, it wasn't bad!' He was a bit crestfallen. 'Well, what do *you* make of it, Sir Denis?' 'My own feeling,' I said, 'is that you

were running a KGB training course, and you put in some idiots who
made a complete mess of it.' 'Oh,' he protested, 'we must take it more
seriously than that!'

The minister promised it would not end there – that it would be
investigated in Moscow and that his ambassador would personally call
on me and give a full account of what Moscow thought had happened. To
this day I have never heard a word.

A senior journalist does inevitably become a sort of ambassador for his
country when travelling or receiving foreign guests. The danger he must
avoid, clearly, is letting such contacts have undue influence on the way
he edits his newspaper. I know I was rather hurt when one of my
journalists, Hugo Young – whom I had recommended to Rupert
Murdoch as the best successor to Harold Evans as *Sunday Times* editor –
once accused me in print of being a straw man in my dealings with the
government. I was infuriated, because I doubt if any government in our
country since the 1960s has had to show respect to any journalist or editor
for his impartiality, integrity or willingness to stand firm over important
issues more than to me – whether in the case of the Richard Crossman
diaries, the Freedom of the Press struggle (when I was asked by the
national newspaper editors to represent them in opposing Michael
Foot's proposed closed shop for journalists), Devaluation, or the
numberless issues over which the *Sunday Times* and the *Times* challenged
the Government over the years. It is not the journalist who shouts loudest
whom a government fears: it is the journalist with honesty and judgment.

Of course, backbiting is itself an endemic disease among journalists,
and has been since coffee-house days. Gratitude is rare – I remember
once I paid Randolph Churchill £10,000 to buy the serial rights of his
early autobiography – a book on the lines of Beverley Nichols's *Twenty-
Five*. As soon as I'd done the deal Randolph rang Roy Thomson and said
that if I'd been a better business man I could have had the rights for
£5,000! It was a typical dirty trick, in a profession which *is* often dirty. It
didn't dent my admiration for him as a writer and a journalist – though I
suspect his own self-contempt contributed to his unhappiness, his failed
marriages, alcoholism and early death. I may have paid too much for his
story and been the butt of ill-informed remarks over the years: but I count
myself lucky as a journalist that I have lived an intensely interesting life,
while enjoying a happy marriage that has lasted forty-eight years and
brought me four loving sons, all of whom have prospered in their lives
and careers.

One explanation, I think, is that I have never sought social
advancement, wealth, or the company of those I did not admire or like. I
have tried to be discreet, a man who could be trusted with confidences,

yet respected for his judgment. I cherish the friendships I have made over the decades – friendships which inevitably terminate in death, yet live on in my memory. The friendship of great men like Field-Marshal Montgomery or Harold Macmillan was humbling, for these were men who stamped their mark on history. I was proud to have served under Monty in battle and that I could, in my own small way, repay a tiny fraction of what our country owed to him, by becoming his adviser and confidant, as well as publisher and editor.

Similarly, with Harold Macmillan I felt a younger man's admiration for his greatness as a political leader and thinker. We both felt fervently on the subject of unemployment; we both saw military service, and the great qualities of the British soldier under fire, far from home. There was a strange bond between us, fostering a warm friendship which lasted to the very end of his life.

I was blessed, too, in certain friendships with fellow journalists that went beyond simple professional camaraderie. With Leonard Russell, husband of the film critic, Dilys Powell, I enjoyed a relationship that was both personal and productive – Leonard being the finest editor of serials I have known. With Robert Harling, writer, typographer and editor, I also enjoyed a close friendship, deepened by the years we had both spent serving in the forces. His two books about life in the Royal Navy remain classics of their kind.

Yet perhaps the most arresting friendship I enjoyed was with Ian Fleming. He also had served in the Navy, at times with Harling, but he'd been trained in the Secret Service before the war, while in merchant banking, and though he cultivated high society and had the entrée to Lord and Lady Kemsley's house and circle, he was desperate to make a more telling impact on his times. As his close friend I had to keep from Lord Kemsley the fact that Fleming was consorting with the wife of Kemsley's fellow newspaper proprietor, Lord Rothermere – indeed was sleeping with Anne Rothermere under Kemsley's own roof. I loved Ian and it hurt me to witness the less pleasant side of his subsequent marriage to Anne – for, although she inspired him to great achievements by the passion he had for her, she was very much a socialite, needed constant company and entertainment in a way that, increasingly, Ian didn't. She would mock his James Bond books, in the hearing of Ian, with people like Cyril Connolly. This social and literary snobbishness I despised – it was everything I wished to avoid as an editor: a silly, old-fashioned élitism.

Cyril Connolly had been at Oxford with Waugh and Acton. He was a brilliant reviewer, with a great depth and breadth of literary reading; but as a human being he was a somewhat repulsive egoist. Ian towered over him physically and in character. And if Ian helped me in my career, both with Kemsley and Thomson, I hope I was able to repay the debt by encouraging Ian as a feature writer on the paper, and as one of the best-selling thriller-writers of the century. Cyril Connolly might scoff – his long parody of Bond betrayed his envy of Ian's success in creating such a legendary literary hero – but Fleming's rise to international best-sellerdom did not happen overnight. I read every manuscript before it went to Ian's publisher, not to advise or correct anything, but as a friend whom Ian trusted, whose approval and respect he wished to earn. From the first novel – over which we tormented ourselves, discussing whether the title should be *Casino Royal* or *Casino Royale* – to the last, I admired Ian's narrative skill and ability to create characters. When the first novels flopped in hardback, the encouragement of his friends meant, I think, a great deal to Ian – as did an arrangement I made with him whereby, although a full-time staff journalist on the Kemsley payroll, it was agreed that he could spend a certain number of months each year in Jamaica, writing his novels.

I remember visiting Ian, at his invitation, at Goldeneye. Ian was a bit naughty, really – he'd bought the plot at the end of the war, overlooking a bay, and had built a shack-like house, without any mod cons – without even a telephone. Yet he went around pretending to everyone that he had this great palace in Jamaica, a miniature Ritz. I think partly it was to keep up his end with Anne, who wasn't going to miss a party in London and always dragged him along. Thus it was that all sorts of people were invited to Goldeneye who were unaware of what they were in for – culminating with Anthony Eden, the Prime Minister, when he fell ill after Suez. It was Ian's fault, he'd sold the Foreign Office a dud, and when the Prime Minister's party reached Goldeneye they found there wasn't a telephone and the place was riddled with snakes and vermin of every kind. You could have sold Fleming stock very cheaply at that moment!

But that was Ian's bravado. I don't suppose Anne would have tolerated the place, except for the fact that Noël Coward was the next-door neighbour, and there was a succession of illustrious visitors. Ian loved the underwater swimming – there was a charming bay with a jetty where small ships could take off bananas from the plantations. Anne grumbled about how awful the place was and how she missed London, but Ian was in paradise. It was there that he spun out his impossible yarns, with their schoolboy humour, and unforgettable figures. He was in his element. I remember swimming with him and building on the beach an artistic pile of rock and bits of wrecked ships that had drifted in from Cuba after a storm. Noël Coward arrived from next door. He sauntered down to the beach, where he saw us at work on this construction. He looked down at us, over his cigarette holder, and uttered the immortal words: 'Fleming's last erection!'

I was taking a Sunday Times conference one Tuesday when Ian suddenly keeled over. I thought he was dying because he was a deathly white; I tried to get him out of the stuffy room, but he resisted. I said, 'Come on, Ian, you'll bloody well do as I tell you! We'll go out and I'll get you a doctor.' I summoned a car to take him home and arranged for his doctor to be waiting there – that was all he'd agree to. He had suffered a massive heart attack and was put in the London Clinic within minutes of the doctor seeing him. He was so ill I wasn't allowed to visit him at first, but he'd smuggle out handwritten letters, which I still have and treasure.

Nothing could stop him from living his life to the full. 'I'm 54 and I'm not giving up now,' he said, insisting on his double-whiskies and his golf. Often I'd go to his flat, of an evening, where he'd show me the latest addition to his collection of first editions. Then one day I was standing on the quayside at Dieppe, with one of my children, when I saw an English newspaper at a stall, with the headline: 'Ian Fleming Dies on Golf Course.' He was dead by the time they got him to hospital; I did not have the chance to say goodbye.

It was Ian's nudge, above all, which got Roy Thomson to put me in as editor of the *Sunday Times*. He had courage and he faced the trials of his life with manliness and humour. I miss him, as I do many others who gave colour and sinew to Fleet Street in the post-war years.

# POSTSCRIPT

# AN HONOURABLE
# PROFESSION

IN A HALDANE LECTURE, I ONCE ATTEMPTED TO ANSWER THE QUESTION: 'Who is to own the British Press?' The talk was widely reported and reprinted, even by one of the main printing unions: for the answer concerns us all, whether we are newspaper readers, journalists, or employed in newspaper production. The conclusion I reached in my lecture was that our system of private ownership, though far from perfect, does in fact guarantee a plurality of views and reporting that would inevitably be diminished under other systems of ownership or control. We have, after all, some five quality national daily newspapers printed in London, three Sundays, as well as a variety of tabloids of varying status. A Monopolies Commission safeguards us against too great concentration of newspaper power, and a Press Council, with a number of distinguished men and women on its committee, investigates complaints of unfair or untruthful journalism. New technology has already added new titles as the traditional use (or misuse) of union power wanes. In that respect, I am confident newspapers have an excellent commercial future, as well as performing a vital role in the development of a democratic society.

However, neither owners nor technology can of themselves create good or great newspapers. Mrs Thatcher's law on picketing and the fining of unions for contempt of court (or rather, the seizure of their assets until they comply with the law) made possible Eddie Shah's newspaper *Today* – but the newspaper itself had to stand or fall in the market-place as a distinctive, readable product, in competition with other similar newspapers. As was clear from the start, achievement of that aim was infinitely more difficult than the financing, production or distribution of the paper. In the end a newspaper is only as good as its editor and his editorial team, assisted by management and other staff. It was for this reason that I held out against those who recommended dismissing our journalists during the Times Newspapers shutdown – and I note with interest how many journalists on the new national newspaper the *Independent* come from the old Thomson stable.

I am proud that, although we failed in our struggle with the unions, we managed to nurture so much journalistic talent – although, with the exception of the *Independent*, I do not think the standard of editing or editorial team-work in British national newspapers is currently outstanding. There are too many shrill voices, shouting instant opinions, instead of well-considered, well-researched and well-written journalism. Like the old *Sunday Times* under Lord Kemsley, the sum of too many newspapers today is less than their parts, the judgment of their editors too weak and the standard of leadership too low. Yet the history of Fleet Street has shown that great editors do emerge every so often, and men of the calibre of Gordon Newton will, I'm certain, rise again in time. To them, were I asked for my advice, I would say this:

The role of the newspaper editor is an honourable one. An editor is a leader – not only of his staff of journalists, but in society.

Never forget that the secret of a good newspaper is the quality of the journalists you have under you, and recruit. There is no short-cut. I made this my priority as a commanding officer in 1943 and 1944 before I took my battalion into battle, and in Kemsley and Thomson Newspapers and Fleet Street thereafter. You can do anything with good raw material. It is not simply a matter of getting people in and giving them an office and a large salary. Recruiting people entails being clear about what you want them to do, and supporting and encouraging them in doing it. They need to be given their head, yet also to have access to you for advice.

What makes a good journalist? Predominantly, hard work, and self-motivation – the ability to think ideas out for himself and to pursue leads in getting the story. A good editor must back him in this: with encouragement, resources, and the freedom to get on with his job.

Apart from journalists, a good editor must have, engraved in his heart, a clear idea of his market, the people he is aiming to inform and to entertain. He must have courage in serving that market: the courage to face up to his proprietor where necessary, or others who may seek to deflect him from his task. He needs to be sensitive to his readers' changing or evolving interests. Above all he needs, amid the ever-flowing stream of news and opinion, to show firmness of judgment: judgment that will inspire his staff and offer a steadying hand to his readers in their daily lives.

The most creative, innovative editor of our century, in my eyes, was Lord Camrose, who created the *Daily Telegraph* – a creation so solid and distinctive that his son, Lord Hartwell, never sought to alter it (even perhaps when he ought to have done). Camrose created the *Telegraph* out of nothing – just as Andreas Whittam Smith did the *Independent* in 1986. It can be done, and will continue to be done, I am sure, despite or perhaps because of the inroads and distractions of television.

If I had my life to live again, I would still become a journalist. It has often been called the second oldest profession, its practitioners collectively abused because, at its most scurrilous level, the standard of journalism is so low: deliberately dishonest, intrusive, salacious. The gutter press is the gutter press.

But no journalist has to work for such newspapers. The standard of provincial newspapers and of the quality national press in this country is high enough to encourage any hard-working, honest and inquisitive school-leaver or university graduate to train as a journalist, and in time to rise to the top of his profession. In doing so he or she will learn to write cogently, to track down a story, meet people from all walks of life, and exercise his or her judgment both of people and events. I hope my own life, recorded in outline in these pages, demonstrates that it is quite possible for a journalist from the humblest of origins to succeed in newspapers; moreover, that it is perfectly possible to follow high ideals: to be a man of your word, and to produce journalism which is informative, truthful and even educative, yet which 'sells'. My experience in editing the *Sunday Times* in the 1960s – in starting the colour magazine, Insight, the 'Big Read', the Business News – or in creating the *Times Higher Educational Supplement* in 1970 are cases in point. Of course, a journalist has to learn to accept setbacks too – as every mature individual must in life.

I can only hope that those readers who have retraced with me the path of a professional journalist from Teeside to the *Times* will have found these recollections worth preserving.

# INDEX